BOMBERS

PHILIP KAPLAN

AURUM PRESS

For Neal and Hargi

First published in Great Britain 2000 by
Aurum Press Ltd.
25 Bedford Avenue
London WC1B 3AT

Text copyright © 2000 by Philip Kaplan

Page 236 is an extension of this copyright page

A catalogue record for this book is available from the British Library.

ISBN 1 85410 680 5

1 3 5 7 9 10 8 6 4 2
2000 2002 2004 2003 2001
Printed and bound in Singapore by Imago

CONTENTS

Below: Bicycles of airmen attending services in the base chapel of the 381st Bomb Group (H) at Ridgewell, England on 31 October 1943. Previous spread: Eighth US Army Air Force airmen in World War II England.

INTRODUCTION

IN WAR the innocent suffer along with the guilty. In his vision of the future, Italian Air Force General Guilio Douhet wrote in 1921: "No longer can areas exist in which life can be lived in safety and tranquility, nor can the battlefield any longer be limited to actual combatants . . . there will be no distinction any longer between soldiers and civilians."

The earliest indicator of what would become the most significant military concept ever was virtually a non–event. In a row between Italy and Turkey in 1911, the Italians sent six scout planes across enemy lines. One of them tried, for the first time, the concept of aerial bombing from a fixed–wing aircraft. Dropping a few small hand grenades on the terrified Turks did little damage, but provoked considerable world press comment on the evils of air attack. 34 years later another attack by a single airplane, an American B-29 Superfortress called *Enola Gay* after the pilot's mother, dropped one bomb which was detonated over the city of Hiroshima in southern Japan. This first use of a nuclear bomb led directly to the ending of a war that had cost more than 200 million lives. The use of this new and untried weapon was authorised by US President Harry Truman in the belief that it would work and in so doing would persuade the Japanese to surrender unconditionally to the Allied Powers. The war would thereby come to an end without requiring an invasion of Japan's home islands, which most military strategists of the time believed would cost the Allies up to an additional one million casualties.

Near the end of the First World War, the true heavy bomber aircraft began to evolve. Until then aerial bombing had been limited to the tossing of tiny token explosives from the scout planes of the day. Little damage was done to those on the ground. Of much greater concern to the British and French were the attacks by German Zeppelin airships which began almost as soon as that war was declared. The effect of these eerie night raids was far more frightening than damaging, but showed the Allies how vulnerable they were to such attacks. The Zeppelins were vulnerable too, and by 1917 were replaced over London by the highly–touted and much–feared Gothas, the first of the successful heavy bombers. By the end of the war air bombing was still a fumbling, ineffectual affair. But the writing was on the wall.

The world shuddered at the prospect of the mighty bombing force which General Douhet had predicted would carry the attack deep into enemy territory to destroy both its cities and its industrial centres. Others who shared his views included US General William E. Mitchell, the father of American military aviation, and Air Marshal Sir Hugh Trenchard, for ten years Britain's Chief of Air Staff. They were prophets, but as is often so with prophets, they had little honour in their time. Trenchard could barely maintain the independence of the Royal Air Force into the 1930s, and the career of Billy Mitchell came apart in 1926 when he antagonized powerful elements in the US armed forces. He was court–martialed for insubordination, found guilty, and suspended from the Army for five years. He resigned before the sentence could take effect, but his doctrine that great fleets of heavy bombers could destroy an enemy's means of making war by hitting his centres of production, was accepted by many in American and international military circles.

The influence of Douhet, Trenchard and Mitchell persisted, both in Britain and the United States, as did the long–running agitation for heavy bombers. In the US, Mitchell's disciples finally managed to create a small force of true, long–range, strategic bombers in the early 1930s. The Martin B-10 spearheaded that force and was soon followed by the four-engined B-17 Flying Fortress, a bomber with a 2000–mile range, and in 1936 the B-24 Liberator. At the same time, Germany was rearming in the name of a "new order" dedicated to redressing its World War I grievances, while the Allies of that conflict were striving for a new world without arms. The 1932 League of Nations Disarmament Conference was a final effort to achieve such agreement, and in the decade of the '30s most nations allowed their defences to deteriorate. Japan, Italy and Germany

Below: Poster by E. Montaut for the first international air display, Paris, 1909.

6

Below: First Lieutenant Raymond W. Wild, back row centre, and his 92nd Bomb Group (H) crew at Podington, Bedfordshire, England in early 1944.

Horsham St Faith, Ridgewell, Horham, Snetterton Heath, Thorpe Abbotts, Knettishall, Framlingham and Wendling detailed the times for briefing and take–off for the crews who would fly the mission that day. In the early hours of the 14th, additional field orders arrived which defined the mission requirements in greater detail for the participating bomb groups. Earlier orders had instructed the groups as to the bomb loads they were to take and the other items essential to such strategic attacks.

Ground crew personnel were occupied for the next several hours in fuelling the B-17s and B-24s taking part in No. 115. In addition to aviation gas,

the bombers had to be supplied with ammunition, oxygen, extra clothing and shoes, sandwiches, first–aid kits and maps.

At Debden and Boxted, at Bodney and Raydon, the P-47 Thunderbolt fighters of Eighth Fighter Command were alerted and readied shortly after two in the morning of the 14th for their vital escort role. To have much chance of returning safely to their English bases from this complex, demanding and extremely hazardous operation, the bombers would require substantial protection by their little fighter friends.

By 2 a.m. every bomb group commander was in

chose a different course. The alarm sounded in Britain in 1938 as the German threat loomed. The Royal Air Force was rapidly reorganised with a planned expansion: a secret radar defence network was being developed, a large new force of four–engined heavy bombers was ordered and, after British Prime Minister Neville Chamberlain's Munich appeasement of Adolf Hitler, the RAF bomber capability began to grow dramatically. In the United States, the concept of strategic bombing was still under attack as being both barbarous and unnecessary. With the Munich crisis, however, and the appointment of General Henry H. Arnold, an ardent disciple of Billy Mitchell, as Chief of the US Army Air Corps, the future of the American bomber programme was suddenly assured.

Hitler's invasion of his European neighbours in September 1939, and the Japanese attack on the US naval base at Pearl Harbor, Hawaii in December 1941, had ignited World War II in the east and west, and both tactical and strategic bombing quickly became important. In the air forces of all the combatants, organisation, training, recruitment, planning, equipping, conveying and actual operations went ahead with unparalleled urgency. During the war the United States alone produced a staggering 300,317 military aircraft. The US Army Air Force accepted 188,880 planes, among them 61,221 bombers, the most significant of them being the Boeing B-29 (3760), the Boeing B-17 (12,677), and the Consolidated B-24 (18,188). At the end of the war contracts for an additional 31,000 military aircraft were on US manufacturers' books and were quickly cancelled. Many thousands of British Lancaster, Halifax, Stirling, Wellington and other bombers were built for the RAF in that war, and the major aircraft manufacturers of Germany, Japan and Italy contributed mightily to their nations' bomber arsenals as well. Aerial bombing had come of age.

The main job of the men who flew in the Blenheims, Bostons, Fortresses, Gothas, Halifaxes, Hampdens, Heinkels, Junkers, Lancasters, Liberators, Marauders, Mitchells, Mitsubishis, Mosquitos, Savoia–Marchettis and the other bombers, was to strike at and attempt to destroy the military targets of the enemy. For the most part they did this with courage, skill and determination. Most of them liked to fly, though many disliked their job as bombers. Most believed in the cause they served. Most were young — in their late teens and early twenties. Many were too young to vote, but not too young to die.

The debate on the wisdom, morality and effect of the bombing in World War II, Korea, Vietnam and later conflicts will probably never end, but there can be no doubt about the price paid by those who did "the work." More than 100,000 RAF and USAAF bomber aircrew died in the air campaigns of World War II, as did many more thousands of bomber crew of Germany, Japan and scores of other nations in that war. They may have been young when it began, but those who survived were old when it ended. Those who lived had no more illusions about the glamour of the "wild blue." Their job had taken them five miles above the earth into an environment where they faced double jeopardy. They endured the risks of the ground soldier and, when the shooting started, there were no foxholes in the sky, nowhere to hide. They had to sit there and take it. The harmless–looking, indiscriminate little puffs of flak that appeared randomly around their aircraft taught them an unforgettable lesson in the law of chance. There was no real defence and the enemy fighters they faced pressed their attacks with ferocious intensity, though at least with the fighters, they could fight back.

There were few "war lovers" among the hundreds of thousands of men who went to war in the bombers. They understood that it had to be done. They *had* to go. They couldn't let the side down. Fortunately most were equipped with that odd rationale that went: "Sure, the guy on my left may get it, and the guy on my right, but nothing's gonna happen to me." They were wrong, but they believed it, and it kept them going back again and again. It was the one great adventure of their lives.

It was during the Spanish Civil War, on 26 April 1937, that the world first witnessed the deliberate large–scale terror bombing of civilians. Luftwaffe Kondor Legion GeneralMajor Hugo Sperrle's Heinkel bombers were ostensibly attacking an important bridge on the River Oca at the Basque town of Guernica. They were operating in support of Nationalist forces near the town. In fact, the German aircrews were participating in an experiment in terror. Their mission was to attempt to destroy the morale of the Government troops and their civilian supporters. They carried great quantities of incendiary ordnance, a weapon clearly unsuited for use against a stone bridge. The bombers attacked the town for 3 1/2 hours in poor visibility. It was Monday, market day in Guernica, and Sperrle sent the raid at noon when most of the population of 7000 was outdoors. In addition to the incendiaries, the bombers brought high explosives, and followed the raid with strafing attacks. 1654 people were killed and 889 were wounded. The town lay in ruins and the event was later remembered in the great painting *Guernica* by Pablo Picasso.

This is a damned unnatural sort of war; / The pilot sits among the clouds, quite sure About the values he is fighting for; / He cannot hear beyond his veil of sound,

He cannot see the people on the ground; / He only knows that on the sloping map / Of sea–fringed town and country people creep/ Like ants—and who cares if ants laugh or weep?
— from 'Unseen Fire'
by R. N. Currey

JUST A HAULING JOB? NOT QUITE.

"War is a nasty, dirty, rotten business. It's all right for the Navy to blockade a city, to starve the inhabitants to death. But there is something wrong, not nice, about bombing that city."
– Marshal of the Royal Air Force Sir Arthur Harris

Right: Ordnance men of the 93rd Bomb Group (H), Eighth USAAF fit tail fins and insert a fuse into a 1000–pound bomb in preparation for a B-24 mission from their base at Hardwick in Norfolk, England, April 1943. Above: Fifteenth USAAF B-24 pilot Stan Staples in the aircraft he flew on his last World War II mission, a supply drop to a British P.O.W. camp near Villach, Austria.

The tumult and the shouting have died away. The B-17s and B-24s will never again assemble into strike formation in the bitter cold of embattled skies. Never again will the musical thunder of their passage cause the very earth to tremble, the source of sound lost in infinity and seeming to emanate from all things, visible and invisible. The great deep–throated engines are forever silent . . .
– from *Heritage of Valor*
by Budd J. Peaslee, USAF (Ret)

COLONEL PEASLEE, air commander of the Schweinfurt attack of 14 October 1943, wrote those words in tribute to the men of the Eighth US Army Air Force who participated in what many historians consider the most savage air battle in history, the second mighty US bombing raid on the Vereinigte Kugellager Fabrik (VKF), Kugelfischer AG (FAG), Deutsche Star Kugelhalter, and the Fichtel and Sachs ball and anti–friction bearing works at Schweinfurt, Germany.

Why did Allied planners conclude that these targets at Schweinfurt were of such importance to the war effort that a maximum effort attack had to be mounted that October day, even though the Eighth Air Force had suffered its worst losses ever when attempting a similar strike on the German town just two months earlier? Virtually all aircraft, tanks, warships, submarines, machines and precision instruments were utterly dependent on anti–friction bearings in their performance. Like the weather, friction was a formidable enemy, as surely as any declared political foe. Germany's entire war machine (like the Allies') literally ran on these bearings, and it consumed them by the multi–millions.

It was known to the planners of Eighth Bomber Command that most manufacturers of Germany's military industrial complex maintained only a small on–hand stock of finished bearings. They knew, too, that an effective attack on the German bearings industry would undoubtedly result in

8

Right: A tense, exhausted crew of an Eighth USAAF B-17G. Just back from a combat mission, they must still attend an interrogation session, always the final duty of the day for Allied bomber crews on their return.

one effect of particular importance to the Eighth Air Force itself . . . a nearly immediate and crippling disruption of German fighter aircraft production. The American planners found that the German anti–friction bearings industry was highly concentrated geographically, with some 73 per cent of her entire bearings output generated by plants in just six cities. Schweinfurt alone produced 42 per cent of all bearings utilized in the German war effort and, as a target, was irresistible.

On 17 August 1943, one year to the day after the first US Eighth Air Force B-17 operation of the war, the first major American bombing raid on the German bearings industry was mounted as part of a two–pronged attack. A combined force of 376 B-17s took their bombs to Schweinfurt, and to Regensburg, where the target was a large and vital Messerschmitt fighter factory. On that day, 315 of the bombers successfully attacked their targets, delivering a total of 724 tons of bombs. Thirty–six heavy bombers of the Regensburg force and twenty–four from the Schweinfurt force (a total of 600 American airmen) fell to enemy flak and fighters, for a staggering 19 per cent loss to the attacking force. Bombing results at Regensburg were judged good, with every significant building in the manufacturing complex badly damaged. The Schweinfurt effort, however, was not as successful, and those responsible for target selection at Eighth Bomber Command knew that the Yanks would have to go back to that town and try again.

The effort of 17 August, while useful and fairly effective, had resulted in losses that were clearly unsustainable. For nearly two months the heavy bomb groups of the Eighth lay incapacitated, unable to bring war to German targets. Grievously wounded, the Eighth slowly regathered strength and, by the second week of October, prepared to return to the fight with a renewed will and greatly increased firepower. On the morning of 8 October it sent a force of 399 heavy bombers to attack targets at Bremen and Vegesack with a loss of thirty aircraft. On the 9th 378 B-17s and B-24s were dispatched to hit targets at Danzig, Gdynia, Anklam and Marienburg, with a loss that day of twenty–eight of the heavies. It was followed on the 10th with an attack (the third major US raid in as many days) by 236 bombers on the city of Münster where another thirty aircraft were lost. Then came a three–day rest, a breathing spell in which the crews of the Eighth could regroup for what they were to face on 14 October. The survivors would always remember it as "Black Thursday."

The decision to return to Schweinfurt on the 14th was made by General Frederick L. Anderson at Eighth Bomber Command Headquarters, code–named Pinetree, at High Wycombe, Buckinghamshire. It was referred to simply as Mission 115. Anderson and his little committee of specialist officers had many factors to consider in its planning: the importance of the target relative to all others, the routes and timing of their attacking force, the German anti–aircraft and fighter defences *en route*, the relative vulnerability of the target factories, the predicted weather for England, the weather for the routes to and from the target and for the target area itself, the types and categories of bombs to be delivered, and the size and nature of the fighter escort needed to shepherd the heavy bombers both outbound and back.

Once Anderson had made the decision to attack Schweinfurt for a second time in a maximum effort, a Warning Order was issued by teletype to the air divisions of the Eighth Air Force across England, alerting them to begin preparations for the raid.

At twenty–five minutes to midnight on 13 October, Field Order 220 clattered from teletype machines at the various Eighth Air Force heavy bomber stations in the English Midlands and East Anglia. The message received at Great Ashfield, Chelveston, Polebrook, Podington, Thurleigh, Bury St Edmunds, Bassingbourn, Alconbury, Grafton Underwood, Molesworth, Kimbolton, Hardwick, possession of the complete Combat Order for Mission 115. The Order provided them with the information that would be the core of the briefings their crews would receive in a few hours, including, but not limited to, the schedules for starting engines, take–offs, assembly times and altitudes, the Initial Point, Mean Point of Impact, Rally Point, routes, bomb loadings and weights, the anticipated enemy flak and fighter opposition.

Lieutenant Raymond W. Wild was a B-17 pilot with the 92nd Bomb Group (H) stationed at Podington, Northamptonshire in the autumn of 1943. Ray was one of the first Eighth Air Force veterans I met and in the course of our many long conversations he was exceptionally articulate in relating his vivid and colourful memories of missions against German targets in what was the most difficult, dangerous period for the American bomber crews in the European Theatre of Operations. Mission 115, the second great Schweinfurt raid, was the third mission of Wild's tour of duty.

"We arrived at Podington and the 92nd Bomb Group in September 1943 and they had us shoot some landings right away. At Podington the runways were built right into the farm, and the farmer was still farming it. The farmer was there, and the farmer's daughter was there. He'd be there farming when we left on a raid, and he'd still be farming when we came back.

"They checked out our crew and assigned us to a squadron, the 325th. They had a wall with names on it — twelve missions, fourteen missions — and MIA, KIA. None of us knew what that meant. They showed us that and then they took us to the ready room, and there was a certain kind of dust in there; I don't know what the hell it was, but I sneezed eleven times in a row. We took our crew out flying formation for a short period of time, according to how fast they needed replacement crews to fly missions.

"When I got to Podington one of the first things I did was to look up an RAF pilot who had been a classmate of mine during training in the States. He and I went out and had a couple of beers with some of his buddies. They felt that we Americans were out of our minds. They had tried daylight bombing and it just wasn't feasible. They said we'd get the hell shot out of us. They were right: on the first few raids we did get the hell shot out of us. But those Limeys did something that sure would scare me — night bombing. They'd come in over a target a minute apart, one guy this way, another guy from another point in the compass. This would scare me to death. They had tremendous intestinal fortitude. They were also realistic in that they couldn't bomb by daylight. Those Lancs were built to carry bombs, and not to protect themselves, while we could. So long as we stayed in tight formation, we could throw a lot of lead out in the right direction at the right time.

"The frightening times of a raid for me were before take–off and after you got back down. In the ready room you were with a bunch of other guys, and you were wisecracking to ease the tension.

"I remember that just before my first raid — the one where you are really frightened to death — I went into the john in the operations tower. Didn't have to go, but just went in and sat on the john. That was when the song 'Paper Doll' had just come out and somebody had written all the words on the wall. Just through nothing but being nervous I sat there and memorized those words. The mission was the 8 October 1943 raid, and it was a rough one. This day I was being sent as co–pilot with Gus Arenholtz, a helluva nice guy who later became a good friend of mine. They were sending me to be oriented by him. We took off in the foulest weather and, when we got over the middle of the Channel, and I was really scared, Gus said to me, 'Take it a minute'. I said 'OK', and took the wheel. We were flying in formation and he reached down and put on flak gloves, a flak suit and a flak helmet, and said, 'OK, I've got it.' So, I reached down and said,

"On arriving at our equipment room we were issued our Mae West life vest, parachute and harness, goggles, leather helmet, gabardine flying coveralls, heated suit, and a steel helmet that had hinged ear flaps to cover our radio headset. We were also given felt heated inserts to cover our feet inside our sheepskin-lined leather flying boots and silk insert gloves to wear under our heated heavy leather gloves. We also picked up our escape kits which contained a silk map which was highly detailed and could be folded quite small to take up very little space. The kit also held a razor, high-energy hard candy, a translation sheet in Dutch, Flemish, French and German, and a plastic bottle and water purification tablets. We left behind our .45 calibre Colt Automatic and shoulder holster which had been issued to us to protect us from the German civilians and the SS. Intelligence had learned that our crew members who carried the weapons were sometimes shot because the presence of the gun gave the enemy an excuse to shoot them. In addition to all of our other gear, we brought our oxygen masks, headsets and throat microphones, all of which were kept in our footlockers. After picking up our flight equipment, a six-by-six truck took us as a crew to our dispersal area and the hardstand where our B-17 was parked. It was about a five minute ride from the hangar and our equipment room. On the way out to dispersal, everyone was quiet. We all had our own thoughts."
– Roger Armstrong, formerly with the 91st Bomb Group (H) Eighth USAAF

'Where the hell is mine?' He said, 'Didn't you bring any?' I said, 'You're breaking me in!' 'Well, don't worry about it,' he said. 'It's gonna be an easy raid.' I said, 'OK, *I'll* hold it a minute,' and he replied, 'No, I've got it.' And I said, 'No, I'll hold it. You take that stuff off. If it's gonna be an easy raid, give it to me.' 'Like hell I will,' he said. Our ship got back with a two–foot hole in one side, one engine shot out, three of the six elevator control cables shot in two, and our radio operator wounded. Because we got back safely and all the crew survived, from then on I sat in that same john every morning, and I still know every word of 'Paper Doll'.

"Many of my mission memories are associated with particular odours. The first time it hit me was in that ready room. It was damp and musty–had probably been that way for months. Then when you went into that briefing hut, and the briefing officers checked you out, you would always smell shaving lotion on those guys. It bothered the hell out of me. You had these heavy boots, heavy pants and jackets, and you opened them up and there was body smell then — not really unpleasant, but not pleasant, because it was connected with the raid. Then we might sit, waiting in the airplane for thirty, forty minutes, and there was a heavy smell of gasoline, but there was a ready room smell in there too, every time. I guess it was the odour of fear. On the runway, and for the first thousand feet or so, there'd still be the gasoline, and the smell of burnt cordite from the Channel on, from the test firing of our guns. The cordite smell was so strong that you'd keep asking the top turret and ball turret gunners to check the engines because you thought of fire. There always seemed to be a kind of haze in the airplane, from the guns going off. But it probably wasn't true.

"Everything was connected to emotion, I guess. You hated to get up in the English fog. You hated to be briefed. You hated to be told where you were going. You wore heavy woollen socks 'cause your feet perspired and they turned to icy–cold sweat if you didn't. You climbed in the truck and they took you over to the officer's mess and there was the odour of powdered eggs. God damn, that was horrible! If you were flying you got fresh eggs. The guys who weren't flying ate the powdered eggs.

"The cold at altitude was incredible. The gunners wore electric suits—blue bunny suits—which they plugged in at their stations, but sometimes the suits would short out and then they were in trouble. Up front we had a heating unit which didn't work too well. At altitude you were nervous and frightened and you would perspire. If you didn't wear gloves the throttles would freeze and get slippery. I used thin kid gloves. They also had fleece–lined gloves, but they were impractical for flying. Coming back we'd take off the oxygen mask and smoke a cigarette, and there was *that* smell, and always the cold sweat smell, until we got back on the ground. But after we landed, there was no gasoline smell, no cordite, no sweat — nothing that wasn't nice. It was all connected with fear and non–fear, I guess."

14 October. "Believe me, I never hope to go through anything comparable to this again and live to write about it. If anyone were to sneak up behind me and bellow 'Schweinfurt' I would probably run screaming down the road. Those of us who were lucky enough to return know now how much body and soul can endure. When you have enough people trying to take that last little hold you have on life away, you really get down to some honest to goodness fighting and will use any measures to strengthen your grip.

"My friend, James 'Tripod' McLaughlin, said to Budd Peaslee, who was the Eighth Air Force commander in the air for this Schweinfurt raid, 'I don't think we are going to make it.' In his heart, I think he knew he was going to make it, or he wouldn't have gone. If someone tells you to get in an airplane, you're gonna bomb Schweinfurt today and you're not coming back . . . Jones is, Smith isn't, Brown isn't . . . hell, you wouldn't go! Who would go? If they'd say, 'Two out of three of you guys will not be coming back today,' you'd look at the guy on your left and the guy on your right and you'd say, 'You poor guys.' That was the whole concept it was built on. Pride made you get into the airplane, more than anything else. Certainly not bravery.

"You were either *stood up* or *stood down*. Stood down meant get drunk because you weren't flying the next day; your name wasn't on the list, which would go up at nine, ten, or eleven p.m. the night before a raid depending on when the word came through from Eighth Bomber Command. You went on the weather over Germany, not the weather over England. Your weather could be really bad, but if the weather over there was good for visual bombing, you went. Sometimes, of course, it wasn't good for visual bombing and you did it by radar.

"Normally, we would be awakened at, say, 1:30 a.m. When you got up and knew you were gonna fly a mission, you hadn't slept all that well. Some will tell you they had, but they hadn't. The deepest sleep you'd get was five minutes before they would wake you. We'd put on our coveralls and shoes and then flying boots over them. We wore our fur-lined flying jackets in to breakfast, as well as our 'hot-shot Charlie' hats—the garrison hat with the grommet removed to give it the 'fifty–mission–crush' look. They would tell us that the truck would be outside in twenty minutes, and we'd go eat breakfast at 2 and be at the briefing at about 2.45. Then we'd go down to the ready room and the navigators went to their own briefing. The enlisted men went to their briefing, which was much shorter than ours. After that, our co–pilot went down with the crew and shaped them up for the mission; made sure they all had their Mae Wests, parachutes and other gear; that the plane was ready to go. He had two to three hours on his hands in which to check things. The pilots just

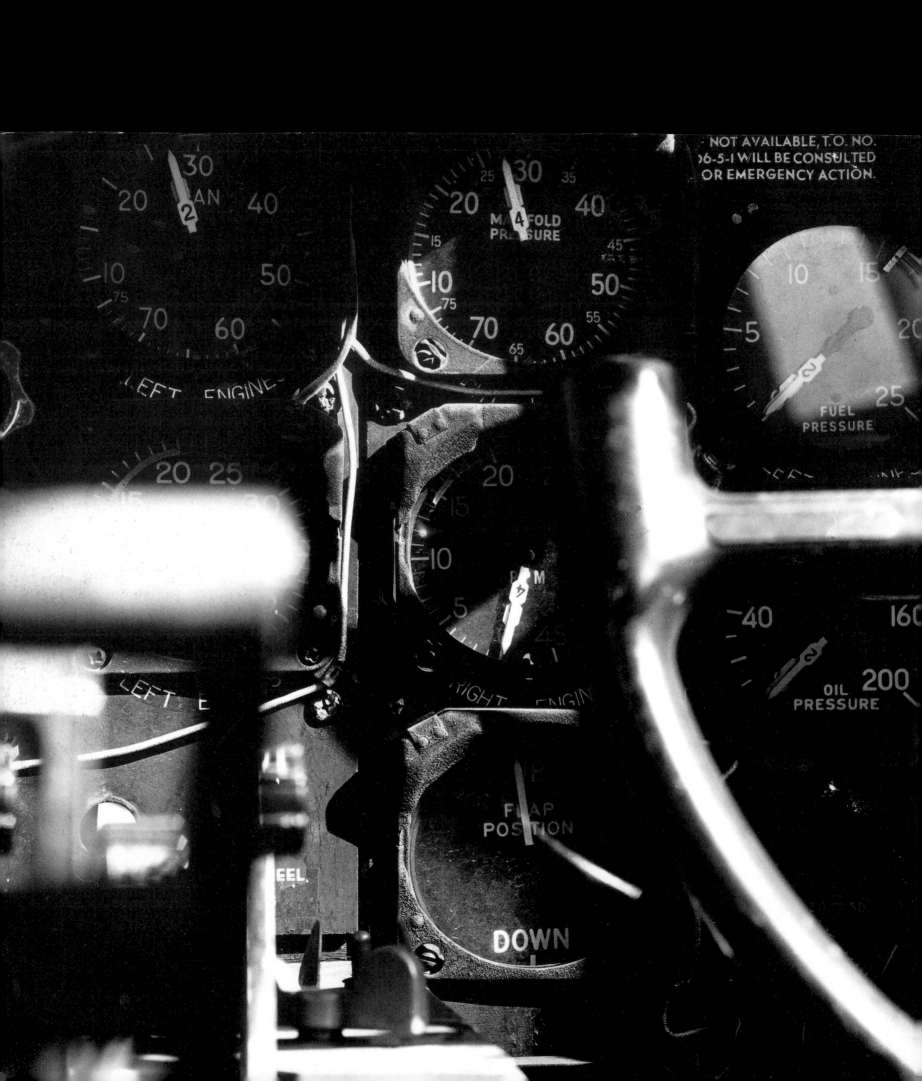

hung around the ready room, shootin' the bull and hoping the mission would be scrubbed and they wouldn't have to go. Then we'd be told that take-off would be at, say, 5 a.m.; the start-engines and taxi times when we all went out and weaved around through the taxi strips, following a certain airplane according to the order for take-off.

"When your turn came to take off, you lined up so that one guy would take off from this side of the runway, and the next guy from the other side. That way you had a better chance of avoiding each others' prop wash.

"The B-17 was a very consistent, dependable airplane. You went down the runway, you hit a hundred and ten, you pulled the wheel back and it would take off. You'd come in over the fence at a hundred and ten, it would stall out at ninety-two, ninety-three. Shot up or in good shape, they were pretty consistent. It was amazing, but it was also a tremendous feeling of comfort.

"The throttle quadrant on a B-17 is shaped like an 'H' with a closed top. The top two are the outboard engines; the bottom two are the inboards. There is a circle a few inches in diameter where half on the right is the number three engine, bottom right is the number four, top left is number one and bottom left is number two . . . so you could just roll 'em going down the runway.

"And boy, did it take punishment. It would fly when it shouldn't fly. There was no reason for it to fly and it would fly. Everybody in the '17 knew that the plane would get back. If they could stay in it, and stay alive, they knew they'd get back. We all had tremendous confidence in the airplane. My crew were convinced there was no other airplane like the B-17, and I could be the worst pilot in the world and they were convinced I was the best. What they were doing, I guess, was convincing themselves that they'd get back.

"I called every B-17 I flew *Mizpah*, Hebrew, meaning 'May God protect us while we are apart

from one another.' The name was actually only painted on the first plane I flew. I flew a total of nine different B-17s. If you got one shot up, maybe they'd repair it or use it for spare parts, and the next day you'd be flying a different airplane. It could have flown ninety-two missions, or this could be its first, but the ground crews were so great, it didn't make much difference.

"They would truck us to the ready room where we would yak, go to the john fifteen times and pick up our Mae Wests, parachute back or chest packs. Most of the pilots and co-pilots wore chest 'chutes because movement in the airplane was so restricted. You kept your harness on but stowed your 'chute right behind your seat so you could grab it and hook it on just before you had to get out. You also picked up your flak suit, which was like a baseball catcher's chest protector. Every time we would change planes, my engineer would change the armour plating under the seats because most of the flak would come up from underneath. A lot of the wounds were castration, so we'd put armour plating under our bodies. Some guys wore a flak helmet. I didn't. I took the inner lining shell out of an infantry helmet and used that. I carried a .45. All the officers . . . the bombardier, navigator, pilot and co-pilot, had .45s. The chief engineer had a tommy gun and the other

Left: Part of the instrument panel of a Boeing B-17G bomber. Below: First Lieutenant Robert F. Cooper, a co-pilot with the 385th Bomb Group (H), Eighth USAAF at Great Ashfield, Suffolk, England in 1944.

Over storm-torn clouds' reflected livid glow / At cold wastelands of dead darkness down below. / That his hellfire may consume this night of horror / He pours pitch and brimstone down on their Gomorrah.
– from 'War'
by Georg Heym

five enlisted men had carbines. We took them, but I
was against them because we had been told that if
you got knocked down, you shouldn't give up to
civilians because they had probably lost a mother,
father, brother, sister, in a bombing raid and would
pitchfork you to death. If you saw military and were
caught, you should give up to them.

"There isn't anybody that wants to get killed.
You'd go into the briefing room and you'd get the
weather officer, intelligence, flak positions, and so
forth. They'd pull the curtain back and you'd see
this line going to the target and you'd think, 'Oh,
boy, I'm not going on this, this'll kill me.' And
then you'd say, 'What I'll do is, I'll wait a while and
then I'll go on sick call and get out of it.' Then
you'd go down to the airplane and you'd figure,
'Well, I'll go on sick call later.' And then you'd see
everybody get in their planes and you'd know they
were just as frightened as you were, and you'd
think, 'What the hell, I'll go about a hundred miles
and find something wrong with the airplane.' But
they had this tradition that an Eighth Air Force
sortie never turned back from the target. So, in the
end, you didn't dare turn back. Pride made you go.

"On instruments, we took off a minute apart;
visually, thirty seconds apart. On instruments we
would take off and go straight ahead until we
broke clear. The weather reports were real bad
because we had so little information. The Germans
weren't gonna give us any. But most of the time,
the reports were fairly close, and when we broke
through we did a circle and looked for the
coloured flares of the squadron and group leaders.
We'd form on the squadron first, then the
squadron commander would form on the group.

"We were off to a comparatively early start
Thursday, October 14th. We reached altitude and
got over the French coast. Somehow, we failed to
pick up the low group of our wing. As we were
lead wing, the Colonel decided we had better fall
in with another group. We did a three–sixty over

the Channel and, seeing a 'bastard group' of
fifteen planes ahead of us that didn't seem to be
attached to anyone, we just tagged along with
them. We picked up enemy fighters at just about
the time our own escort had to leave due to fuel
consumption. We had P-47s and they could only
take us a certain distance in, and you could see
the Hun fighters circling out there, waiting for our
escort to leave. From that moment, it was an
unbelievable horror of fighting. For at least three
hours over enemy territory, we had between 300
and 400 enemy fighters shooting tracer and
rockets at us. You could see those rockets coming.
They were about eighteen inches long, and when
they hit they would explode and set a plane on
fire. Some twin–engined jobs at about a thousand
feet above us were dropping bombs on the
formation. There was no way they could aim at any
one bomber — they were just dropping bombs
into the group. And they were dropping chains or
cables to foul our propellers.

"We were riding Ray Clough's left wing when he
got hit. He dropped out and, I believe, burst into
flames because twenty seconds later I looked
under my left wing and saw a burning wing
floating lazily downward. Oliviero was riding
Brown's wing when Brown got hit by a rocket and
disintegrated: a great sheet of flame and then a
hole in the formation.

"At this point I took over the lead of the second
element just prior to going over the target. Major
Ott was riding on three engines and had to drop
behind. I never saw him again. Even over the
target, the enemy fighters came on through the
flak. It was one of the few times they did that.
They were really first team, those guys. They had
guts and they were damned good fliers. They'd
come in close, and if you straggled by as much as
fifty yards, you'd had it. You'd get hit by three or
four guys. The German fighters normally attacked
you from the best position they could get in,
usually from above. At Schweinfurt, most of them

WESTERN UNION

A. N. WILLIAMS
PRESIDENT

NEWCOMB CARLTON
CHAIRMAN OF THE BOARD

J. C. WILLEVER
FIRST VICE-PRESIDENT

The filing time shown in the date line on telegrams and day letters is STANDARD TIME at point of origin. Time of receipt is STANDARD TIME at point of destination

T3 S5 GOVT WUX WASHINGTON D C 11:08P JUNE 2 1944

MRS ANNA J JOHNSON
1660 INDIANA AVE
LOUISVILLE KY

REPORT JUST RECEIVED THROUGH THE INTERNATIONAL RED CROSS STATES THAT YOUR SON STAFF
SERGEANT CHARLES W JOHNSON IS A PRISONER OF WAR OF THE GERMAN GOVERNMENT PERIOD LETTER
OF INFORMATION FOLLOWS FROM PROVOST MARSHALL GENERAL

DUNLOP ACTING
THE ADJUTANT GENERAL

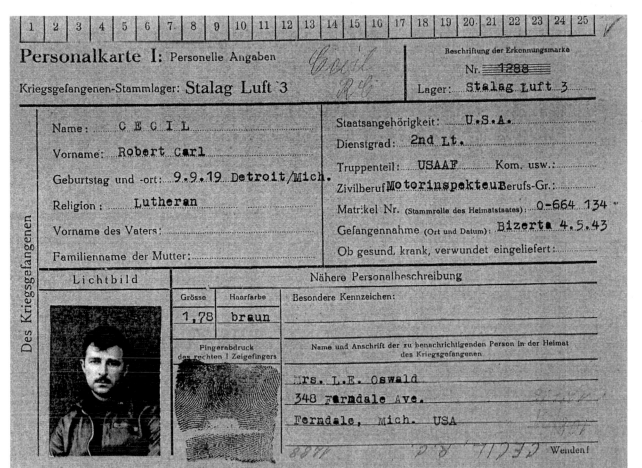

1	2	3	4	5	6	7	8	9	10	11	12	13	14	15	16	17	18	19	20	21	22	23	24	25

Personalkarte I: Personelle Angaben

Beschriftung der Erkennungsmarke

Nr. 1288

Kriegsgefangenen-Stammlager: **Stalag Luft 3**   Lager: **Stalag Luft 3**

Name: **CECIL**

Vorname: **Robert Carl**

Geburtstag und -ort: **9.9.19 Detroit/Mich.**

Religion: **Lutheran**

Vorname des Vaters:

Familienname der Mutter:

Staatsangehörigkeit: **U.S.A.**

Dienstgrad: **2nd Lt.**

Truppenteil: **USAAF**   Kom. usw.:

Zivilberuf **Motorinspekteur** Berufs-Gr.:

Matrikel Nr. (Stammrolle des Heimatstaates): **0-664 134**

Gefangennahme (Ort und Datum): **Bizerta 4.5.43**

Ob gesund, krank, verwundet eingeliefert:

Des Kriegsgefangenen

Lichtbild

Nähere Personalbeschreibung

Grösse	Haarfarbe	Besondere Kennzeichen:
1,78	braun	

Fingerabdruck des rechten I Zeigefingers

Name und Anschrift der zu benachrichtigenden Person in der Heimat des Kriegsgefangenen

Mrs. L.E. Oswald
348 Ferndale Ave.
Ferndale, Mich. USA

Wenden!

see these guys coming in and I'd scrunch down behind the skin of the airplane, which seemed like about 1/10,000th of an inch thick. They'd come in and the rate of closure would be between 400 and 500 miles an hour and I would always wonder if they were gonna break or collide with us. They'd come in shooting. You could always see the wings 'blinking' and you knew they weren't saying 'Hello Charlie' in Morse code. It was worrying because you'd think, if they hit my wingman then I've got to do something about that, but at the same time my oil pressure is up and my cylinder head temperature is up, and I just have too many things to worry about to be frightened . . . except I WAS. That rate of closure. Boy, they were coming in through a hail of lead, and they'd keep on coming. You'd see a wing break off one and he'd spin in, but the rest of them kept on coming. 'My God, he's not gonna break off, he's not . . .' Then, finally, he'd barrel–roll and go over or under us. They pressed home real good.

"The *most* frightening thing about the enemy fighters was not so much their pressing of the attack, but knowing that, having pressed in once, they would peel off, go out to the side, line up and press in again!

"As soon as you hit the coast of France, the first burst of flak would be right off your nose. I don't know how the hell they knew where you were going to be, but they knew. A flak burst that was a near miss produced a sound like pebbles bouncing off a tin roof, and you'd hear a crackling through the airplane where you were getting shrapnel coming through. In an actual hit, you wouldn't be there. With a near miss, there would be a 'whoomf' sound, and the blast effect moved the airplane. Mostly, we only heard the sound of our own engines, except for the 'whoomf' of the near–miss flak bursts, and, of course, the sound of our guns firing. They were REAL loud. Going over the Channel, I'd tell the crew to clear their guns, and this would really break you up! Especially the

came in from the front, forty or fifty abreast. They'd peel off and another forty or fifty would come in from the front, fire and peel off. They were close . . . real close.

"I called out 'friendly fighters' by mistake one time. I couldn't identify an airplane. God, I was horrible at it. Gene Logan, my co–pilot, was real good at identifying 'em. Many times they would barrel–roll through the group. About ninety per cent of the time they weren't shooting at individual airplanes, just going through and pouring into the group . . . unless you straggled. Then they would come get you. The one exception was our lead plane. They always tried to knock down our lead plane because there were usually only two bombsights in a group . . . the leader and the deputy lead plane, and I guess they knew it. I'd look up and chief engineer's turret right behind us. We'd *feel* that. There was a lot of conversation over the intercom . . . 'twelve o'clock level', 'three o'clock high', etc. You couldn't talk across to your co–pilot without using your throat mike. It was even tough when you were down low. The B-17 engines were slightly behind you, but boy, they were noisy.

"The German 88mm guns which were, I think, mostly used for flak . . . they were tremendously accurate, just fabulous. They used two types. One was *predetermined*; the other was *box barrage*. In barrage, there'd be a flock of guns and they'd shoot at one spot in the sky and keep shooting at it. The other was predetermined, aiming at planes. The most frightening was the indeterminate one where they were shooting at a spot in the sky. You had to get through that spot when they weren't shooting. Emden, Kiel, Wilshelmshaven, Munich, Berlin . . . I think they did both at all five of those targets. But Schweinfurt was murder. I'm sure they shot barrage because they had so damned many guns. The German fighters stayed pretty much out of the flak, but on Schweinfurt they *did* come through it. It's one of the few times they flew through their own flak, but they were probably under orders. They were expending themselves. There was no reason for it, really.

"Evasive action? I don't think you can do it against flak. Certainly not against the barrage type. Where are you going to go? Off the target? You can't win, except through luck. Now, for the group as a whole flying up to a flak barrage, if the leader says 'Use evasive action' as the group is starting to get hit, and the group turns off a bit, that's 'evasive action', but I don't think that the people in the low squadron would believe it. Still, for the group it's the best thing you can do.

"That indeterminate flak that was coming up, there was nothing you could do about it. You could take no evasive action against a box barrage. This was something that was gonna happen. It was impersonal as hell. There was only one way to

counteract it, and it began, 'Our Father who art in heaven . . .'

"The main thing was, the lead bombardier did a beautiful job on the target. You were flying on the code of the day, to be at certain points at certain times . . . the Initial Point and then the Mean Point of Impact. You had to fly straight and level for six, seven minutes . . . I've seen it up to twenty–two minutes. You flipped on the automatic pilot and the plane flew wherever the bombardier aimed his bombsight . . . he was flying the plane, really. If the bombing altitude was to be 25,000 feet and the speed 150 indicated, all you did was control the throttles and altitude and he controlled the direction. There was no evasive action. The point was to drop the bombs on the target, and the Germans knew it.

"About three minutes after dropping our bombs we got hit in number three engine. Due to loss of the prop governor control, we couldn't feather it and we began to sweat. We had to use maximum manifold pressure and 2,500 revs to stay in formation. A flak burst just off my side of the nose cracked my windshield into a million pieces. A piece of flak about an inch long and a half inch wide was right in line with my face, but fortunately we had a bullet–resistant windshield and it stuck in the glass. I had the engineer dig it out for me after we landed. We limped home with the formation as far as the Channel and started to let down into the nearest field. We got into Biggin Hill, south–east of London. Seven Forts set down there and they were all shot up. Several had wounded aboard and one had a dead navigator. We had fifteen holes in the ship and only about sixty gallons of gas left.

"There were always runways somewhere in the neighbourhood. If you were coming back from a raid in trouble and needed a field in a hurry, or if you were in soupy weather and couldn't find one, you'd just fly a circle while saying 'Hello Darky, Hello Darky', three times, and give them the code

"During my first [Vietnam B-52] tour in Guam, we were scheduled to be a runway spare, rather than fly the primary mission one day. We would only launch if one of the primary aircraft aborted within fifteen minutes after take off. One of the primary aircraft had an 'unsafe gear' indication and was going to abort if recycling [the landing gear] did not cure the problem. While he was performing this action, we taxied to the end of the runway and were within one minute of launch when the primary called to tell us that his problem was fixed. We were released and taxied back to the parking area. The aircraft we had been about to fly was scheduled as a primary for the evening mission, and we were at an outdoor movie when that mission launched. As the number two bomber lifted off, the left wing fell off and [the plane] exploded in a fireball that was visible over most of the island. I was stunned to learn that the aircraft we had almost launched in earlier in the day was the one that had been lost. None of the crew was ever recovered as the plane went down in the Marianas Trench."
– Larry Henderson, formerly with the 97th Bomb Wing, Second USAF

Above left: Eighth Air Force B-17s dropping their bombs through flak over their German target. Below left: Bombardier Paul Connolly, a member of the 94th Bomb Group (H), on the completion of his 35th mission, the last of his tour, 9 March 1945.

and call letters of the day on your radio. Then this English voice would come on and say 'Hello, Yank! How was it?' He'd be kidding you about it but within thirty seconds he'd have you on radar and would say something like, 'Fly 270 degrees for ninety seconds, then left for 30 seconds on 180 degrees, and there will be an airfield right under you.'

"The papers said we lost sixty Forts on this Schweinfurt trip. At one time all you could see were burning airplanes and parachutes. But then, we knocked a little hell out of them too. My crew got two fighters, giving us a total of three. After Schweinfurt, I thought the rest of our missions would seem easy."

Major–General John M. Bennett, Jr was a commander of the 100th Bomb Group (H), and a Colonel in the Eighth USAAF, based at Thorpe Abbotts, Norfolk in World War II. During his stay there he wrote a series of letters about his war experiences to his father in Texas. These formed the basis of his book *Letters From England*. According to Harry Crosby, former Group Navigator of the 100th and author of *A Wing and A Prayer*, an excellent book about that group, Bennett "came in and quietly but with a glint of steel explained how it was going to be. We would maintain discipline, on the ground and in the air. New crews would be checked out before they could fly. Stood–down crews would have practice missions every day. Pilots who could not fly formation would become co–pilots. Gunners who did not do their duties would become latrine orderlies. Passes, promotions, and medals would be given as rewards, not as routine."

"Back at Thorpe Abbotts, we never understood him. I never saw him take a drink. He never took part in the bragging and flight talk in the Officers Club. I don't think he ever took the grommet out of his hat. He even sat erect."

Major–General Bennett: "The telephone in my quarters rang at five o'clock. I stumbled out of bed and groped my way across the room. 'Briefing at six o'clock, sir.' That was the Duty Officer who had been instructed to call me one hour before briefing.

"This was my first combat mission so my feelings were rather confused. I was very anxious to make the trip, but I was pretty nervous about the whole idea. I put on my heavy underwear and my heavy GI shoes. These shoes are very important in case you have to jump. They won't pop off when your 'chute opens. In case you land in an occupied country and are fortunate enough to escape capture, there will be plenty of walking to do. Breakfast at the Combat Mess is difficult to remember. I recall passing some inconsequential remarks with other flyers around me, but don't believe I ate very much. This is unusual, as breakfast is my favourite meal.

"The briefing room is right next to operations. It resembles a crude theatre with benches lined up one behind the other. There is a guard at the door who checks each individual who enters to see that he is authorized to be there. The end wall of the building is covered with a huge map of Europe. One can see a great deal of detail as the scale is one inch to eight miles. The Intelligence Section has marked in red those areas where anti–aircraft guns are located. Cities like Berlin, Hamburg, and others show up as large red spots. However, the largest red area on the whole map is the highly industrial Ruhr Valley. Naturally, the Germans are making every effort to protect this important district from Allied bombing.

"Up until this time the map is not visible to the combat crews as it is covered by a curtain. There is coughing and shuffling of feet as the crews make themselves comfortable. Suddenly the room comes to a dead silence as the group intelligence officer pulls back the curtain covering the map. Outlined in tape on the map is our course to and from the target for today. The suspense is broken

Above: Major–General John M. Bennett, Jr, a group commander of the 100th Bomb Group (H) in World War II. Far right: A patch of the 713th Bomb Squadron, 448th Bomb Group (H), Eighth USAAF, which was based at Seething, Norfolk. The squadron patches were normally worn by American airmen on their A2 leather flying jackets. Far right bottom: A Royal Air Force recruiting poster of the 1920s.

by a groan from all sides. The target is right in the middle of the Ruhr Valley.

" 'Happy Valley', as it is called by the Eighth Air Force, has a greater concentration of anti–aircraft guns than any other area of equal size in the world. This explains the general sound of disapproval which was expressed at the briefing. Our only comfort was that this was to be a Pathfinder Mission. This means that the target would be covered with clouds and the anti-aircraft gunners cannot actually see you. Of course, they still have their radar–controlled guns which are plenty accurate. Our target was to be the synthetic gasoline plants at Gelsenkirchen.

"After the intelligence officer finished, the operations officer, Lieutenant Colonel Jack Kidd, gave us the time for take-off and instructions for group, wing and division assemblies. He also went over our route into the target and out again, explaining where we would meet our fighter escort for invasion and withdrawal. Next the weather officer gave us complete data on clouds, direction of winds at various altitudes and temperatures. This was followed by the communications officer who gave us the various frequencies and channels to be used on the radio: group frequency, wing frequency, division channel, fighter to bomber channels for air–sea rescue, and many others. You really need a blonde switchboard operator in a Fortress. All of this is followed by the warning, 'Don't use any of these unless absolutely necessary for the success of the mission.' Colonel Harding, the group CO, then gave a few final words of advice about flying in close formation and how to exercise the super–charger regulators in order to keep them from freezing up at 27,000 feet, our bombing altitude.

"The next two hours were the toughest part of the raid. I believe the Bard of Avon expressed it, 'Thus conscience does make cowards of us all.' One is inclined to think of all of the terrible things which might happen. Since this was my first raid, I

Flying in a tail turret is like being dragged backwards in a goldfish bowl. You sit in frustrated silence while the others speculate about what can be seen ahead, and when at last you see what was being discussed, and can give your opinion, everyone else has lost interest.
– from *The Eighth Passenger* by Miles Tripp

GET A GOOD RISE
BY
JOINING THE
R.A.F.
PAY 3/- to 18/- a day

was to fly with Ollen Turner whose home is in Dallas. The engineer–gunner was Sergeant Bennett whose home was in Terrell, Texas. He was very proud of his ship, 'Skipper.' I was told that this was the thirteenth trip for Turner and Sergeant Bennett and also for the airplane. The tail gunner, Sergeant Weatherly from Amarillo, was making his 25th raid. Since this was my first mission, we struck an even balance, one man finishing, one man starting, and two men about halfway through. The rest of the crew were non–Texans (almost foreigners in the Eighth Air Force). These two hours were spent in checking the airplane, collecting personal equipment and putting the guns in the turrets. Everyone is nervous and almost over–polite in attempting to be considerate of the feelings of others.

"It's now 7.40 so we start the engines and at 7.45 we start taxiing. We line up in proper position and at last, at precisely 8:00, the first ship, the Pathfinder, starts rolling. The group assembly is good and we start to climb to altitude. All of this climbing is done over England. As leader of the high squadron, we are in good position to observe the formation. With a heavy bomb load it takes almost one hour and a half to reach 27,000 feet. I have kept myself busy by checking the oxygen of all crew members at 2,000 foot levels above 10,000 feet. This is done by calling on the interphone. Each man checks in, beginning with the tail gunner. If someone doesn't call in, you have to get the 'walk around bottle' of oxygen and go and see what happened, maybe he has passed out. Today everybody seems OK. The rest of the time I spend checking the settings on the turbo–superchargers. These babies are rather temperamental at high altitudes when they get cold. Occasionally I relieve Turner at the controls. However, he does most of the flying. I think that he does not like my formation flying.

"After what seems like years, we reach our altitude. The lead ship fires some identification flares and we assemble with two other groups to form a wing. The wing, in turn, gets into position with the other wings in the division. The division leader likewise must find his proper place in respect to the other divisions. The Eighth Air Force is really out today. Now we are on our way. We leave the English coast just three minutes ahead of scheduled time. The sun is shining brightly and the sky is filled with bombers as far as you can see in all directions. This must be what Seversky means by 'Air Power.' As we near the Dutch Coast, clouds begin to form beneath us. That's good protection from the anti–aircraft; just as we were told by the weatherman.

"High above us at about 35,000 feet we can see some small specks in groups of four. Each of these tiny dots has a white tail feather. This is the most beautiful sight in the world, because we realize that they are Thunderbolts, our fighter escort. The white plumes are vapour trails. We truck drivers really love these boys. They do a swell job. Their rendezvous with us is right on time. In their groups of four, they skate across the sky above us, weaving back and forth. Unfortunately, for them, there's not very good hunting today. Occasionally, a fighter dives down to about 20,000 feet to have a look below. He either sees nothing, or frightens away the enemy because he zooms back up to join his brothers.

"We are now over the Zuider Zee, having flown just north of Amsterdam to avoid the flak. Josh Logan '31 wrote the book for the Triangle Club show, Zuider Zee. Well, no time for Princeton memories now. We are turning to the south–east which will take us into Happy Valley. Something is wrong; cloud cover below is opening up. Hell, it's clear weather ahead. The anti–aircraft gunners will be able to see us plainly. 'Not tho' the soldiers knew, someone had blunder'd.' Tennyson's famous lines do not apply, because we know all right; only too damn well.

"The clear weather becomes artificially cloudy at

About 140 of us crowded into Eglin's Operations Office. We sat on benches and window sills and, when we were more or less quiet, Doolittle began to talk.

The first thing he said was, "If you men have any idea that this isn't the most dangerous thing you've ever been on, don't even start this training period. You can drop out now. There isn't much sense wasting time and money training men who aren't going through with this thing. It's perfectly all right for any of you to drop out."

A couple of the boys spoke up together and asked Doolittle if he could give them any information about the mission. You could hear a pin drop.

"No, I can't–just now." Doolittle said. "But you'll begin to get an idea of what it's all about the longer we're down here training for it. Now, there's one important thing I want to stress. This whole thing must be kept secret. I don't even want you to tell your wives, no matter what you see, or are asked to do, down here. If you've guessed where we're going, don't even talk about your guess. That means every one of you. Don't even talk among yourselves about this thing. Now, does anybody want to drop out?"
– from Thirty Seconds Over Tokyo
by Captain Ted W. Lawson

Left: B-17F Flying Fortresses of the 390th Bomb Group (H), Eighth USAAF, are accompanied by their fighter escort "little friends" while attacking a German target in 1943.

'O curséd were the cruel wars
that ever they should rise! And
out of merry England pressed
many a lad likewise; They
pressed young Harry from me,
likewise my brothers / three,
And sent them to the cruel
wars in High Germany.
– 'High Germany'
Anonymous

our altitude. A huge black cloud, made up of smaller ones, boils up in front of us. This is barrage–type flak. The enemy guesses our target and makes some calculations. He figures where we will have to fly to release our bombs to hit the target. He then aims all his guns at this bomb–release point and fires as rapidly as possible. They seem to be throwing up every bit of scrap iron in the Ruhr. There is a burst directly in front of us and the sound of hail on a tin roof. The bombardier has been knocked down by a jagged piece which does not penetrate his flak suit. The cockpit is filled with smoke and smell.

"Things are beginning to happen in rapid succession. The Pathfinder has been hit and is knocked out of the formation. Our No. 2 supercharger has started to runaway. There is a whirring sound like a siren. I quickly grab the throttle to No. 2 engine. We are now flying on only three engines. We are deputy–leaders so we have to take over. Where the hell is the target? The navigator says we have passed it. During the confusion of changing lead ships, we have missed our aiming point. Turner calls the bombardier to aim at any town or industrial center in the Ruhr. This is our secondary target. Bombs are away. We are now making a turn to the left. 'Let's get the hell out of here,' shouts Turner. With three engines laboring, and by losing a little altitude, we can maintain our air speed. The tail-gunner reports that another plane in our squadron has been hit, has an engine on fire and is diving out of the formation. A few minutes later, far down below us, eight parachutes are reported opening.

"We are now out of the Ruhr. I have flown through 'the valley of the shadow of death'. The 23rd Psalm notwithstanding, I feared plenty of evil. Maybe I should go to church more often."

Dan deCamp was born in Oakland, California in 1960, the son of a navigator who had flown for World Airways and later for Flying Tiger Airlines.

As a teenager he knew that he wanted to be a US Air Force pilot, and joined the Civil Air Patrol where he learned to fly light aircraft and quickly soloed. In 1978 he began studies at the US Air Force Academy at Colorado Springs where he received a degree in aeronautical engineering. From Colorado he moved on to Sheppard AFB, Texas where he earned his wings in the Euro–NATO Joint Jet Pilot Training organisation. Instruction at Sheppard was provided by pilots from nearly all the NATO member nations and Dan trained with student pilots from Germany, Norway and the Netherlands.

His first assignment after pilot training was to the A-10 Thunderbolt program, initially at Holloman AFB, New Mexico, and then at Davis Monthan AFB, Arizona. He flew the A-10 for four and a half years including a posting to RAF Bentwaters/Woodbridge, in Suffolk, England, and finished on that aircraft at Suwon Air Base, Republic of Korea. While at Bentwaters/Woodbridge Dan became aware of the F-117 stealth programme and his interest in joining it was sparked. He was later selected for it and his initial training in the programme was at Tucson, Arizona on the A-7, and from there to the Tonopah Test Range base (TNX) in Nevada, to begin flying the F-117.

"By the time I arrived at TNX, the program had started to emerge from the black world [of Air Force secrecy] into the grey world. In October of 1988 the Air Force had released that first grainy front quarter photo of the F-117, had given some limited details about the airplane and it had acknowledged the existence of TNX as a USAF base.

"Training in the F-117 was a well–conducted affair with civilian instructors presenting the systems classes, as well as about 25 hours in the simulator, which culminated in a check–ride. After that the basic syllabus involved nine rides in the airplane including four basic aircraft handling and instrument sorties for familiarization, one air–refuelling ride, and four surface attack rides in which we practised the core mission of the aircraft: medium altitude laser–guided bomb delivery. These nine sorties were all flown in daylight [unlike in the earlier history of the plane] and accompanied by a T-38 chase plane. With only a few minor exceptions, the F-117 flew very well, with its fly–by–wire control system.

"On 30 November 1990, I was on my way to Langley AFB, Virginia, to meet up with our jets and continue on to King Khalid AB, Khamis Mushait, Saudi Arabia. Khamis Mushait is in the high desert of south–west Saudi Arabia about 75 miles north of the Yemeni border. There, we were outside of Saddam Hussein's SCUD missile range, and well away from Riyadh and Dhahran. Our base was state of the art. The hardened aircraft shelters were pristine, having just been finished by the Dutch contractor. They had not yet been turned over to the Saudis when we occupied them. Each group of shelters included living space, showers, large briefing rooms, and common areas as well as the aircraft shelters and maintenance areas. One of the shelters housed all the administrative functions of the Wing including the Wing Operations Center, Intelligence, and the Mission Planning Cell where I spent all of my extra time.

"I was half asleep when I was awakened and told that I didn't have to worry about the remainder of my alert shift. The Mission Planning Cell was getting quite busy and I began to realize that we were definitely going [to war], and the Air Operations Center (AOC) headquarters in Riyadh for all Desert Storm air operations was obviously going [to war] because we were suddenly faced with numerous target changes.

DESERT STORM – NIGHT TWO "My first turn and it was a failure. It should be noted that all F-117 missions were flown in strict radio silence and I like to think it was much tougher the second night as we had made the Iraqis very angry the previous evening. About half way between my pre–strike refuelling and the target, a security apparatus building on the

Was none who would be foremost / To lead such dire attack; / But those behind cried 'Forward!' And those before cried 'Back!'
– Thomas Babington Macaulay

Left: The patch of the 548th Bomb Squadron, 385th Bomb Group (H), Eighth USAAF, top, which was based at Great Ashfield, Suffolk, and below, that of the 570th Bomb Squadron, 390th Bomb Group (H), based at Framlingham, Suffolk. Above: A World War II RAF aircraft compass.

Below: Eighth Air Force crash crews sweat out the return of their heavy bomb group from a raid in March 1944.

This is the story of *Uncle Tom's Cabin*, a 498th Bomb Group B-29 participating in a raid against Tokyo, on 27 December 1944. It was the lead ship of the third element of nine B-29s of the 72–plane force on that raid. The crew were flying to the target at altitudes varying from about 28,000 to 34,000 feet and were experiencing moderate to intense enemy anti–aircraft fire, but it was fighters, not flak, that ruined their day. Less *continued*

east side of Baghdad, I had an apparent fuel transfer malfunction which would have left me with no fuel just at the point of crossing the border. I immediately turned south–east and headed directly to the tanker. My biggest fear was that I was now no longer following the planned route and that someone on our side might decide that I was a possible hostile. I climbed into our sanctuary block, the airspace block between 22,000 and 24,000 feet, in which our guys were not to engage during the time of our ingress to egress, and hoped for the best. I climbed and slowed down a bit, and the tank started feeding again, leaving me feeling quite sheepish. By this time, however, I was so far out of the flow that there was no longer any hope of turning back and trying to make it to the target.

"My second mission was a comedy of errors. I

found the tanker and then headed for the border. The weather *en route* was horrendous. I spent most of the flight in formation off the number four engine of the KC-135 tanker while the rest of that big airplane intermittently disappeared in the heavy cumulus build–ups. It was the best way for an F-117 to get through areas of thunderstorms or heavy precipitation, as we had no special radar for flying through heavy weather.

"Dodging weather, and accomplishing my last fuel top–off delayed my getting started on the mission. My wingman, who was flying the same route and going to hit the same target group, was supposed to be about seven minutes behind me. I was flowing through the target area with about five other airplanes, all of them flying different routes, but all assigned to hit targets in the same general area.

"Before the mission I had selected an update point on the route at which to correct any navigational errors that might accumulate in the two hours of flight time to the target. I had typed these new co–ordinates into my inertial navigation system (INS) during the pre–flight of my aircraft. Somehow I had mis–typed the update point by a full degree, or about 60 miles north of the intended point. I finally discovered the error when I was about half–way between the group I was supposed to be flying with and my own wingman. My error put me three minutes behind the group. As they attacked the target, the Iraqi anti–aircraft artillery (AAA) opened up and continued to shoot for about five minutes. I got the full force as I came across the target and was lucky to get away with it. I was doing the same thing to my wingman who was now just three to four minutes behind me instead of the five to seven minutes as briefed. I'd screwed up, and probably deserved to face the music.

"The target was a C2 bunker near the town of Abu Gurayb. I was then to make a 100–degree left turn followed by 45 seconds of wings–level time before hitting a second target, another bunker near Taji. The AAA began to die down just as I overflew the target, but then my engine noise triggered it again. I glanced to the rear through each side window and saw what looked like a boat wake of AAA fire spreading out behind the aircraft. In spite of the various distractions, the target was easy to find, and I put the cursors on the Desired Mean Point of Impact (DMPI) which was about ten metres from an entryway to the bunker. I got the weapon off and tracked the target for the terminal guidance phase of the laser–guided bomb, and watched the thing go about twenty metres beyond the cursors and miss the target completely.

"With no time to dwell on the miss, I selected the next waypoint and started that big turn toward the next target. It was a fairly steep banked turn and while in it I looked through the canopy at the barrel of what seemed to be a 37mm gun blasting away at me. I was mesmerized by the sight and thought that turn would never end. I checked my head–up display and it appeared that I had turned about 25 or 30 degrees past the correct heading. In a weapons–delivery mode, the airplane will follow the turrets of the infra–red (IR) targeting system, wherever they are looking. They should be directing at wherever the inertial navigation system thinks the target is. The target was 90 + degrees to my left and, when I changed to the next waypoint, the IR system attempted to look all the way to the left and it jammed in that position. The airplane would have flown in circles all night, so I knocked off the autopilot and turned the plane back towards where the INS said the target was.

"I turned off the offending upper turret and, like magic, the target area popped up in the sensor display through the lower turret, with about ten seconds to go until release point. This target was not so easy; a dirt–covered bunker in an area of dirt with no distinguishing road patterns. I let fly with a 'wish bomb'—wishing that the target would show up between release and when the weapon required guidance before impact. Another miss. In retrospect, it was a pretty callow thing to do, but it was not a populated area, and I was a little jangled having just been shot at for the first time in my life.

"The same crummy weather I had experienced on the way in had now moved up into our post–strike refuelling track. Luckily, I found the tanker and got into contact position while popping in and out of the clouds. Just then another F-117, apparently looking for any port in a storm, stumbled on to our tanker and stayed with me for the rest of the mission. My poor wingman, meanwhile, had to make an emergency fuel divert. Fortunately, he then met another tanker en route and was able to make it back to Khamis Mushait.

"I had been shot at, survived crummy weather and aircraft malfunctions, and had done my share of stupid pilot tricks. Finally, with my third mission I hit paydirt."

than one minute from the bomb–release point Uncle Tom's Cabin was rammed by a Tony flying a frontal attack. The enemy fighter's wingtip opened a gash along the right side of the B-29 from the nose to the leading edge of the wing. The crippled bomber began to slip behind and below the formation and was quickly set upon by several more Japanese fighters. In the next moment she was again rammed by a Tony. This time the bomber lost pieces of her right wing and parts from both engines on that side. She was now descending, massively damaged and nearly out of control when a third fighter, approaching this time from below, rammed her. She entered a spin, but almost miraculously, her pilots managed to regain a measure of control and bring her out of the spin and back onto their intended course, though well below their formation. In the next seven minutes Uncle Tom's Cabin was savaged by more than 30 enemy fighters until finally she could no longer maintain stable flight. With all control lost the big bomber fell vertically from more than 20,000 feet and impacted a few miles outside of Tokyo. Observers in other aircraft of the bomber force saw no parachutes emerge from Uncle Tom's Cabin, but confirmed that, in their final mission, her crew had put up an amazing fight and destroyed at least nine Japanese fighters before being brought down.

– adapted from Aerial Gunners: The Unknown Aces of World War II
by Charles A. Watry and Duane L. Hall

BUMF

Right: Examples of the propaganda leaflet materials dropped over German–occupied Europe by British and American air crews in World War II.

WITH THE GERMAN INVASION of Poland in September 1939, US President Franklin D. Roosevelt made an ardent appeal to the nations involved in the war, and to those about to become involved, to avoid the bombing of undefended cities and towns, and of any targets where civilian casualties might result. Britain, France and, a few weeks later, Germany, all agreed and gave their assurances. RAF Bomber Command found itself encumbered by a bombing policy that was, to say the least, bizarre. It was ordered to refrain from attacking targets of any type on German soil due to the nearly impossible challenge of identifying the purely military ones, and thus avoiding any possibility of hitting civilians. What they could attack were German naval ships moored in harbours or steaming at sea, though not those in port alongside a wharf. They were also allowed to operate over Germany in order to drop propaganda leaflets prepared by the Political Intelligence Department of the British Foreign Office. So, they could hit the German fleet when they could find it, providing no civilian lives were at risk, and they could practise psychological warfare. A joke making the rounds at the time had bomber crews being warned to be sure to untie the leaflet bundles before dropping them lest they hurt someone below. Still, for the leaders in Bomber Command, this odd approach to military engagement came with a silver lining of a sort . . . it bought them time to build strength in manpower, aircraft and ordnance and to attain some vitally needed reconnaissance and training experience.

Bomber Command desperately required reliable intelligence about the German enemy and set out to make the best use of this period during which they were prohibited, for the most part, from doing what they were designed to do. They began, instead, on the first night of the war to carry out long–range reconnaissance flights to Germany, and they continued this intelligence–gathering activity throughout the bitter winter of 1939–40. Flying deep penetration sorties into the German homeland, Armstrong Whitworth Whitley bombers, as well as some Vickers Wellingtons and Handley–Page Hampdens, were utilized to obtain and confirm information about potential bombing targets such as industrial factories, aerodromes, air defences, power stations, roads and rail centres. These trips provided invaluable training and experience for the aircrews in extremely demanding conditions over what for them was largely unknown terrain. The missions were ostensibly for the purpose of distributing anti–Nazi propaganda leaflets over selected German towns. After a week of this pamphleteering, the British public expressed its anger over the policy of bombing the Nazis with leaflets while the Nazis were busy bombarding Poland with the real thing. The reaction brought the leaflet campaign to a swift halt. It was resumed a few weeks later, however, though by that point the British government had concluded that its bombing offensive would have to be cranked up a notch or two. The degree to which the leaflets influenced German public opinion is debatable, but not so the importance to the Royal Air Force of the military intelligence and aircrew experience gained through the missions.

In the effort to deliver some 74,000,000 of the leaflets, the Whitley crews found and brought back urgently needed reconnaissance data. This data, combined with that obtained by the Advanced Air Striking Force in its own reconnaissances over western Germany, greatly aided those who would plan and organize the major attacks that Bomber Command was soon to launch. Operationally, they helped to show that even target cities in the most distant parts of Germany could be reached and hit by the British bombers. RAF navigators faced the challenge of finding their way to and from a range of target sites with a foretaste of the troubles they would encounter many times on future raids. Crews had to operate frequently in dense cloud cover, extreme cold, the murky German black-out, the nerve–wracking enemy searchlights and anti–aircraft fire.

TALIA FARA DA SE

SAFE CONDUCT

The German soldier who carries this safe-conduct is using it as a sign of his genuine wish to give himself up. He is to be disarmed, to be well looked after, to receive food and medical attention as required, and is to be removed from the danger zone as soon as possible.

PASSIERSCHEIN

An die britischen und amerikanischen Vorposten:
Der deutsche Soldat, der diesen Passierschein vorzeigt.

MESSAGE URGENT

du Commandement Suprême

des Forces Expéditionnaires Alliées

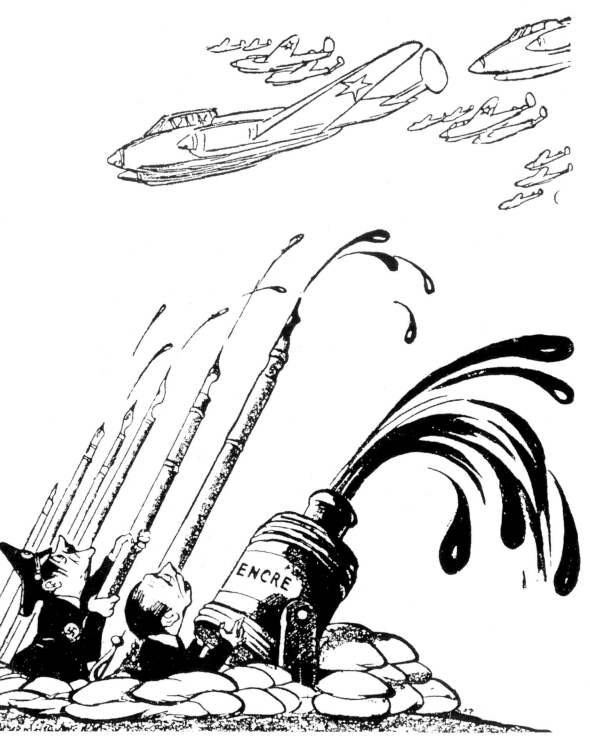

They contended with these difficulties but suffered most from the icy effects of that particularly savage winter. They found that ice would collect to a thickness of six inches on wings and windscreens. As it accumulated, it gradually caused controls to stick, sometimes rendering the aircraft uncontrollable. They were equipped with de–icing gear but it was often ineffective in the conditions they experienced. Equally ineffective was the heating equipment provided in the aircraft. Added to this was the strange phenomenon of fine, rime ice that would penetrate the aircraft, covering the crew with a white powder that froze on their clothing and equipment. Flight instruments became encrusted with the opaque crystalline ice and frequently froze up.

Another aspect of the leaflet raids was the level of endurance they demanded of the crews. Flown at night and in varying conditions, the raids lasted between six and twelve hours and were unequalled as tests of both navigation and endurance.

According to an Air Ministry account of the leaflet offensive, nearly all of the Whitley bomber crews experienced one common problem: it was all but impossible to lower the turret from which the pamphlets were discharged due to the intense cold. The temperature varied between minus 22 and minus 32 degrees centigrade. In one aircraft the starboard engine had to be shut down when it caught fire. The Whitley was then in heavy cloud and approximately six inches of ice had formed on its wings. The aircraft went into a dive and it required the strength of both pilots to pull it out at 7000 feet. They then found that the elevators and rudder were immovable. The wireless operator sent a signal to say that one engine was on fire, and tried to get an immediate "fix" but could not be certain that he was actually transmitting as the glass covering his instruments was thick with ice.

At this point the Whitley was relatively stable but

losing altitude at the rate of 2000 feet a minute. The port engine was stopped and the crew estimated that about four inches of ice was protruding from the inside of the engine cowling. The propeller, the wing leading edges and the windscreen all had a thick ice coating. The pilot ordered his crew to abandon the aircraft but he got no reply from either the front or rear gunners and immediately cancelled the order. It was later discovered that both gunners had been knocked unconscious in the dive and subsequent recovery.

The plane then began a shallow, high–speed dive and the pilots opened the top hatch and a side window to see where they were going. The Whitley broke from the cloud into heavy rain at a height of only 200 feet. The crew saw only thick forest with a small grey patch in the middle, for which they were heading. They skidded the bomber through the treetops and managed to drop it into the small clear field. It careened through a wire fence and skidded broadside into the trees at the far side of the clearing. The engine fire was now extreme and the crew quickly got out of the fuselage and attempted to put out the flames. The pilot found that the extinguisher they carried in the cockpit had discharged in the crash–landing. The wireless operator attacked the fire with the extinguisher from near his crew station.

The bomber had come down in France and, after spending the night in their airplane, the crew was cared for by local inhabitants.

Another Whitley on the leaflet mission that night developed a defect in its oxygen system creating a shortage of supply to the crew. They successfully dropped their propaganda but by that point both the navigator and the wireless operator were suffering from insufficient oxygen and had to lie down and rest on the floor of the fuselage. The cockpit heating was inoperative and the entire crew was suffering from extreme cold and distress. The pilot and the navigator were experiencing the agonizing onset of frostbite as well as a lack of oxygen. On the homeward journey they descended to 8000 feet, but the icing grew worse. All windows were covered. The crew heard ice as it was whipped off the propeller blades against the sides of the nose. The pilot had to move the controls continuously to keep them from freezing up. Still, they made it to base and the bomber landed safely.

A third Whitley on this particular night raid also made a forced landing in France. It was an especially heavy landing and the rear gunner was badly shaken. He emerged from the aircraft and made his way to the nose to have a word with the pilot and found that he was alone. The rest of the crew had bailed out on command of the pilot. Evidently, the intercom had failed and the rear gunner had not heard the order to abandon the airplane, which had somehow landed itself with no one at the controls.

The gunner made his way to a nearby village and came upon his entire crew safe in a café there. They talked about their experiences and the front gunner told how he been unconscious during his parachute descent. He regained consciousness on his back in a field among a herd of curious but friendly cows. The wireless operator, too, managed to land in a field — of curious and definitely hostile bulls. In full flying kit, the radioman rapidly made for and cleared a four–foot fence. The pilot landed unhurt and the navigator incurred only a sprained ankle. After their reunion in the café the crew were taken to a French hospital where they were treated and released. They were returned to their unit that same day.

Clearly, the principal danger faced by the crews on these early leaflet raids was weather, but there was the occasional interference by a German night fighter. In an incident where a Me 109 closed to within 500 yards of a Whitley whose leaflets were about to be dropped, the rear gunner reported the presence of the enemy fighter to the pilot. The pilot instructed the rear gunner to hold his fire while the navigator and wireless operator

"We cannot tell whether Hitler will be the man who will once again let loose upon the world another war . . . or whether he will go down in history as the man who restored honour and peace of mind to the great Germanic nation and brought it back serene, helpful and strong, to the forefront of the European family circle."
– Winston Churchill, 1935

"I give you my word that there will be no great armaments."
– Stanley Baldwin, Prime Minister, October 1935

"War will not come again . . . [Germany has] a more profound impression than any other of the evil that war causes; Germany's problems cannot be settled by war."
– Adolf Hitler, August 1934

"In spite of the hardness and ruthlessness I thought I saw in his face, I got the impression that here was a man who could be relied upon when he had given his word."
– Neville Chamberlain, Prime Minister, September 1938

"Peace with honour . . . I believe it is peace for our time."
– Neville Chamberlain, Prime Minister, September 1938

"There will be no great war in Europe in 1939."
–[London] Daily Express, 2 January 1939

"No enemy bomber can reach the Ruhr. If one reaches the Ruhr, my name is not Göring. You can call me Meyer."
– Hermann Göring, addressing the German Air Force, 1939

Left: Editorial opinion by the Soviet cartoonist team, The Kukriniksi, in 1941.

completed the leaflet drop. After a bit the rear gunner reported that it would no longer be necessary for him to take action against the 109 as it had flown into the cloud of released leaflets and had dived away.

Flight Lieutenant Tony O'Neill was one of the first RAF pilots to participate in the leaflet raids. R.D. 'Tiny' Cooling, a former Wellington pilot, describes O'Neill's first propaganda attack. "With the outbreak of war not yet twelve hours past, Bomber Command had already launched penetration raids over Hitler's Reich. The first, by a Blenheim IV of No. 139 Squadron, was a photo–reconnaissance mission to Wilhelmshaven. That same night ten Armstrong Whitworth Whitley crews were briefed for sorties to Hamburg, Bremen and the Ruhr; their task to drop thirteen tons of paper, some six million leaflets, on these cities in north–west Germany. In part it was a propaganda mission, in part a demonstration to the population that the Royal Air Force could roam freely through German skies notwithstanding Hermann Göring's boast that no enemy bomber would ever penetrate the airspace of the Fatherland.

"Preparation began three days before. A runway was being laid at Linton on Ouse, home to No. 58 Squadron's Whitley Mk IIIs, so ten aircraft, three from No. 51 Squadron and seven from No. 58, were detached to Leconfield to take on their paper load. Code–named 'Nickels' these leaflets would become familiar to bomber crews in all theatres of the War. In obscure Oriental languages they would flutter down over Japanese–occupied territories; over North Africa and the Western Desert they would invite Axis troops to surrender; over occupied Europe they took the form of mini–newspapers like *La Revue de Monde Libre* or its equivalent in Dutch, Flemish and German. On 3 September it was a warning addressed to the German people, a forecast of things to come.

"The Whitley was a twin–engined bomber which

34

had entered RAF service in 1937. The Mark III was powered by Armstrong Whitworth's 845 hp Tiger engines which had a disconcerting habit of blowing off cylinder heads, even complete cylinders, punching holes in the long chord cowlings. Deliveries of the later and much more reliable Merlin–powered Mark V had only begun days before in August.

"Briefing was in the late afternoon, take–off at dusk. The route ran from Leconfield to Borkum, an island off the estuary of the Ems, south along the frontier of Holland to Essen and then along the Ruhr Valley, scattering bundles of leaflets through the flare chutes of the bombers. The weather forecast, unaffected by security, stemmed from observations less than twelve hours old. Intelligence was a different matter. Information about searchlights, guns and balloons was based on conjecture and deduction. Navigation would be by dead reckoning aided by any trustworthy radio bearings coaxed from the atmosphere. Release height was set at 16,000 feet. Into the gathering darkness the Whitleys crossed the Yorkshire coast and headed out over the North Sea on their way, for the first time, to Germany.

"The island of Borkum lay below, a black shadow fringed with a grey lace of surf. Cloud covered the German coast, spreading across the hinterland. An unpractised searchlight crew probed their beam through a distant break in the stratus sheet. Flight Lieutenant O'Neill sat watching the instruments glowing green in the dark, glancing at the port engine and its spinning propeller. Gradually, G–George climbed to the selected height. The crew were in their oxygen masks, which were uncomfortable but bearable, and it was cold.

Four hours out and the Whitley was over the Ruhr. A few heavy shells burst in tiny red sparks in the distance. Inside the gloom of the long metal fuselage the crew began posting bundles of leaflets through the flare chute. There was no oxygen in its vicinity and there were no portable oxygen bottles.

In less than ten minutes the two men were exhausted. Two others took their place while those relieved went forward to plug into the main oxygen supply and refresh themselves for a further spell. It was then that the port engine showed the first signs of failure.

"The choice was clear. Two hours to the southwest lay France and friendly territory. There was no point in risking aircraft and crew in a flight through hostile air space, steadily losing height, then to face the North Sea on a single engine. O'Neill headed towards Rheims, discharging the last few bundles of leaflets as he went. Unfortunately, the route lay across neutral Belgium but an aircraft in trouble could expect more consideration than one deliberately violating the frontiers of a non–combatant nation and total cloud cover beneath would help them. The Whitley droned on across the Belgian border, past Liège, into France, descending slowly. Then the port engine failed completely, its propeller windmilling in the slipstream (the day of the feathering airscrew still lay in the future). The starboard engine began showing signs of strain. A landing could not long be delayed, but it was still dark. The cloud layer stretched above them now and ground detail was almost invisible. O'Neill launched a flare. In its light he identified one field large enough for a wheels–up landing. It was nip–and–tuck to line up and creep in over the hedge. A railway embankment loomed up but he was committed. With a loud thump, and the tearing of metal, G–George skated across a vegetable patch. Group Captain O'Neill, DFC, now retired, recalls cabbages bouncing about the cockpit like short–pitched cricket balls as the broken bomb–aiming window sheared them off like a harvester's knife. The crew emerged unharmed. They had been in the air for seven and three quarter hours.

"The silence was profound, almost oppressive. An erratic ticking from metal contracting within the cooling engine and the subdued voices of the crew

"The Americans cannot build aeroplanes. They are very good at refrigerators and razor blades."
– Hermann Göring, to Hitler, 1940

"I'm an experienced fighter pilot myself. I know what is possible. But I know what isn't too... I officially assert that American fighter planes did not reach Aachen... I herewith give you an official order that they weren't there."
– Hermann Göring, when told that an American fighter had been downed over Germany, 1943.

"Defeat of Germany means defeat of Japan, probably without firing a shot."
– President Franklin Roosevelt, July 1942

"The entry of the United States into the war is of no consequence at all for Germany . . .The United States will not be a threat to us for decades- not in 1945 but at the earliest in 1970 or 1980."
– Adolf Hitler, 12 November 1940

Above left: A 1943 RAF leaflet in a "news journal" format for the people of France. Below left: RAF personnel preparing an Armstrong Whitworth Whitley bomber for a leaflet raid early in World War II.

were the only sounds. As the daylight increased, some men emerged from the darker edges of the field and approached cautiously.

"G–George lay inert. The Whitley's tailplane was festooned with leaflets in German gothic script where the slipstream had trapped them. It was some time before the group of French farmworkers could be persuaded that it was the Royal Air Force which had dropped in on them. From then on the warmth of the welcome became overwhelming. They had landed close to the village of Dormans, near Epernay in the heart of the Champagne country. As news spread, the village was *en fête*. Eventually transport was found to ferry the fatigued crew to Rheims where a telephone call to Linton notified the squadron of their situation. Finally, the bliss of bed and sleep. On 5 September, a DH Rapide flew Flight Lieutenant O'Neill and his crew to Harwell and they were soon back at Linton. Only G–George did not return.

"On 9 April 1940 German forces invaded Denmark and Norway; the 'Phoney War' was almost over. Since that first sortie the number of leaflet raids had risen to 69. Fourteen aircraft were lost. Severe weather caused a four–week break in operations, and over ten days around Christmas and the New Year, Bomber Command flew only shipping searches, but on the night of 12–13 January 1940, Whitleys carried nickels to Prague and Vienna. At the same time Wellingtons and Hampdens joined the fray, in their initial night operations. On 10 May the Western Front erupted as the Luftwaffe savaged Rotterdam. On 11 May Bomber Command carried the first bombs to mainland German targets. Leaflets now took second place. But these operations had been immensely valuable. At low cost a basic cadre had been created upon whose experience the development of the bomber offensive was to build. That warning carried by Tony O'Neill was to prove justified."

"On the night of 8–9 September 1942, I was flying as

navigator in Wellington 1342. The target was Frankfurt. Crossing the city we were coned in searchlights and came under intense anti–aircraft fire. We were hit and the starboard engine lost power. We were unable to maintain course. We were hit again and found that we were losing fuel rapidly. We could not maintain altitude and it was obvious that we wouldn't make England and our base. We crossed out over the coast and took up ditching positions. The wireless operator sent out a distress signal on the Mayday wavelength and clamped down his key. Shortly thereafter, as we were still airborne, he went back to his seat and tapped out the SOS again. I reminded him to bring his Very pistol back with him. While climbing over the main spar he slipped and must have squeezed the trigger as a couple of stars shot past my face, burnt through the aircraft fabric and, in so doing, set fire to some leaflets which had blown back during the dropping operation. Between us, we beat out the flames and again took up our ditching positions.

"It was quite misty, and, while holding off just above the water, the starboard engine suddenly cut out; the wing dropped and struck the water, and the poor old Wimpy broke her back. The lights went out and the IFF blew up in a blue flash. I was trapped, but eventually managed to struggle free and was washed out of the fracture in the middle of the fuselage. As I emerged, a couple of packages floated up beside me and I tucked them under each arm and pushed off on my back.

"In my hand was a Woolworth's torch which was switched on. I heard voices calling but I couldn't tell from which direction. The pilot, bomb aimer and wireless operator had got into the dinghy and, guided by my torch, came alongside me. The wireless op seized me by the hair and the others hauled me into the dinghy. Apparently the rear gunner had gone down with the tail.

"It was now 4.30 a.m. and quite dark. We baled water from the dinghy and made ourselves as comfortable as possible. At about 6.30 we heard the sound of an engine and saw a launch in the distance. Not knowing whether it was one of ours or a German, we fired off a marine distress signal. We assumed the launch hadn't seen us or our signal, as it turned and disappeared from view. Five hours later we again heard and saw a launch. The bomb aimer tried to fire another distress signal, but the igniting tape broke so he used his thumb nail to ignite the flare, and burnt the palm of his hand in so doing. The launch saw our signal and headed towards us. As it approached we saw the RAF roundels on the hull. The launch crew put out a scramble net over the side and with assistance we climbed aboard. They told us that when we first saw them at 6.30, they were recalled due to a naval action taking place in the vicinity (about ten miles from the Channel Islands). When they got back to their base, their CO sent them out again immediately. They had plotted our position from our Mayday signal. We were given dry clothes, rum and hot coffee by the launch crew as we headed for the Needles on the Isle of Wight."
– John Holmes, formerly with Nos. 102 and 142 Squadrons, RAF

"The bus made its way slowly to Madingley along the winding country roads, through villages undisturbed by the passage of time, full of mellow stone and thatched cottages. It was raining fitfully and as I peered through the raindrops on the bus window, my mind was straining to remember the events that led up to fifteen Cheddington airmen being buried in that military cemetery, and two more being listed on the Wall of Missing. Nine of those still buried there had been from my unit, the 406th Bombardment Squadron, Eighth US Army Air Force.

"There was Lieutenant–Colonel Earle J. Aber, Jr, our squadron commander. I don't think anyone who had been in the squadron will ever forget how his remains had come to be buried in this hallowed ground, which had been donated by Cambridge

I know that I shall meet my fate
Somewhere among the clouds above;
Those that I fight I do not hate,
Those that I guard I do not love;
My country is Kiltartan Cross,
My countrymen Kiltartan's poor,
No likely end could bring them loss Or leave them happier than before. Nor law, nor duty bade me fight,
Nor public men, nor cheering crowds,
A lonely impulse of delight
Drove to this tumult in the clouds;
I balanced all, brought all to mind,
The years to come seemed waste of breath,
A waste of breath the years behind
In balance with this life, this death.
– 'An Irish Airman Foresees His Death'
by W. B. Yeats

In its psychological warfare operations in World War II, the US Eighth Army Air Force dropped a total of 1,493,760,000 propaganda leaflets over German–occupied Europe.

Left: In late January 1945 the Eighth Air Force carried out a raid in which its heavy bombers first dropped their bombs on a target at Merseburg, Germany, and then released containers of propaganda leaflets. The containers were set to burst at an altitude of 6000 feet, scattering the leaflets over the target area. The bomb explosions on the ground are visible between the leaflet canisters.

Above: Captain Brian Gunderson was a navigator and radar bombardier and was assigned to the 406th Bomb Squadron, 492nd Bomb Group (H), Eighth USAAF. Their black–painted B-17s flew night leaflet operations from Cheddington, Buckinghamshire. Far right above: R.D. "Tiny" Cooling, a Wellington pilot in WWII and in 1999. Far right: 422nd Bomb Squadron, 305th Bomb Group (H) Lieutenant Colonel Earle Aber (left) and two members of his crew at their Chelveston base in Northamptonshire.

University to the American Battle Monuments Commission. Just as the bus arrived at the cemetery, the rain stopped and the sun broke through and shone brightly on the 3811 white crosses and Stars of David headstones marking the graves of American servicemen from every state, the District of Columbia, Puerto Rico, and the Philippines.

"As I wandered along the paths, looking at each perfectly manicured plot for the graves of the airmen who had been stationed at Cheddington, I found that my task had been made easier by the thoughtful Cemetery Superintendent and his staff who had marked all fifteen graves with a miniature US flag. I found the simple white cross with the inscription EARLE J. ABER, JR., LT. COL., 406 BOMB SQ., 305 BOMB GROUP (H), WISCONSIN, MAR. 4, 1945. What it didn't say was that he had been born on 19 June 1919, in Racine, Wisconsin. Young in years, he had been endearingly known as 'The Old Man' by all of us in the squadron. Like so many squadron and group commanders in Eighth Air Force units during World War II, he had catapulted to the top as the result of a combination of circumstances. He had been a top–notch pilot who had survived almost fifty night combat missions. Group and Wing Headquarters had recognized his operational and leadership qualities by making him the Operations Officer and promoting him to the rank of Major. And finally, and this happened all too often during the war, he had become the Squadron Commander when his predecessor had crashed and was killed. In Lieutenant–Colonel Aber, the 406th had an outstanding leader with infectious energy and inspirational leadership. He was well liked by all his personnel, in spite of the high standards and constant demands for excellence on the part of air crew and ground crew alike.

"I had flown my 51st, and last, combat mission as his navigator on the night of 5 February 1945 when we went to Frankfurt. We had been targeted against one of the largest and most heavily

defended cities in Germany and had expected to encounter intense anti–aircraft fire and nightfighter activity from the Luftwaffe, but it turned out to be a relatively uneventful flight, for which I was extremely grateful. That was not the case a month later, on the night of 4 March, when Lieutenant–Colonel Aber decided to fly with a 'make-up' crew (personnel who usually flew with a regular crew, but had missed a previously scheduled mission for some reason, and were trying to catch up with their fellow crew members so they could finish their tour together).

"This mission was expected to be a 'milk run' (an easy trip) to the Netherlands, dropping leaflets on Amsterdam, Utrecht and Rotterdam. The flight out of England and over the targets was routine, and the crew could visualize the news leaflets fluttering down to be eagerly picked up the next morning by the Dutch people.

"Only two weeks earlier, on 14 February, the Dutch Prime Minister, Pieter Gerbrandy, had visited Cheddington and, in a highly emotional speech, told the 406th Squadron how much it meant to the Dutch populace to receive the leaflets with their accurate recounting of war events.

"Shortly after Lieutenant–Colonel Aber had turned the B-17 westward, after the last leaflet bomb had been dropped, and started the slow descent toward the designated entry point into England at Clacton–on–Sea, a series of events came together to produce one of the most ironic endings to an Eighth Air Force bomber mission of the war. In the days preceding this mission, the German Air Force had cleverly used Ju 88s at night to make hit–and–run bombing missions against airfields just inside the east coast of England, usually when RAF bombers were returning from their own raids, in order to add further confusion to the situation. After several nights of such activities, the British anti–aircraft batteries along the coastline were understandably tired, frustrated, and 'trigger–happy'. Unknown to Lieutenant–Colonel Aber and his crew, which included co–pilot Lieutenant Maurice J. Harper, and the navigator, Captain Paul S. Stonerock, who also planned to make this flight his last mission, the Ju 88s had carried out another attack and were heading back to Germany.

"As the B-17 passed through 10,000 feet on the descent, a loud noise was heard and the plane shook violently. The crew didn't know what had happened. They first thought that they had collided with another aircraft. Then the plane was hit again, and all aboard quickly realized that the British anti–aircraft batteries had zeroed in on them instead of on an outgoing Ju 88. With engines on fire and flight controls shot away, Lieutenant–Colonel Aber and Lieutenant Harper struggled to keep the plane in level flight. Finally, Aber, in a strong, unemotional voice, directed the crew to bail out. Miraculously, one by one, the crew was able leave the bomber. In some cases, their parachutes opened only seconds before they touched down on the marshy land near the cold and unforgiving North Sea. All, that is, except Aber and Harper. Time had run out for them before they could leave the plane. The rest of the crew saw a fireball as the stricken aircraft crashed into the ground nearby. The next day, when search crews went to the crash site, all they found of this great airman and outstanding commander was a hand with his ring on it.

"As I prepared to leave Lieutenant–Colonel Aber's grave site to rejoin the others, I found myself saluting and saying a few words of prayer. After we had climbed aboard the bus for the return trip to Luton, I looked back across this beautifully landscaped and very special bit of England, and Thornton Wilder's words came to mind: 'All that we can know about those we have loved and lost is that they would wish us to remember them with a more intensified realization of their reality. What is essential does not die but clarifies. The highest tribute to the dead is not grief but gratitude.' "
– Brian Gunderson, formerly with the 305th Bomb Group (H), Eighth USAAF

39

LEARNING CURVE

At the start of the Battle of Britain in July 1940, British Prime Minister Winston Churchill, still smarting from the setback at Dunkirk, wrote to Lord Beaverbrook, his Minister of Aircraft Production: ". . . when I look round to see how we can win the war I see that there is only one sure path . . . and that is absolutely devastating, exterminating attack by very heavy bombers from this country upon the Nazi homeland. We must be able to overwhelm them by this means, without which I do not see a way through."

Right: *Yankee Doodle* was a popular song of the American Revolutionary War. It was also the name of a B-17 of the 97th Bomb Group (H), one of twelve that took off from an airfield at Grafton Underwood in Northamptonshire on 17 August 1942 to attack the rail yards at Rouen, France in the first American heavy bomber raid of World War II. In addition to its bomb load, *Yankee Doodle* carried Ira Eaker, the General officer commanding Eighth Bomber Command, the US strategic bombing force in the European Theatre of Operations.

SHORTLY BEFORE SEVEN in the evening of 17 August 1942, all twelve of the 97th Bomb Group B-17Es that had taken off from a base at Grafton Underwood, Northamptonshire 3 1/2 hours earlier, were sighted from the control tower. They approached Grafton from the west and in the next few minutes all landed, having returned safely from the US Eighth Army Air Force's first heavy bombing raid of World War II.

Their target that summer afternoon had been the huge Rouen—Sotteville rail marshalling yards near the French coast. Twice in the preceding week the raid had been scrubbed due to what the mission planners decided was unacceptable weather.

The B-17s on the Rouen mission that day all had nicknames. They were called *Yankee Doodle, Dixie Demo, Johnny Reb, Big Punk, The Big Bitch, Heidi Ho, Birmingham Blitzkrieg, Butcher Shop, Prowler, Baby Doll, The Berlin Sleeper* and *Peggy D*. Colonel Frank Armstrong had led the mission in *Butcher Shop*, which was piloted by Major Paul Tibbets. In a touch of irony Tibbets was to be instrumental in ending the war when, on 6 August 1945, he commanded the B-29 *Enola Gay* on the mission to drop the first atomic bomb on Japan.

Flying in *Yankee Doodle* was Brigadier—General Ira C. Eaker, Commander of Eighth Bomber Command, the new kids on the block, untried and unproven. It was Eaker whose speech at a dinner in his honour shortly after arriving in England had consisted of, "We won't do much talking until we've done more flying. We hope that when we leave, you'll be glad we came. Thank you."

Ira Eaker had come to England in February 1942 at the head of a small group of US Army Air Force officers to work with the British in arranging for the presence of the first American combat flying units to be based there. He and his staff focused immediately on three needs:

1. To mount a bomber offensive against German—occupied Europe in conjunction with the RAF.

2. To begin fighter operations in conjunction with the RAF — at first in defence of the British Isles and later in the escort of daylight bombers.

3. To organize the logistical support required to meet the first two needs.

He was soon to become embroiled in a heated controversy over the method the USAAF intended to use in its bombing activity. He and Major—General Henry "Hap" Arnold, then head of the US Army Air Forces, were key advocates of daylight bombing, a thing that had been tried by the Royal Air Force and rejected after painfully unsuccessful efforts and their attendant losses.

British doubts about the American daylight bombing approach were publicly expressed on 16 August by Peter Masefield, air correspondent of the *Sunday Times*. Masefield welcomed the prospect of the Americans joining the British in the air war against Germany. He struck out at the B-17 and B-24, though, as being, in his opinion, unsuited for bombing over heavily defended enemy territory: "American heavy bombers — the latest Fortresses and Liberators — are fine flying machines, but not suited for bombing in Europe. Their bombs and bomb loads are small, their armour and armament are not up to the standard now found necessary and their speeds are low." In that the American bombers were certainly not suited (nor designed) for night bombing, Masefield concluded that the best use to be made of them would be Atlantic anti—submarine and shipping patrols. The next day Hap Arnold read the Masefield column and wired Major—General Carl Spaatz for the facts as Spaatz knew them. Timing being everything, Spaatz was, on this occasion, in a position to answer Arnold with an actual combat report for the Rouen mission, and a relatively good one at that.

One British newspaper took the position that "it was a great pity the Americans hadn't seen fit to build Lancasters, Britain's finest bomber, and fly them by night instead of clinging to the discredited theory of daylight raids." Prime Minister Winston Churchill agreed, and managed to convince

Right: World War II commander of the US Army Air Forces, Major–General Henry H. Arnold. Below: Brigadier–General Ira C. Eaker, who led Eighth Bomber Command in the European Theatre of Operations. Below right: Air Officer Commanding–in–Chief, Air Marshal Sir Arthur Harris, Royal Air Force.

"When the mission has gone the ground crews stand about looking lonesome. They have watched every bit of the take–off and now they are left to sweat out the day until the ships come home. It is hard to set down the relation of the ground crew to the air crew, but there is something very close between them. This ground crew will be nervous and anxious until the ships come home. And if the *Mary Ruth* should fail to return they will go into a kind of sullen, wordless mourning. They have been working all night. Now they pile on a tractor to ride back to the hangar to get a cup of coffee in the mess hall. In the barracks it is very quiet; the beds are unmade, their blankets hanging over the sides of the iron bunks. The pin–up girls look a little haggard in their sequin gowns. The family pictures are on the tops of the steel lockers. A clock ticking sounds strident."
— from *Once There Was A War* by John Steinbeck

President Roosevelt to halt the daylight bombing. Lieutenant–General Ira Eaker wrote: "My most unforgettable meeting with the Prime Minister occurred at the Casablanca Conference. A cable had come to me at my Eighth Air Force Headquarters near London from General H.H. Arnold, Commanding General of US Army Air Forces, directing me to meet him at Casablanca next day. When I arrived after a night flight and reported to him, I could see at once that he was unusually disturbed and unhappy. There was no vestige of the normal, smiling disposition which had won for him the nickname of 'Hap' while a cadet at West Point. He said, 'Churchill got an agreement from President Roosevelt that your Eighth Air Force will stop daylight bombing and join the RAF in night bombing . . . what do you think of that?' I said, 'General, that is absurd; it represents complete disaster. It will permit the Luftwaffe to escape. The cross–Channel operation will then fail. Our planes are not equipped for night bombing; our crews are not trained for it. We'll lose more planes landing on that fog–shrouded island in darkness than we lose now over German targets. The million men now standing on the "Westwall"— anti–aircraft, fire wardens and bomb repair squads— can now go back to work in the factories or make up another sixty divisions for the Russian front. Every time our bombers show on radars, every workman in the Ruhr takes to the shelters. If our leaders are that stupid, count me out; I don't want any part of such nonsense.'

"When I paused for breath, Arnold said, 'I know all that as well as you do. As a matter of fact, I hoped you would react that way. The only chance we have to get that disastrous decision reversed is to convince Churchill of its error. I have heard him speak favourably of you. I am going to try to get an appointment for you to see him; stand by and be ready.'

"That evening I was advised that I was to see Mr. Churchill at 10.00 a.m. the next day. Shortly after I was admitted to his villa, he came down the stairs, resplendent in his Air Commodore's uniform. I had been told that when he was receiving a naval person, he wore his Navy uniform — the same for the other services — but this was the first time I had seen him in Royal Air Force uniform. This struck me then as a good omen.

"The P.M. said that he understood from General Arnold that I was very unhappy about his suggestion to our President that my Eighth Air Force join the RAF Bomber Command in night bombing, abandoning the daytime bomber effort. Without awaiting my response, he continued, 'Young man, I am half American, my mother was a US citizen. The tragic losses of so many of your gallant crews tears my heart. Marshal Harris tells me that his losses average 2 per cent while yours are at least double that and sometimes much higher.'

"I replied to Churchill that I had learned during the past year, while serving in Britain, that he always heard both sides of any controversy before making a decision and for that reason I wished to present a brief memorandum, less than a page long (it was well known that he seldom read a 'minute' of greater length, having it 'briefed' instead). This I hoped he would read.

"Mr. Churchill motioned me to a seat on a couch beside him and began to read, half aloud, my summary of the reasons why our daylight bombing should continue. At one point, when he came to the line about the advantages of round–the–clock bombing he rolled the words off his tongue as though they were tasty morsels. When he had finished reading the memo, he handed it back and said, 'Young man, you have not convinced me you are right, but you have persuaded me that you should have further opportunity to prove your contention. How fortuitous it would be if we could, as you say, 'bomb the devils round the clock.' When I see your President at lunch today, I shall tell him that I withdraw my suggestion that US bombers join the RAF in night bombing and that I

"For us the war was very new. The word was that the average life expectancy for a tail gunner in combat was thirty seconds. All kinds of rumours were floating around. England was very different from the US. It had already suffered three years of war, but the people were very friendly and helpful. We had to get used to a different monetary system, and I found out that Brussels sprouts and some of the other food they gave us were not the best things to eat when you were going to fly at high altitude in an unpressurized airplane. I bought a bike and, though I didn't get off the base as much as some of the guys, I really enjoyed myself when I did. I had a 36–hour pass in London and had a cab driver take me for a tour. I liked the scotch, but could never get used to the dark warm beer. England has the most beautiful countryside to fly over. We did a lot of that."
– Ed Leary, formerly with the 97th Bomb Group (H) Eighth USAAF

Above: A Military Police guard checks the identity of an airman at the door of the briefing room at Grafton Underwood, home of the 384th Bomb Group (H), Eighth USAAF, in WWII. Right: Eighth Air Force bomber air crews are briefed for a mission. The Eighth normally flew raids in daylight, and were briefed for them in the middle of the preceding night.

now recommend that our joint effort, day and night bombing, be continued for a time.'

"When I reported to General Arnold the result of this meeting, he said, 'Apparently you accomplished the mission I had in mind. Now I suggest you return to England at once and make sure you prove our case for daylight bombing.'" Churchill did as he had promised Eaker, and thereafter, found many occasions to refer to "bombing round the clock" until it became a standard expression of the time.

General Eaker and his staff were stationed at RAF Bomber Command Headquarters, High Wycombe, Buckinghamshire, so they could rub elbows with and learn something of the procedures and methods then in use by the RAF. The Americans were headquartered in what had been a girl's school before the war years. At war's end the

complex reverted to its former role.

Eaker clearly recognized and valued RAF Bomber Command's knowledge born of experience and set about to take full advantage of their proximity, even though he disagreed entirely with the British position on American daylight bombing. He then patterned the organisation of Eighth Bomber Command on that of RAF Bomber Command to ensure maximum co–operation between the two forces. His assignment to England had come when Major–General Carl Spaatz, a top commander under Hap Arnold, was given overall charge of the Army Air Force in Great Britain. It was at the suggestion of Spaatz that the American air combat presence in the UK be constructed around the fledgling Eighth Air Force, only recently activated and as yet lacking a mission. Arnold agreed and Spaatz then ordered Eaker to England to get the show on the road. Arnold and Eaker decided that this was their golden opportunity to prove the doctrine of high–altitude daylight precision bombing.

Eaker faced an early and pressing need for airfield and base facilities for the American air combat units that would be arriving in Britain. For some time before the Pearl Harbor attack and the US entry into the war, British and American military officials had been in conversation about arrangements for such units *should* the US come into the War at some point, and such accommodation had already been considered. Thus, when the US did go to war, the Air Ministry could implement a vital, large–scale airfield construction programme almost immediately. The Americans were planning an ultimate strength of some 3500 aircraft based in Britain by April 1943. These included sixty combat groups composed of seventeen heavy, ten medium and six light bomber; twelve fighter, seven observation and eight transport groups. Certain airfields in the English Midlands were already under construction for RAF Bomber Command in 1942 and these were quickly turned over to the

Americans. As the American air build–up in Britain increased, their airfield requirement was also reassessed and increased, with the majority of the bases and sites allocated for the use of USAAF units in East Anglia.

Another problem requiring General Eaker's urgent attention was that of adequate supply and maintenance capability for his forces in Britain. In addition to the on–going, ever–increasing need of his units for food, clothing, coal and many other domestic requirements, operationally they needed enormous quantities of aviation and motor fuels, ordnance, spare parts, oil, lubricants and other consumables, as well as the massive inventory of items essential to keep such a dynamic military organisation up and running. Here again, the British stepped in to meet the needs of their American cousins, providing both temporary and permanent facilities for depot storage, aircraft repair and maintenance, and technical support.

In line with Eaker's determination that the Eighth Air Force profit from the experience and learn the procedures of the RAF, it was decided that the Americans must adopt the RAF systems for air traffic control and communications. The British were wholly generous in sharing what they knew about the German enemy, and they provided instructional staffing for the USAAF personnel who were to attend training sessions at special units called Combat Crew Replacement and Training Centres. Primary among these was a new RAF base at Bovingdon, Hertfordshire, and its satellite at Cheddington, Buckinghamshire, which were both near Eaker's headquarters, and were promptly leased to the Yanks. It was apparent early on that the American crews had, in the urgency to mobilize, been insufficiently trained for the task they were to meet in the coming bombing campaign. This added to the doubt and polite scepticism, impatience and curiosity focused on them and their daylight offensive by the British. Gunners, especially, were found

Top: 452nd Bomb Group (H) bombardier Sam Young. Top right: An American .50 calibre machine gun round found at Deenethorpe, Northamptonshire in 1967. Above: A B-17 fuel filler cap found on the airfield at Polebrook in 1976. Right: The author found this leather flying glove at the edge of a hardstand on the former 384th Bomb Group base at Grafton Underwood, in 1971.

Left: A hardstand at Grafton Underwood in 1976. Below: Remains of the bomb dump at Grafton Underwood in 1999.

A journalist will say anything to earn a fast buck. I get my information from the horse's mouth, not from the rear end where they do.
— Marshal of the Royal Air Force Sir Arthur Harris

wanting and required additional training. The British, whose early experience with the B-17 Flying Fortress was unsatisfactory in the extreme, had grave misgivings about the equipment to be used by the Yanks.

It was the English weather, however, that proved the greatest challenge to the US crews who had done most of their flying training in the clear, blue skies of Texas and the American west. They were having to learn to cope with the rapidly changing weather conditions in the UK and flying much of the time in poor visibility. The frequently nasty weather of England and the Continent tended to work against their efforts to fly high-altitude daylight precision raids, complicating Ira Eaker's job considerably.

Getting the first aircraft and crews to the UK was yet another concern of the American General and his staff at High Wycombe. In June the first transport unit to provide logistical support for the Eighth Air Force, the 60th Transport Group, operating C-47s, completed their training and prepared for the move to England. On 18 June the first combat air units of the Eighth were staged to Presque Isle, Maine to be made ready for their departure east. Their first leg was some 570 miles to Goose Bay, Labrador, and the first fifteen B-17s arrived there in the late afternoon of 26 June, where they were refuelled. They left that same evening for Bluie West 1, a landing field on south-west Greenland about 775 miles from Goose Bay. At Bluie West 1 the arriving bombers were unable to land owing to extremely poor visibility and had to elect to either return to Goose Bay or go on to another landing site, Bluie West 8, about 400 miles further along the Greenland coast. One B-17 went on to land safely at BW8, while eleven others returned to Goose Bay. The other three planes became lost and, out of fuel, were eventually forced to crash-land on the Greenland coast. All of the crews survived and were rescued. Additional B-17s, navigating for a large group of

P-38 fighters, began the long trip on 19 June and by 27 July, 180 aircraft, B-17s, P-38s, and C-47s, the Eighth's first major ferrying movement of the War, had arrived at Prestwick, Scotland. In the movement, six P-38s and five B-17s were lost, but all of the crews were saved.

Eighth Fighter Command headquarters, under the command of Brigadier-General Frank O'D. Hunter, was established at Bushey Hall, near Watford in Hertfordshire, quite near its counterpart, RAF Fighter Command headquarters at Bentley Priory. Gradually, the important fighter support for the bombers of the Eighth was taking shape.

By the beginning of August 1942 Generals Spaatz and Eaker believed the Eighth was ready for action at last, and soon committed an admittedly tiny force to the Rouen raid, Mission No. 1. Getting to 17 August, and the actual launch of that first American heavy bomber raid against a German target, had been a test of patience strained nearly to the breaking point for Eaker. Continuing delays in supply and in the arrival of crews and equipment; the wholly inadequate training his crews had received prior to embarking for the UK, relative to the realities of the air war with the German enemy, and the often poor weather, mitigated against his determined effort to bring the new Air Force into the war.

General Spaatz had decided early in the Eighth's UK tenure that it was more important to bring the first heavy bomber crews and equipment to England as soon as they were organized, equipped and trained well enough to negotiate the ferry route, than to give them the more thorough training Stateside that they would so desperately need. Tight formation and high-altitude flying was all but completely missing from the repertoire of his first bomber pilots and co-pilots to arrive. Many of the radio operators were unable to either send or receive Morse code. And the previously mentioned deficiencies of most of the arriving gunners were, perhaps, most worrying of all. Those in the top echelon of the Eighth were convinced that the only

We walked toward the ship through nacreous pools of oily water on the asphalt parking area. Visibility was less than a hundred yards. We couldn't begin to see *Erector Set* and *Finah Than Dinah*, the Forts that were parked on hardstands on either side of ours on the perimeter.

It was stations time, a quarter to ten, and we went into The Body. The pearly ground fog had lifted; low clouds were running down to the eastward like suds in a rocky river bed. From my seat in the cockpit I could see the cubical control tower in the far distance, and I could even make out some tiny figures — members of the operational staff — on the iron-railed balcony of the tower. Eight or ten Forts were visible, scattered at their hardstands along the perimeter track, dark and squat, imponderable, rooted to the ground by their tail wheels. A big camouflaged RAF gasoline lorry and trailer moved slowly along the main road toward the hangars. Jeeps busy-bodied up and down the perimeter track.
— from *The War Lover* by John Hersey

Left: A view of the Rouen–Sotteville rail marshalling yards (arrow) during an attack by the Eighth USAAF on 28 March 1943.

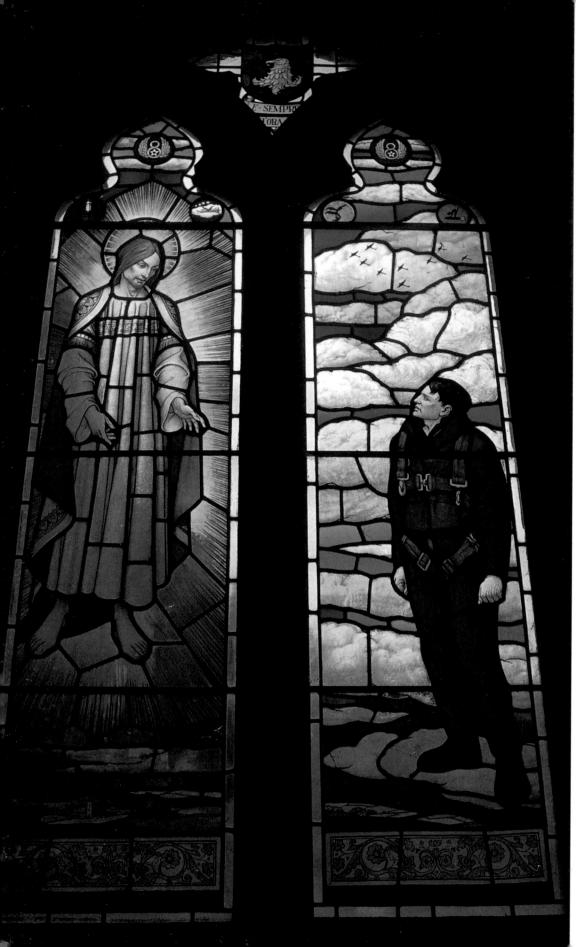

way their bombers could hit and destroy enemy targets by daylight without suffering prohibitive losses was through being able to defend themselves effectively against the enemy fighters.

Carl Spaatz stood on the roof of the flying control tower at Grafton Underwood with several Eighth Air Force and RAF staff officers and approximately thirty members of the US and British press. They had gathered to watch the take–off of the twelve American bombers of the 97th Bomb Group, the first and only heavy bomb group of the brand new Eighth US Army Air Force. This first raid was vitally important to Spaatz, Eaker and to Hap Arnold back in Washington — all of whom were betting the whole kitty on the concept of daylight bombing in the manner they intended to practise it. After months of frustrating delays, set–backs, and the scepticism of the British and American publics and nearly everyone else involved in the war against the Germans, their day and opportunity to get into the fight and show what they could do had finally come.

All twelve B-17s were airborne from Grafton by 3.40 that afternoon, as were six more from the base at Polebrook, Northamptonshire. The Polebrook planes were to act as a diversion for the main force.

Ira Eaker was riding in *Yankee Doodle*, the lead ship of the second flight of six bombers, to see for himself how this first mission would go.

The Rouen target was important to the Germans because of its major repair shops and large locomotive depot, as well as the many hundreds of freight cars there and the links it provided to the Channel Ports and the west of France. The aiming points for the bombers were the locomotive workshops and the Buddicum rolling stock repair shops.

The RAF, for its part, contributed a great many Spitfires to provide close air support for the B-17s — four squadrons of Mk IXs going with the bombers to the target, and five squadrons of Mk

Vs for withdrawal support.

The weather co—operated too with excellent visibility for the attacking force, and all twelve planes dropped their loads of general purpose bombs, 36,900 pounds, from an altitude of 23,000 feet. Official records indicate reasonably accurate bombing with approximately half the bombs falling in the general target area. Results were surprisingly good for a small, inexperienced force, with direct hits on two large trans—shipment sheds in the heart of the marshalling yards, with significant track damage and the destruction, damaging or derailing of quite a lot of rolling stock. There was one direct hit on the locomotive workshop. In all, however, the damage caused was, while sizeable, not sufficient to seriously impair rail operations there. Clearly, a much larger bombing effort would be needed to take out the Sotteville yard.

Neither the attacking or diversionary forces suffered any losses and incurred only minimal damage. The Germans were barely responsive to the attacking forces with only slight flak damage to two aircraft. The Luftwaffe did respond with an attack by three Me 109s with no damage resulting. There were no injuries to the bomber crews apart from the bombardier and navigator of one plane who were slightly injured when the plexiglass nose of their B-17 was shattered in a bird strike on the return flight to England.

In a letter to General Spaatz on 19 August 1942 Ira Eaker observed that the crews on this initial American raid were alert and enthusiastic, but nonchalant to the point of being blasé. They needed more drill in the use of oxygen equipment and, in general, better discipline. The formations needed tightening for improved defence against enemy fighters. Other items requiring considerable immediate attention included the timing of the rendezvous with fighter escort, navigation, bombing training, and gunnery. Pilotage needed a lot of work with the aim of refining formation flying to the point where tight and manoeuvrable formations could be flown with the shortest possible level bomb run on a target, thus minimizing exposure to enemy flak and fighter opposition. As to the ability of the bombers to defend themselves against enemy fighters, it was too soon to know. Certainly the Rouen raid had not provided any meaningful test of that, and both Spaatz and Eaker determined to tread with utmost caution in committing their bombers to subsequent missions that required much deeper penetration into German—occupied territory.

On 18 August General Eaker received the following message from Air Marshal Sir Arthur Harris, Air Officer Commanding—in—Chief, RAF Bomber Command: "Congratulations from all ranks of Bomber Command on the highly successful completion of the first all—American raid by the big fellows on German occupied territory in Europe. Yankee Doodle certainly went to town and can stick yet another well—deserved feather in his cap." To paraphrase Mr Churchill, for General Eaker and his staff, it was, perhaps, the end of the beginning.

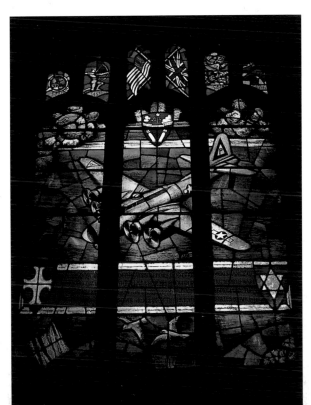

Presently he turned off on a side road, propped his bike against a hedge and strode slowly a hundred yards out onto an enormous flat, unobstructed field.

When he halted he was standing at the head of a wide, dilapidated avenue of concrete, which stretched in front of him with gentle undulations for a mile and a half. A herd of cows, nibbling at the tall grass which had grown up through the cracks, helped to camouflage his recollection of the huge runway. He noted the black streaks left by tires, where they had struck the surface, smoking, and nearby, through the weeds which nearly covered it, he could still see the stains left by puddles of grease and black oil on one of the hardstands evenly spaced around the five—mile circumference of the perimeter track, like teeth on a ring gear. And in the background he could make out a forlorn dark green control tower, surmounted by a tattered gray windsock and behind it two empty hangars, a shoe box of a water tank on high stilts and an ugly cluster of squat Nissen huts.
— from *12 O'Clock High!* by Beirne Lay, Jr and Sy Bartlett

Far left: A memorial church window in the village of Quidenham in Norfolk, to the WWII airmen of the 96th Bomb Group (H), Eighth USAAF, who were stationed at nearby Snetterton Heath. Left: A window in the church at Grafton Underwood dedicated to those who served at the base there.

As they watched it the bomber seemed to swell up very gently with a soft whoomph that was audible far across the sky. It became a ball of burning petrol, oil and pyrotechnic compounds. The yellow datum marker, which should have marked the approach to Krefeld, burned brightly as it fell away, leaving thin trails of sparks. The fireball changed from red to light pink as its rising temperature enabled it to devour new substances from hydraulic fluid and human fat to engine components of manganese, vanadium, and copper. Finally even the airframe burned. Ten tons of magnesium alloy flared with a strange greenish blue light. It lit up the countryside beneath it like a slow flash of lightning and was gone. For a moment a cloud of dust illuminated by the searchlights floated in the sky and then even that disappeared.
– from *Bomber*
by Len Deighton

"NIGHT BOMBING towards the end of 1916 and early 1917 was carried out mainly with Sopwith 1 1/2 Strutters, in which the rear seat was removed to accomodate a honeycomb bomb rack taking twelve French Le Pecq liquid 20lb bombs. The two old twin Anzani– engined Caudron G IVs were also used and they carried an observer or bomb aimer as well as a pilot. One took off down a paraffin flare path usually about two hours before dawn and on return waited until sufficient light enabled one to see the ground clearly before landing. Our usual night targets were the docks and shipping at Ostend, the docks and submarine pens at Bruges, and the Mole and shipping alongside at Zeebrugge. All three were heavily defended by AA and rocket batteries and bristled with searchlights, while more searchlights were spaced along the coast right up to the Dutch frontier, especially at Westende, Middlekerke, Wenduyne and Blankenberghe.

"A truly wonderful fireworks display attended us on our night stunts, the long chains of vivid jade– green balls which streaked up, invariably reaching

DELIVERY SYSTEMS

"We brought tea along but we didn't want to drink too much because then we'd have to use the Heinz bean tin. That's all we had. We'd use the bean tin and then out the window or down the window chute. I would have to hold the tin for the pilot. We did have a loo, but it was right down in the back of the plane and, on a Lancaster, you couldn't necessarily get to that thing whenever you needed to go."
– Jack Clift, formerly with No. 463 Squadron, RAAF

Left: One of the finest images made by the great aviation photographer Charles E. Brown: No. 9 Squadron, RAF, Wellington bombers en route to the Brussels Aero Exhibition in 1939. The Wellington design was begun in 1932 and the prototype first flew in 1936. The aircraft's impressive resistance to battle damage stemmed from the geodetic construction used by Dr Barnes Wallis in his concept for the unique new aircraft from Vickers.

53

Top: Ted Richardson flew as a WWII RAF navigator with Nos. 61 and 463 Squadrons in Lancasters. Above: Reg Payne was also in Lancasters, with No. 50 Squadron at Skellingthorpe in Lincolnshire. Right: The Battle of Britain Memorial Flight Avro Lancaster at its Coningsby, Lincolnshire base. At top left, the cockpit, nose turret and bomb aimer's position, top right, the wireless operator's station, and right, the pilot's instrument panel.

one's height before falling away and dying out, were a magnificent sight providing they didn't come too near. They must have been in the nature of a rangefinder as they always seemed to come to, or slightly above one's level, whatever one's height, before fading out, and were immediately followed by HE bursts pretty well on target. We called them 'Flaming Onions' and at first imagined they were connected by wire which would entangle one's propeller; but of course they were not, their regular spacing, like a glorious jade–green necklace, being due to some sort of machine mortar from which they were fired. I never heard of their doing any damage but occasionally one fell on a wing, being quickly swept off by the airspeed and slipstream, the fabric only showing a slight scorching, but I wouldn't have welcomed one in the cockpit. The advantage of coastal targets was that one could creep up the coast two or three miles out to sea without being heard, then turn in when approximately level with the objective, so giving the defences very little warning of one's approach. If one was heard the signal went up from Nieuport and was repeated all the way up the coast, on came the searchlights and the guns were ready for you."
– from *Bomber Pilot 1916 – 1918* by C. P. O. Bartlett

During the winter of 1916, the Germans decided that, as their airship raids over London had become impossible to sustain, they should launch a campaign of bombing attacks by airplane against the British. Their new strategic battle squadron 3, *Englandgeschwader,* was assigned the long–range attacks on British war industry, coastal ports, transport, and communications. The squadron was equipped with Gotha G–series bombers powered by two 260 hp Mercedes six–cylinder in–line engines. For the time, the Gotha operated in relative safety from attack by British fighters, as it bombed from an altitude of 16,000 feet and was

then able to climb even higher for its return trip to base. On 13 June 1917, in a bold daylight attack on the heart of the British capital, a force of 14 Gothas dropped a total of 72 bombs on the area of Liverpool Street Station in London, killing 162 people and causing a profound psychological reaction among the populace and a heated debate on the organization of the home defence. All of the attacking force returned safely to their base at Gontrode in Belgium. By October, however, the British defences got the better of the Gothas, with much improved anti–aircraft and fighter opposition, and the Germans switched to night bombing. This offensive included a few significant incendiary raids, the beginning of a planned campaign of fire raids which was called off shortly before negotiations to end World War I began. The psychological effect on Britons by the Gotha offensives remained after the end of the War. Fearful memories of being bombed from the air were to be long–lasting.

It fell upon its victims while emitting a terrifying shriek. An icon of the Nazi *Blitzkreig*, it typified the 'lightning strike' of the hard–charging German forces at the beginning of World War II. All across Poland, Czechoslovakia, the Low Countries and France, the siren scream of the Ju 87 Stuka announced the imminent arrival of Hitler's legions. The dive–bombing of the Stuka was as much psychological warfare as anything else.

The Stuka's command of the skies was relatively short–lived, however. The Hurricanes and Spitfires of the Royal Air Force saw to that rather quickly and without much fuss. It was no match for the Merlin–engined fighters and fell to them in great numbers throughout the summer and fall of 1940. While it was still to perform with some distinction against Allied shipping in the Mediterranean and their convoys sailing the arctic route to Russia, in the Balkans and against Crete, it was no longer the threat it had once been.

The name Stuka came from the German term

Above: A fine study of a B-17 Flying Fortress, by Third Air Division, Eighth USAAF photographer Major Mark Brown. Many who flew in the Fort believed it was the finest bomber of the War. In his excellent book *Flying Fortress*, Edward Jablonski stated: "With wings punctured and ablaze, tail surfaces shredded, with chunks of its graceful body gouged out by cannon fire, flak, or mid–air collision, the B-17 brought them home. With an almost human will to live this great plane, shattered and torn beyond the limits of flyability, carried them to safety and, for some, to life itself."

Sturzkampfflugzeug, referring to dive–bombers. The Germans were fascinated with the concept and potential of aerial dive–bombing as early as the late '20s, and in the Ju 87 they produced a rugged, if somewhat ugly and slow two–man machine, capable of terrifying the folks below in the target area while doing damage as well.

The plane was significantly improved through the development and production of several later marks, making it formidable to Germany's opponents right up to the summer of 1940 when reality struck in the form of RAF Fighter Command, and the heyday of the Stuka was over.

The Bristol Blenheim was a pioneering effort in the British aircraft industry; the first all–metal stressed–skin cantilever monoplane bomber. It gave the Royal Air Force just the edge it needed, and brought an end

to the older, prevailing philosphy about bomber aircraft design. It was a bomber of the 1930s capable of outpacing most fighters of the day.

The Blenheim had its detractors, and was certainly not one of aviation's greatest achievements, but in its time it met a need of the RAF and, in a sense, kept them in the game until the bigger, better, more capable bomber types came on stream.

Powered by two Bristol Mercury XV air–cooled radial engines rated at 995 hp each, the Mk IV Blenheim was the best of the breed. It cruised at 259 mph at 15,000 feet with a normal cruising speed of 198 mph and it carried a normal bomb load of 1000 pounds.

The Blenheim was widely used and performed commendably, and while it was not particularly outstanding among all the bomber aircraft of the war, it did represent an important transition for

RAF Bomber Command.

The Vickers Wellington carried the brunt of RAF Bomber Command's night bombing offensive against German–occupied Europe in World War II until the coming of the new heavy bombers. Known affectionately as the Wimpy, after the character J. Wellington Wimpy in the Popeye comic strip, it served effectively throughout the War. Much of its success was due to its geodetic construction, a revolutionary "basket weave" structure employed by the engineer Barnes Wallis, who also designed the "bouncing bombs" utilized in the Dam Busters attack of May 1943. This construction technique resulted in an amazing combination of high strength and low weight, and an airplane able to take terrific battle damage and still bring its crew home safely.

The Wellington B.Mk.X had two Bristol Hercules VI radial engines rated at 1585 hp for take–off, a cruising speed of 180 mph and a service ceiling of 24,000 feet. Its range, with a 4500–pound bomb load, was 1325 miles.

While a solid performer, the Wellington also demonstrated conclusively to the British Air Staff the futility of daylight bombing raids without fighter escort when the enemy had obvious air superiority. At one point two raids cost the RAF 21 Wellingtons of a total force of 36 despatched. From that day the daylight bombing campaign of the RAF was abandoned.

They sounded odd . . . out of sync, the Daimler Benz DB 601 (and later the Junkers Jumo) engines of the Heinkel He 111s that visited London and other English cities on so many nights during the great Blitzes of 1940 – 41 and after in World War II. The He 111 had good flying characteristics and was presented to the German public initially in early 1936 in the form of a ten–passenger commercial airliner. It was clear to aviation experts, however, that this was a mean machine intended for a far more aggressive role than that being conducted by Deutsche Lufthansa.

This relatively light and fast medium bomber cruised at 224 mph at 16,400 feet and had a service ceiling of 25,500 feet, but a range, with a maximum bomb load, of only 760 miles.

The 111 broke its maiden in the skies over Spain with the bomber element of the German Air Force's Legion Condor in 1936 and, though lightly armed with only three 7.9 mm machine guns, was quite effective and suffered only negligible losses in the Spanish Civil War. Daylight bombing, however, always a tricky prospect for any air force, proved too much for the Heinkel when it ran into the Spitfires and Hurricanes of the RAF in the Battle of Britain. It was undergunned and not really fast enough to put up much of a struggle against the excellence of the British fighters and their extraordinarily courageous pilots who had the added incentive of defending their island against Nazi invasion. The Germans scrambled to improve the armament of the 111 but, by the final phase of the Battle, were forced to withdraw the bomber from day raids and put it on the night shift.

In the mid–morning of 3 February 1940 a Heinkel He 111 had the dubious distinction of being the first German warplane to fall on English soil in World War II. The bomber was under the command of pilot Hermann Wilms and carried a crew of four, all Unteroffiziere, Peter Leushake, Johann Meyer and Karl Missy. Their airplane, No. 3232, was operating with 2nd Gruppe, KG 26 "Lion" Geschwader from Schleswig–Jagel, a base north of Hamburg. Their assignment that frigid winter morning was to attack an enemy convoy off the northeast coast of England. Shortly after 9 a.m. Blue Section of No. 43 Squadron, RAF, got the call at Acklington and in a few minutes Flight Lieutenant Peter Townsend and Sergeants Tiger Folkes and Jim Hallowes were climbing to intercept the hapless Heinkels. Their Hurricanes joined with the German planes of the Schleswig

Flight and Wilms' bomber was badly shot up by Townsend. It crash–landed near Whitby.

The front–line heavy bomber of the Japanese Army Air Force for most of World War II was the Mitsubishi Type 97 Ki.21-IIb, known to the Allies as the Sally. Dating from 1937, it was a twin–engined aircraft with a 236 mph cruising speed at 16,400 feet and a top speed of 297 mph at 13,000 feet. It had a 1350–mile range with a maximum bomb load of 2200 pounds. Its power was provided by two Mitsubishi Ha.101 Type 100 radial engines rated at 1490 hp each. The Ki.21 was operated by a four–man crew: a pilot, co–pilot/navigator, radio operator/gunner and a bombardier/gunner.

Initial combat operations for the Ki.21 came in August 1938 when the first units to receive the aircraft, the 60th and 61st *Sentai*, began flying it in Manchuria against the Chinese, where it showed that it was not up to the task at hand. It was being flown to its objectives without escort, and, with insufficient defensive armament, could not adequately defend itself and suffered alarmingly high losses in this, its first trial by fire.

Subsequent models of the bomber, produced with features such as improved fuel tanks, increased armament and enlarged flaps, replaced the older, inferior model in early 1941, giving a new, but unwarranted, sense of confidence and security to the Japanese crews who flew it. This confidence was soon dispelled when they encountered fighter opposition from the P-40s of General Claire Chennault's American Volunteer Group, the Flying Tigers, and RAF Hurricanes. In an engagement with the AVG and the RAF on 20 December 1941 over Kunming, the Japanese lost twenty of their attacking force of 60 bombers.

After the fall of Singapore in mid–February 1942, Japanese units flying the latest version of the Sally were assigned to hit British and Canadian garrisons at Hong Kong, which they did very well, albeit with no enemy fighter opposition.

With the increasing presence of US and British high performance fighters in the western Pacific, Ki.21 losses rose sharply and its days in the region were numbered. The Sally was thought to be a comparatively easy target by Allied fighter pilots, with its inadequate defensive armament. The bomber fared no better in the China–Burma–India theatre of the War where, despite operating with significant fighter protection, its losses continued to climb. A pattern began in which the Sally was withdrawn from front–line units until, finally, its role was reduced to transport and suicide attack.

Widow Maker, Flying Torpedo, Flying Prostitute, Martin Murderer, and One-a-day-in-Tampa Bay... all were references to the B-26 Marauder medium bomber. It had "a reputation" among American pilots learning to handle it. US Government investigators convened on four separate occasions to consider discontinuing its development. The unusually small wing area and the resultant high wing–loading led to the Marauder's bad name. Ultimately, though, it rose above it all. By 1944, the US Ninth Air Force was operating Marauders in the European theatre with a lower operational loss rate than that of any other American aircraft type.

With a 1100–mile range at maximum cruising speed, a 283 mph top speed at maximum weight, and a service ceiling of 19,800 feet, the Martin bomber was not the most impressive of performers, but it got the job done. It began to make a name for itself beginning with the run –up to D–Day when it was the first USAAF aircraft in the European theatre to operate at night. Its ability to hit and destroy bridges and other targets requiring a high degree of precision was exceptional. The B-26 flew more than 29,000 sorties in its first year of combat in Europe, dropping 46,430 tons of bombs and incurring a relatively tiny loss rate for the effort. 5157

Marauders were made at Martin by the end of the war, and, despite the views of its early detractors, it was in fact a good, reliable airplane, if one that demanded pilots of a high standard.

Among the most interesting and successful of all bombing aircraft is the De Havilland Mosquito, whose designers believed that the airplane could accomplish its mission and defend itself primarily by relying on its great speed to outrun enemy fighter opposition. They were correct and, as if more proof were needed of the adage that 'an airplane that looks right will fly right', the Mosquito was as graceful and elegant of line as she was swift, powerful and a joy to fly. Her secrets were a small, highly practical airframe, a wonderful aerodynamic aesthetic, an amazingly high power–to–weight ratio, and energy from two superb and reliable Rolls–Royce Merlin engines.

The De Havilland design team was working on a high–speed bomber concept as early as October 1938. When war broke out in September 1939, the British Air Ministry began to show serious interest in the idea of a bomber capable of "fighter" speeds. It asked De Havilland if they could come up with a design for such an aircraft that could carry a 1000–pound bomb load and have a range of 1500 miles. The manufacturer agreed to have a go and was given latitude to take a revolutionary approach to the problem. The Air Ministry was thinking 'unarmed' high–speed bomber, but the airplane maker had other plans, and proceeded to design an aircraft with provision for guns or cameras, as well as bomb–carrying capability, with an eye to making their new bird a model of versatility as well as one of supreme performance. It would, they thought, be as competent in the photo–reconnaissance or fighter roles as it would be in the bomber role. Not only would it be the fastest bomber in the world, and brilliant in its other capacities, it would be made of WOOD. The designers incorporated the timely advantages of a

She went into that little field with so much class that it made your heart jump. It was a strange feeling, rolling across the snow at 90 or 100, taking off every time we hit a bump under the snow. It was the best landing I ever made, or, now, ever will. But it was the B-25 more than I. It was things like this that made me love that ship. It helps itself more than any plane I ever worked on or flew. It is so much more than an inanimate mass of material, intricately geared and wired and riveted into a tight package. It's a good, trustworthy friend.
– from *Thirty Seconds Over Tokyo*
by Captain Ted W. Lawson

Above left: A Vickers Virginia, a type which helped meet the bomber requirement of the RAF from 1927 through the mid–1930s. Below left: North American Mitchell IIs of No. 180 Squadron, RAF, at their Foulsham, Norfolk airfield, by aviation photographer Charles E. Brown. The RAF operated 800 of these bombers on daylight raids with No. 2 Group of Bomber Command. They were also used in close air support with the 2nd Tactical Air Force during the Allied advance through the Low Countries in 1944.

Below: No. 102 Squadron, RAF, bomb aimer Nick Brown, who served at Pocklington in Yorkshire. Above right: The fourth production Stirling Mk I was built at Belfast by Short Brothers and is seen here in July 1940. It served with No. 7 Squadron. Below right: A Canadian crew and their Handley–Page Halifax.

new process for fabricating the plane from wood laminates, and when it was finished, the 'wooden wonder', as the Mosquito was often referred to, was indeed a 400 mph airplane that cruised at well over 300 mph, climbed to 15,000 feet in less than eight minutes, had a service ceiling of 37,000 feet and a range (with a 4000–pound bomb load) of 1370 miles at 245 mph. As a bomber the "Mossie" normally went to its target at an economical cruising speed of 300 mph at about 22,000 feet, or down around sea level at a similar speed.

The airplane was extremely successful in a wide range of activities, not least being the vital Pathfinder role later in the war.

5584 Mosquitos were built by the end of World War II in Britain, Canada and Australia. The outstanding performance and legendary combat record of the Mossie assure its place among the great planes of all time.

Another twin–engined medium bomber of World War II remembered for its excellent and highly efficient performance, as well as its fine handling characteristics, is the North American B-25 Mitchell. Just as the famous Dam Buster raid by No. 617 Squadron, RAF, provided an immense psychological boost to the British public, so too did the 1942 attack on Tokyo, Kobe, Yokohama and Nagoya by sixteen B-25s under the command of Jimmy Doolittle, inspire and raise the spirits of the American people. Flying from the deck of the USS *Hornet* on 18 April 1942, Doolittle's raiders provided a wake–up call the Japanese would long remember.

The final version of the Mitchell, the B-25J, bristled with thirteen .50 calibre machine guns; it had a short–range bomb load capacity of 4000 pounds, a maximum speed of 275 mph at 15,000 feet and a normal operating cruise of 200 mph. With a 3200–pound bomb load it had a cruise range of 1275 miles.

The Mitchell was operated effectively on every major battle front in World War II, earning an exceptionally fine reputation and high praise wherever it served.

Considered the backbone of the Luftwaffe in World War II, the Junkers Ju 88 was easily the best German bomber to serve in that conflict. Conceived in 1935 as a medium bomber with the speed of a fighter, the Ju 88 was produced from 1939 to 1945. A total of 15,000 were built; 9000 of them as bombers.

Although the plane performed reasonably well in the Battle of Britain, this experience led to a lengthy series of modifications and improvisations resulting in a much–improved bomber. Her defensive armament was significantly increased as was the length and size of her wing. Better armour protection for the four–man crew was added; the undercarriage was made stronger and, through provision for rocket–assisted take–off, the maximum bomb load capability was increased to 6600 pounds.

As with other bombers of the time, by mid–1943 many Ju 88s were simply too slow to operate successfully in daylight without a fighter escort. Several more modifications and model changes continued the development of the line, including the Ju 188 and Ju 388, both of which incorporated bomber versions. Under development at the end of the war was the Ju 488, an essentially new aircraft intended as a high–altitude, four–engined bomber/ reconnaissance plane operated by a crew of three. The Ju 488 was expected to have a maximum cruising speed of 385 mph at 42,000 feet and a range of nearly 1300 miles. The two prototype Ju 488s were destroyed in an Allied bombing attack on their construction site at Toulouse in early 1945.

The first of the important RAF jet bombers was the English Electric Canberra, initially a purpose–built radar bomber. The maiden flight of the prototype took place on 13 May 1949. Like the World War II Mosquito, the Canberra has served both the Royal Air Force and the US Air Force in a variety of roles from night intruder and interdictor, to high–altitude photo reconnaissance, to tactical bomber in Vietnam, where its USAF designation was B-57. The versatile, highly effective Canberra bridged the gap for the RAF between the last of its piston—engined heavy bombers, the Avro Lincoln and the Boeing B-29 Washington, and the first of its strategic nuclear strike bombers in the mid 1950s. A subsonic light bomber, the Canberra proved to be a very capable weapon operating at extremely high altitudes with great manoeuvrability. The American version was built by the Martin Company and General Dynamics. Fitted with a range of special night sensors, the RB-57E was especially suited to the task of locating hidden enemy bases and depots along the Ho Chi Minh Trail in the Vietnam War. The two—seat bomber had a maximum speed of 582 mph at 40,000 feet, a service ceiling of 48,000 feet and a combat range of 2300 miles.

The Douglas A-1 Skyraider entered service in 1946; too late for World War II, but in plenty of time for Korea. It was probably the most sophisticated, unique and utilitarian single piston—engined combat plane in history. Capable of carrying a load of bombs whose weight was greater than its own empty weight, the Skyraider was employed extensively in Vietnam by the US Air Force, US Navy and US Marines, as well as the South Vietnamese Air Force. It has flown in the service of France, Britain and Cambodia, as well as for Chad and the Central African Republic.

Several squadrons of the A-1E version, a two—seat aircraft known as *Spad* or *Sandy*, were flown by the USAF in Vietnam in ground support activity with considerable success.

3180 A-1s had been manufactured by the Douglas Aircraft Corporation by 1957 when production ceased. The big plane had a maximum speed of 318 mph and an operational range of 3000 miles. It was able to carry up to 8000 pounds of ordnance on sixteen underwing pylons. Its all—up weight was 25,000 pounds and it was armed with four 20mm wing—mounted cannon. It was heavily

KEEP HIM FLYING

armoured and able to absorb enemy small arms fire with minimal losses. The Skyraider was a no–nonsense muscle–plane, perfectly adapted to its tasks. It went to work behind the power of a huge Wright R-3350 18–cylinder twin–row radial 2700 hp engine. Twenty years after its introduction, the Skyraider was still fighting, this time in Vietnam. It was there because of its unprecedented load–carrying capability, versatility and endurance.

In the Gulf War the Panavia GR.Mk 1 Tornado was a major player. It also suffered the most losses of all the Coalition aircraft, owing largely to the vulnerability that went with its assignments there. These tasks ranged from counter–runway attacks using JP 233 runway denial weapons, to free–fall bombing of airfields and other strategic targets, to defence suppression. With the assistance of British Aerospace/Blackburn Buccaneer aircraft acting as "buddy laser" platforms using laser designator pods, the Tornado GR.Mk 1s were able to deliver laser–guided bombs from medium altitudes on bridges and airfields with great effect. Eleven Tornados were lost in Gulf War–related activities.

From September 1968, when the US Air Force requested proposals from eight American aerospace companies for a new air superiority fighter to replace the F-4 Phantom, through more than thirty years of development and operation, the Boeing/McDonnell Douglas F-15 Eagle has become the universally recognized indisputable air combat master. In the early 1980s development began on what was to be the ultimate and deadliest version of the Eagle, the E model or Strike Eagle, whose mission is all–weather day or night deep interdiction. Airmen call it the Mud Hen. The F-15E has a two–seat tandem cockpit layout and the crew now includes a Weapons Systems Officer.

The Strike Eagle accomodates an impressive range of weaponry, from 500 lb to 2000 lb bombs (free–fall or precision–guided), to AGM-88 HARM or AGM-65 Maverick missiles, to AGM-130 powered guided bombs, to B57 or B61 nuclear bombs. The aircraft is still fundamentally an F-15 air superiority weapon and can also bring the range of air–to–air weaponry employed by the other members of the Eagle family to a combat situation. In the air superiority role the F-15 is formidable, to say the least. In the Gulf War Operation Desert Storm, USAF Eagles scored an amazing 30–0 kill ratio over the Iraqi opposition. The US record, coupled with that of Israeli and Saudi aerial victories, amounts to an unparalleled 90–0 kill ratio in favour of the F-15.

Power for the Strike Eagle comes from two Pratt & Whitney F100-PW-229 engines, with the General Electric F110-GE-129 engine as an option. The latter develops 29,000 lb static thrust, for an amazing total push of some 58,000 lbs.

In addition to the USAF, which has purchased 226 F-15Es, the air forces of Israel and Saudi Arabia fly their own versions of the Strike Eagle, giving them what is probably the most potent attack aircraft in current operation.

The Short Stirling might have been a much better bomber, had it not been for the narrow–mindedness of those who laid down the specifications for the plane. They insisted on a 100–foot wingspan in order to fit the opening of the then–standard RAF hangar doors. This unrealistic demand doomed the bomber to a second–rate career flying ops lower and slower, with less ability to survive flak and to climb properly, as in missions to Italy when it was required to negotiate the Alps. The Stirlings, in this case, had to fly *through* mountain passes when they could not gain sufficient altitude to fly over them. Given a wing of greater span and higher aspect ratio the plane would certainly have had a better performance and achieved a far better operational record.

Indicative of the Stirling's shortcomings was the position it was forced to accept when operating on large–scale raids together with Lancasters and

Above: The Douglas
Skyraider operated in many
roles during the Vietnam
War. It was renowned as a
great workhorse in that
conflict and was used in
interdiction as well as close
support roles. It was highly
effective in rescue operations
as well. This Skyraider is part
of The Fighter Collection at
Duxford, England. Left: An IDS
(Interdiction/Strike) Tornado of
the German Air Force pulls In
for a final ground check near
the end of the active runway
prior to take–off at Schleswig–
Jagel, north of Hamburg.

Halifaxes. While the other heavies were going to the target at 18 to 20,000 feet, it was all the fully–loaded Stirlings could do to reach 12,000. As the war continued, the Stirling was relegated to more and more ancillary assignments including fringe targets and flying–bomb sites in Northern France, supply drops to partisans in occupied Europe, mine–laying, transport, radio counter–measures, glider towing and fuel supply. In these roles, it performed admirably.

Some officials in the British Ministry of Aircraft Production in 1940 wanted to convert the Avro and Metropolitan Vickers factory production lines from the assembly of twin–engine Manchester bombers to building the new four–engine Handley–Page Halifax. This intention angered Roy Chadwick, Avro's chief designer, and the Hawker Siddeley Group directors who devoutly believed in the superiority of their Manchester III, a new four–engined heavy bomber which had been in development for nearly two years and was, they said, ready for production. It could readily be introduced to the existing Manchester production line without the sort of delivery delays that would necessarily follow the

retooling required if the Manchester line were converted to the making of Halifaxes. Not a fan of the Handley–Page plane, Chadwick disagreed with H–P's choice of the Rolls–Royce Merlin X engine for its bomber, and he was critical of the limitations posed by its bomb bay design. In his Merlin XX–powered Manchester III, he had told the MAP bureaucrats, he could deliver vastly superior performance and bomb load capacity to that of the rival product. Ultimately, the argument of Chadwick and the Avro officials won the day. The MAP Director of Technical Development ordered two Manchester III prototypes built in early September 1940.

Avro was committed to produce and test fly the first of the prototypes within four months of signing the agreement, and to make maximum use of the existing Manchester I jigs, fixtures and other components. The initial prototype aircraft, BT 308, made a first test flight from the Avro Woodford facility on 9 January 1941 with Captain H. A. Brown at the controls. Flight test results after that were encouraging. Despite the first test aircraft having to operate with Merlin X engines owing to the limited availability of the Merlin XX, and an obvious need for an enlarged and strengthened undercarriage, as well as a new, twin–finned tailplane, prospects for the new bomber were most hopeful. She was renamed Lancaster.

"Oh! Boy, oh, boy! What an aeroplane! What a piece of aeroplane!" was the tribute Sir Roy Dobson, Chairman of A.V. Roe Ltd, paid Roy Chadwick, designer of the Lancaster, as they watched the initial take–off of their bomber prototype.

By 1945, the Bomber Command Lancaster force numbered fifty squadrons. From mid–1942, the Avro bomber was the backbone of the 'thousand plane raids' and August 1942 saw formation of the elite Pathfinder Force, No. 8 Group, which was founded with No. 83 Squadron Lancasters. Using the navigational aid "Gee", the Pathfinders went to the targets ahead of the main bomber force and marked the aiming points using flares and incendiaries to ease the task of the bombers bringing the high–explosives.

Marshal of the Royal Air Force Sir Arthur Harris wrote to the Avro Production Group at the end of the war: "As the user of the Lancaster during the last 3 1/2 years of bitter, unrelenting warfare, I would say this to those who placed that shining sword in our hands; without your genius and your effort we would not have prevailed–the Lancaster was the greatest single factor in winning the war."

During World War II Avro Lancasters delivered 608,612 tons of bombs to enemy targets, more than 60 per cent of all the bomb tonnage dropped in that conflict by RAF Bomber Command. The Lancaster was a four–engine mid–wing heavy monoplane, purpose–built to be a night bomber. It was manufactured by A.V. Roe & Co. Ltd, Manchester, Woodford, Cheshire and Yeadon, Sir W. G. Armstrong Whitworth Aircraft Ltd, Coventry and Bitteswell, Metropolitan Vickers Ltd, Manchester, The Austin Motor Co Ltd, Longbridge, Birmingham, Vickers–Armstrongs Ltd., Chester and

Castle Bromwich, and by Victory Aircraft Ltd, Malton, Ontario, Canada. It was powered by four 1460 hp Rolls–Royce or Packard–built Merlin XX, 22, 28, 38 or 224, 12–cylinder engines, and one variant utilized 1650 hp Bristol Hercules VI engines. Most Lancasters were operated by a crew of seven. The plane weighed 36,457 pounds, but could weigh as much as 72,000 pounds all–up with the maximum possible bomb load. A Mark III Lancaster with a normal bomb and fuel load had a maximum speed of 287 mph and a cruising speed of 210 mph at 12,000 feet. With a 14,000–pound bomb load the range was 1660 miles. It was armed with two .303 Browning machine guns in a nose turret, two in a dorsal turret and four in a tail turret. In many aircraft the .303 machine guns were replaced by the more potent .50–calibre Browning guns. A total of 7374 Lancs were built.

Historians and aviation fanatics have long debated the relative contributions of the Lancaster and the Boeing B-17 Flying Fortress to the defeat of Nazi Germany in World War II. Considered by many the most efficient, effective bomber aircraft of the war, the Avro machine brought tremendous bomb tonnage to its target cities, wreaking levels of destruction previously unimagined. It was easier to handle and managed to take increasingly heavier bomb loads with fewer accidents and casualties than any other heavy bomber of the war. It was, perhaps, as well conceived and designed as a bomber of that time could be; but the emphasis had always been on the efficient delivery of maximum bomb tonnage on wide–area targets.

The Boeing airplane was made for a different role and, in most respects, performed superbly. That role was high- altitude daylight precision bombing and, in the right circumstances, the B-17 made a powerful impression on the German war effort. It also contributed greatly to the defeat of the German air force both in the air and on the ground.

Of the models produced, the B-17G was easily the

The Stirling, the first of the British four-engined bombers, was underpowered. It flew slower than the later bombers, and its ceiling was considerably lower.

Halifax and Lancaster crews were prone to rejoice when a few squadrons of Stirlings formed part of the bomber stream. Flying several thousand feet below them, the Stirlings served to attract more of the shit from anti-aircraft guns.

Anyone who completed a tour of ops on Stirlings was a rare specimen, and the chances were that he was not only remarkbly skilful but had access to so much luck as to be practically immortal.
– from *Yesterday's Gone* by N. J. Crisp

"The Hampden was a beautiful aircraft to fly, about the nicest I handled in more than twenty years, although, of course, not really up to the job then required of it."
– J. G. Roberts, formerly with No. 106 Squadron, RAF Bomber Command

"The B-47 was a great airplane. You had to fly it by the numbers or it would kill you."
– Ray Fletcher, former USAF B-47 pilot

Above left: The Boeing B-47 bridged the gap between the decade of the B-36 intercontinental piston-engined bomber and the era of the B-52. The swept–wing B-47 set the style for virtually all bombers that followed. In 1958, 29 US Strategic Air Command wings were equipped with a total of 1590 of the planes.

most effective variant of the type. A total of 4035 G models were built in the facilities of Boeing, Vega and Douglas by mid–1945. The US Eighth and Fifteenth Air Forces operated the B-17G from late 1943, as did the RAF, which called theirs Fortress III. The German air force operated captured Fortresses in the I/K.G.200 unit which specialised in dropping and resupplying secret agents. The Germans gave their Forts the phoney designation 'Dornier Do 200.' At the peak of its utilisation, in August 1944, some 4574 B-17s were in the active

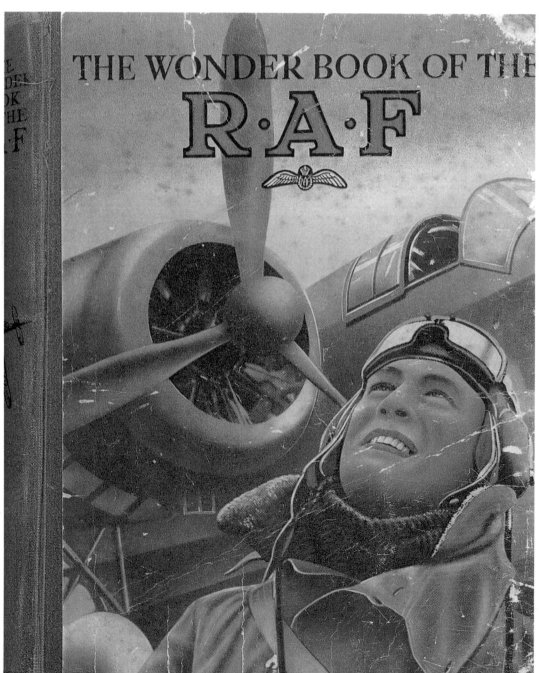

USAAF inventory.

In the design requirements for the heavy and medium bombers of the US Army Air Forces in World War II, crew protection and defensive fire–power were primary considerations. The maximum bomb–carrying capacity of the B-17 (and the B-24) was considerably less than that of the Lancaster, as the two American bombers both required a crew of ten men and were fitted with substantial armour protection. They were mounted with as many as thirteen .50–calibre machine guns and their ammunition. All of this extra weight meant a hefty bomb load penalty, but the Americans believed religiously in the concept of precision bombing in daylight. They felt that they could hurt the enemy more through the surgical placement of fewer bombs on key industrial, supply, and resource targets than the RAF could through its campaign of nocturnal area bombing. Which service was right? Both were, to the extent that the Allied strategic bombing helped bring about the defeat of Germany in the war. By war's end, the B-17 had carried slightly more bomb tonnage to its targets than had the Lancaster; 640,036 tons versus 608,612.

As General Curtis Lemay, a brilliant combat leader in the US strategic bombing campaigns against both Germany and Japan, put it: "The Air Force kind of grew up with the B-17. It was as tough an airplane as was ever built. It was a good honest plane to fly – a pilot's airplane. It did everything we asked it to do and did it well."

General Ira Eaker, who headed Eighth Bomber Command during the height of the US bombing effort against the Germans, said: "The B-17, I think, was the best combat airplane ever built. It combined in perfect balance the right engine, the right wing and the right control surfaces. The B-17 was a bit more rugged than the B-24. It could ditch better because of the low wing and it could sustain more battle damage. You wouldn't believe they could stay in the air."

Of the 12,731 Flying Fortresses produced, 47

survive in 1999 and of these, fourteen are airworthy.

Probably it is fair to say of the Lancaster and B 17 crews that each thought their airplane was the finest, safest, most reliable bomber then flying. Certainly, few of them would have traded places with their American or British counterparts. Most would probably agree that the Lancaster and the Flying Fortress are the most admired . . . and *the* classic bomber aircraft of all time.

She was like the less attractive sister of the beauty queen. The chunky, slab–sided B-24 Liberator was the product of General Hap Arnold's invitation to the Consolidated company to do a design study for a new bomber that would have better performance than the B-17. It was January 1939; war clouds loomed and Arnold wanted an aircraft whose maximum speed exceeded 300 mph, with a ceiling of 35,000 feet and a range of 3000 miles. She lacked the glamour and grace of the Fortress, but she performed brilliantly on more operational war fronts for a longer period and with greater versatility than her sister ship.

By September 1944 6043 Liberators were in active service and by the end of the war 18,188 had been built. They served with the US Army Air Forces, the Royal Air Force, the US Navy, the Royal Australian Air Force, the South African Air Force and later, the Indian Air Force.

The B-24 did slightly out–perform the B-17. She had a maximum speed of 300 mph at 30,000 feet; a maximum continuous speed of 278 mph at 25,000 feet; an initial rate of climb of 1025 feet a minute and a range (with a 5000–pound bomb load) of 1700 miles at 25,000 feet.

The Liberator was designed around a special wing called the Davis high–lift airfoil, which the Consolidated team believed would provide 25 per cent less profile drag at low speeds and ten per cent less at high speeds than conventional wing designs. The wing offered high efficiency and substantial space for fuel tankage. The B-24's power came from four 1200 hp Pratt and Whitney Twin Wasp radial engines.

Liberators were built by Consolidated at plants in San Diego, California and Fort Worth, Texas; by the Ford Motor Company at Willow Run, Michigan (causing more than a few American airmen to refer to bombers produced at the Ford plant as "Willit Run?"); the Dallas, Texas plant of North American Aviation, and a few by Douglas at Tulsa, Oklahoma.

While primarily operated as a long–range heavy bomber, the B-24 was also effective in anti–submarine and maritime reconnaissance roles and as a passenger and freight carrier.

Of all the famous missions flown by B-24s, perhaps the most horrendous and controversial was the Ploesti oilfield raid of 1 August 1943. 177 Libs were sent that day to fly a low–level attack on the Astra Romana, Columbia Aquila, Steaue Romana and Romana Americana oil complexes. A hundred and sixty–three made it to the target area and delivered their bombs. The bombing did a lot of damage, but the attacking force paid dearly with the loss of 54 bombers and 144 airmen.

By early 1945, the Americans were utilizing the bulk of their Liberators in the Pacific and Mediterranean theatres, while in the European theatre, General James H. Doolittle, commander of the Eighth Air Force, clearly indicated his own preference for the B-17 in his operations against German targets. Improvements to its range now made the Fort at least the equal of the B-24 in his estimation. One who stuck with the Lib, though, was Winston Churchill whose personal aircraft, *Commando*, made many historic flights with the British Prime Minister aboard.

The Handley–Page Halifax, with the Avro Lancaster, shared the major responsibility for RAF Bomber Command's night–bombing offensive against German targets across Europe. Forty per cent of the heavy bombers built in the United Kingdom during the war were Halifaxes. More

"It was time for me to transition into flying the ten-engine B-36 intercontinental bomber. I knew how to taxi the aircraft. We would have four engines in reverse and two pushing forward [the six giant piston engines were mounted on the trailing edge of the B-36 wing and operated as pushers. They had nineteen–foot–diameter propellers].

"We had a large steering wheel with a knob on it to help in turning. This knob swivelled in your hand when you grasped it, and as the knob turned, the wheel would turn and then the airplane would turn. For take-off, the engineers sitting behind me would set four engines in reverse at 1300 rpm, and the two forward–pushing engines, numbers one and six, at 1300 rpm. With so much power, I had to ride the brakes a lot to keep the airplane slowed down.

"When making a turn while taxiing, you had to lead the nose almost to the other side of the taxiway to keep the main gear on the cement during the turn. When you came to the run-up pad and taxiied into a hold position, the brakes were applied and a toggle switch was used to put the brakes on and off. It usually took fifteen minutes to run up all six engines. When the engineers said it was OK to go, I would taxi into position and stop. I would then open the four jet engine fuel cocks and actuate the four starter switches. The jets would usually start 'hot' as they were using 115/145 high octane gas from the the wing tanks (we did not carry jet fuel), and were set to idle at 67 per cent power.

"I would advance the number four engine throttle and the engineers would follow me *continued* through to 67 inches of MAP (manifold absolute power) with the other engines. After checking the engine analizer, they would turn the turbo-superchargers of the R4360 Pratt & Whitney engines up to Turbo 10, giving me 3800 horsepower per engine. I would then set the jet throttles over my head to 101.5 per cent rpm and wait for their thrust to stabilize. Taking the steering knob in my hand, I would release the brakes and we were on our way.

The B-36 rolled for about 4500 feet when relatively light at only 375,000 pounds take-off weight. I would lift the nose off the runway and the rudder became effective. At 90 mph I would let go of the steering knob and take hold of the wheel. I put my feet on a large steel bar on top of the rudder pedals and, together, the co-pilot and I would pull the airplane into the air. Normally when the nose wheels came off the runway, the eight main wheels did as well. We would then be airborne for up to thirty hours.
– Joseph Anastasia, former US Air Force B-36 pilot

versatile, if less lovely, than the Lanc, the Handley–Page airplane proved to be a powerful workhorse as a bomber, but also in a maritime reconnaissance role, as a freighter, glider tug, air ambulance and personal transport.

Through a series of design revisions based on the unavailability of some major aero engines of the time, the first two marks of the Halifax were Rolls–Royce Merlin–powered, but the ultimate versions, the B.Mk. III and the final bomber, the B.Mk. VI, were powered by Bristol Hercules engines, giving the aircraft greater energy and enhanced performance.

Halifaxes operated with distinction against Germany, throughout Europe and in the Far East and the Middle East, as well as serving in the airborne operations over Normandy and Arnhem, and the Rhine crossing. 6176 of the aircraft were produced through 1946 by Handley–Page, English Electric, Rootes, Fairey, and the London Aircraft Production Group.

The idea was to develop a strategic bomber able to bring substantial bomb tonnage over great distances, from Northern Ireland and Egypt to Germany, with a new level of efficiency. The plane intended for this job was the Boeing B-29. Called the Superfortress, this successor to the B-17 would in the end find and meet a different challenge.

The B-29 had a top speed of 357 mph at 30,000 feet and an economical cruising speed of 220 mph at 25,000 feet. The range (with a 10,000–pound bomb load) was 3250 miles.

When she was ready she went mainly to the Pacific theatre where she was based in the Marianas Islands. A new Air Force was created and activated for the B-29, the Twentieth. While bases for the big new bombers were also constructed in China and India, it was to be from the Marianas that the major blows against Japan would be struck in the final nine months of World War II.

Initial attacks by the Superfortresses, known to

the Japanese as "Mister B", began in November 1944 on targets like the Nakajima Aircraft Company at Musashino, near Tokyo, with only fair results. In the days immediately following the raid, a B-29 base on the island of Saipan was hit by Japanese bombers in attacks which destroyed eleven of the new American planes, damaged 43 others and killed 45 US personnel, while wounding 200 more. Further B-29 missions were flown to Japanese targets through December and January with varying results. Then on 20 January, General Curtis E. LeMay took charge of Twentieth Bomber Command and immediately began a programme of reorganisation and redirection of its resources. He went with his B-29s on some of the missions to Japan. These were mainly conventional high–altitude precision daylight strikes on point targets—but not entirely. Into this series of attacks he wove two "fire raids" using incendiary ordnance instead of high–explosives. These raids were inspired by his experiences with the Eighth Air Force in Europe, and especially the firestorm attacks on Hamburg by the Eighth and by RAF Bomber Command. Analyses of the two fire raids on Japan resulted in a redefinition of target and attack priorities for LeMay by General Hap Arnold's staff. As of 19 February 1945 LeMay was ordered to prioritise his strikes as follows:

1. Aircraft engine factories.
2. Cities.
3. Aircraft assembly plants.

Importantly, the city targets were to be attacked with incendiaries and approximately sixty Japanese cities were earmarked for such attention.

LeMay was aware of the problems faced by the B-29 crews in their recent high–altitude raids: jet–stream winds of extreme velocity, frequent heavy cloud cover over the targets, engines that were not performing up to specification or reliability standards — "three turning one burning" was a common reference to the Superfort at the time — inability to carry the required bomb load, very strong and determined fighter opposition and heavy exposure to enemy flak. He thought he had the answers to most or all of these irritants. He directed that the '29s would henceforth fly incendiary "fire" raids at low levels by night. His crews would, he believed, be subjected to lighter winds; their engines would run cooler on less fuel and would last longer. They would fly in a bomber stream rather than a formation and would save more fuel. There was little tangible threat from Japanese night fighters, thus reducing the need for defensive firepower on the Superforts to the single tail turret. This alteration alone would greatly cut the weight of the bombers by eliminating excess turrets, gunners and ammunition, and the weight saving would translate into additional bomb tonnage carried.

LeMay used another idea that had been perfected in the ETO: he had pathfinder B-29s fly ahead of the main force to set massive fires on which the rest of the bombers would drop their loads. The first of the great fire raids took place on 9 March 1945 and was the single most destructive air raid in history, including Dresden, Hamburg and both atomic attacks. Twenty–five per cent of all buildings in Tokyo were destroyed. A hundred and fifty thousand inhabitants were dead, injured or missing. One million citizens of Tokyo were homeless. The city could be seen glowing red from forty miles away.

In that time many structures in Japan were made of cedar, bamboo and paper — materials that burned well — and, in the course of many attacks flown by the B-29s, most cities and towns there were turned to ashes. The fire raids continued into August 1945

Below: Known for its great versatility, the Consolidated B-24 Liberator was highly effective as a strategic bomber, in maritime reconnaissance, anti-submarine work, photo–reconaissance, as a flying tanker and for carrying freight and passengers. The US Army Air Forces accepted more than 18,000 Liberators and Liberator variants during World War II. Many were built for the US Navy and the Royal Air Force, and one, named *Commando*, was the personal transport of British Prime Minister Winston Churchill.

with increasing ferocity.

In June the first B-29s to occupy the giant new base at North Field on the island of Tinian arrived. On 6 and 9 August, two of the new atomic bombs were dropped by B-29s of the 509th Composite Group, on Hiroshima and Nagasaki respectively, leading to the unconditional surrender of Japan on 14 August.

She always made the earth move for this writer. She was the Convair B-36 Peacemaker, and was aptly nicknamed, for in the ten–year period in which she roamed the world's skies, peace reigned (except, of course, for occasional small "brushfire" conflicts). The B-36 was big in every respect — 47 feet high and 162 feet long, with a wingspan of 230 feet, dwarfing that of a Boeing 747 jumbo. She cruised at 230 mph, had a service ceiling of 45,700 feet and a top speed of 435 mph. When full of fuel, bombs, ammunition and her crew of sixteen men, she weighed more than 205 tons. She could range 10,000 miles and stay aloft for more than two days carrying up to 86,000 pounds of conventional or nuclear bombs, and was armed with sixteen 20mm cannon. She was driven by the power of six enormous Pratt and Whitney R-4360 pusher–type piston engines mounted on the trailing edge of her wing, each of them producing 3800 hp, and by four General Electric J47 jet engines of 5200 pounds thrust each in twin wing–mounted pods.

Such was the enormity of her noise that, when approaching at low altitude, she often announced her presence as much as a full minute before coming into view. The earth literally shook when a B-36 was in the neighbourhood. Windows rattled and, in San Diego where I lived during the airplane's operational lifetime, cars that had stopped at a traffic light at the intersection near the end of the runway at Lindbergh Field were sometimes "nudged" where they sat if one of the giant bombers was having its engines run up prior to take-off.

Most of the US Air Force B-36s spent several

months in San Diego during the early 1950s having their jet engine pods installed. Flight testing of the jet installation was a part of that project, and I vividly remember a summer afternoon in 1952 when I was fishing from the sandy shore on Mission Bay. I became aware of the approach of one of the big planes through its familiar distant rumble. Something was different this time, though. The sound was somehow incomplete.

I scanned the sky across the bay to the east and spotted her, perhaps six or seven miles out and maybe 6,000 feet up. She was in a slow, shallow descent, and only about half of her engines were running. One entire wing was trailing a sheet of flame at least as long as the airplane itself. It appeared that the crew were doing all they could to guide the great bomber across the densely-populated beach neighbourhoods, over the strand and out to what they must have hoped would be a safe ditching in the Pacific.

I dropped my fishing gear and sprinted the several hundred yards from the bayside across the strand to the ocean's edge and watched as the stricken bomber somehow maintained enough altitude to clear the homes of Mission Beach. Burning more furiously now, she seemed to be heading for an impact with the sea about a mile offshore. Just then a few parachutes appeared from the gently gliding aluminium inferno, and then a few more. In seconds it was over. The great flaming structure knifed into the blue water with a surprisingly slight surface disturbance, like the entry of an Olympic diver. She was gone, leaving only an arcing smoke pillar that didn't last long.

Quite soon a number of small ships and helicopters arrived in the area of the crash. I hoped that all of the test crew had managed to parachute safely from the doomed plane. Most of them survived, but a few, including the pilot, did not. The next morning, and for a week or so after the crash, I walked along the beach and came across many bits given up by the B-36 as she came apart in her plunge to the sea bed.

Pink wodges of insulation, soaked cardboard segments of emergency ration packs, and other stuff... all that remained of what had been a majestic, unforgettable creation.

More than 380 B-36s were built by Convair at Fort Worth, Texas by the end of the production run in August 1954. The bomber never saw combat, a tribute to her role as a peace-keeper.

"I had been flying as first pilot with Major McCullor's crew, learning how to fly the B-36 and how to land it. Our normal landing weight was 257,000 pounds. It was a monster. On landing in a very strong crosswind, there is no one strong enough to hold a B-36 in a crabbed attitude. You couldn't put a wing down because of the jet pods on the ends, so you flew the airplane onto the runway in a crab. When a B-36, even in a thirty-degree crabbed attitude, approached the runway, because the main wheels are aft of the centre of gravity, the airplane would, more often than not, straighten itself out and head down the runway.

"I finally got a crew of my own and, while we could fly training missions, we were not authorized as 'combat ready.' My co-pilot was Reed Mulkey. One day we were on final approach to land and there was a ninety-degree crosswind blowing over the runway, which ran north and south and was 10,000 feet long with 2,000-foot over-runs at either end. It was 300 feet wide. Mulkey was flying the airplane and he had one helluva crab on it. We came over the end of the runway to flare out for landing and as he did, he moved a bit sideways in his seat, to position himself for the crabbed attitude. We hit astraddle of the runway lights and went right off the runway in a large cloud of dust and snow. He caught the yoke and steered the big bomber back onto the runway at more than 150 mph. We were both on the controls, and had our hands full of roaring beast. We were trying to get the six engines into reverse by pushing a little round button, but the ride was so rough that we just couldn't manage it. Mulkey was steering the nose wheel and I was holding aileron and full left rudder

"We climbed on a height test to 17,000 feet, circling a part of England I shall always regard as ours. It was bounded to the north by the Humber and to the west by the silver line of the Trent. To the south it stretched as far as the pale cruciform of Lincoln Cathedral and to the east — that awesome direction — to the North Sea. Though the Halifax appeared to respond well to Geoff's handling, I remembered Doug's words on the ground before we took off. 'They're poor rudders on these kites. The bloomin' things even *look* a bad shape.' The story had already reached us that the Halifax Mark I had a vicious rudder stall and that few of those who experienced it came out alive."
— from *No Moon Tonight* by Don Charlwood

Right: B-29 crewmen check the parachute of the man in front. Right centre: Photo–recon B-29 (F-13) gunner Cliff Shirley in 1943. Below: Ground crews on Saipan in the Marianas Islands at work on the bomb load and ammunition for this B-29 of the 500th Bomb Group (VH).

Far left: A June 1945 photo of Major–General Curtis E. LeMay, then Commander of the Twentieth USAAF in the far east. Left: Fires started in a B-29 attack on the Osaka suburb of Sakai, where factories that were producing ordnance, marine engines, machine tools, chemicals and explosives were hit on 10 July 1945. Below: A B-29 based on Okinawa during the Korean War, 1950.

Top: An Avro Vulcan bomber. Above: A B-2 Stealth bomber in July 1997 at RAF Fairford, Gloucestershire, England. Right: The painting *Hampdens 'bombing up', RAF Waddington*, by Frank Wootton.

for all I was worth. We finally got the engines into reverse and applied full power to get the airplane stopped. We were terrified that something might have gotten broken in the landing, but on inspection, nothing was. One of the engineers remarked that 'it was a good landing.' I still think of it as an arrival."

– Joseph Anastasia, former US Air Force B-36 pilot

They were the V–Force, Britain's bomber delivery system for its Cold War nuclear capability. The Vickers Valiant, the Handley–Page Victor and the Avro Vulcan formed the sharp end of a powerful deterrent force which served effectively into the early 1970s.

Roy Chadwick, Avro's Chief Designer, died tragically in the crash of the Type 689 Tudor 2 airliner prototype in August 1947. His superb delta–wing Vulcan bomber design was accepted by the Air Ministry for production in November of that year. Operated by a five–man crew, the Olympus–powered planes were based on ten UK airfields from the late 1950s. They were assigned a readiness state called Quick Reaction Alert (QRA) during periods of international crisis. Positioned on operational readiness platforms alongside a main base runway, the Vulcans were required to be airborne as a group in five minutes or less.

Vulcans often carried air–launched nuclear weapons on high–altitude missions, but by 1960 it was clear that this role was becoming obsolete and the RAF elected to convert its entire V–Force to an ultra–low–level penetration capability. In this role the big delta bomber was re–equipped with the Yellow Sun Mk 2 nuclear weapon and the WE-177 "lay–down", "off–set" and "over–the–shoulder" weapons. The Vulcan clearly overshadowed its V–Force companions, the Valiant and Victor, both of which experienced serious operational faults and setbacks. By the late 1960s Britain had decided to switch its nuclear deterrent responsibility to the Royal Navy's

Polaris–equipped nuclear submarines. The V–bombers were completely phased out of service at the start of the 1980s, destined to be replaced in the air by the new Panavia Tornado multi–role force that was soon to join the RAF inventory.

It took the gigantic resources of the Boeing Airplane Company to conceive, design, organize, sub–contract and manufacture the plane that has been the mainstay of America's strategic bombing force for most of the period since the end of World War II. Originally planned to carry four B-28 or B-61 thermonuclear gravity bombs in internal weapons bays, the B-52 Stratofortress first appeared in 1952. It answered the call of the US Air Force for a very fast new bomber of great range and load capacity to replace the ageing B-36 intercontinental bomber.

Entering front–line service in 1955, the B-52's capability was linked to the then–revolutionary Pratt & Whitney J57 jet engine; eight of which were needed to drive the huge plane. The J57 developed its great power (10,000 pounds thrust or roughly twice that of most available jet engines of the time) through very high compression, achieved by the use of two compressors in tandem, each turned by separate turbines. Later in the development of the bomber it was re–engined with still more powerful, cleaner and more economical turbofans.

Remembered chiefly for their bombing role in the Vietnam War, black–painted B-52s frequently delivered 84,000–pound bomb loads on jungle guerrilla targets and were said to be the American weapon most feared by the North Vietnamese. The big bomber is the longest–lived combat aircraft design ever produced. It has a top speed of 546 mph and a range of 10,000 miles.

The notion of a bomber able to operate entirely on its own and with virtual impunity against all conceivable air defences is what inspired the US Air Force to pursue the concept, design, funding, development, construction, testing and deployment

Above: Aviation pioneer John K. Northrop, whose work on flying wing aircraft in the 1940s foreshadowed the development of the B-2 Spirit stealth bomber of the 1990s. Right: The F-15E Strike Eagle can operate at night and in adverse weather conditions. It can carry more than 24,000 pounds of external ordnance. Its Hughes APG-63 synthetic aperture radar sees, maps and displays in the cockpit mobile tactical targets more than 20 nautical miles away. This aircraft is carrying twin conformal fuel tanks called Fast Packs, with 10,000 pounds of additional fuel, as well as 22 Mk-82 500–pound bombs. The Strike Eagle also remains a highly capable air-to-air weapon system. Overleaf: A German Dornier Do 217 of KG-2 making its way back to the Continent after hitting a target in southern England a few months after the Battle of Britain. The painting is *Night Crossing* by Robert Bailey

of the B-2 Spirit, the stealth bomber.

Developed through the 1980s, the B-2 is the sharp end of the big bomber triumvirate expected to carry the USAF well into the new century. With the old but still mightily effective B-52, and the highly capable B-1, the stealth bomber provides a comprehensive delivery capability that its advocates see as today's version of Teddy Roosevelt's big stick.

The strange, bat–like wing configuration, the ability to operate on very short notice with no forward basing support, minimal detectability, enviable intercontinental range and the wildly amazing price tag believed to exceed $1 billion a copy, single out the Spirit as one of the most exceptional aircraft (for that matter, man–made creations), of all time.

Originally B-2 production was planned for 132 planes, but many factors, including the collapse of the Soviet Union, whose extensive radar network it was intended to evade, and the staggering unit cost of the advanced bomber, combined to reduce the final quantity (as of 1999) to just 21 aircraft. Surrounded by controversy over its cost, the effectiveness of its stealthy technology, the need for such an apparently extravagant, complex project in a period when the world seemed to be changing so rapidly and unpredictably, the large initial quantity ordered by the Air Force was sliced to the bone. This resulted in a lean and mean operational force which is, its advocates believe, more than capable of delivering on its original broad promise.

The Spirit inherited some of its characteristics from the pioneering efforts in flying wing design and development of Jack Northrop and his Los Angeles–based aircraft company in the late 1940s. Northrop's giant propeller–driven, and later jet–powered wings suffered serious flight stability problems. Some crashes ensued in the flight test programmes which ultimately sealed the fate of the daring and innovative project. Probably the Northrop flying wings were

technologically ahead of their time. In a real sense the B-2 Spirit is their legacy, achieving four decades later what they were unable to do. Northrop, too, is the company that was selected and contracted to design and head the B-2 production effort, which also utilizes major structures and components built by Boeing, Ling Temco Vought, General Electric and Hughes.

The design criteria calling for ultra–low radar observability as well as exceptional aerodynamics, for a uniquely stealthy package, led to one of history's better kept secrets. While it was being developed, the bomber was under management by the US Air Force Aeronautical Systems Division at Wright Patterson AFB, Ohio. Throughout the 1980s the black project was the subject of many rumours. The facts of its existence, capabilities and special design, however, remained secret until the Air Force decided to show it to the press and public in a November 1988 factory roll–out before the flight test phase of development. Jack Northrop, however, was given a special briefing and was shown the B-2 shortly before his death in 1981.

The Spirit can deliver a variety of conventional and nuclear weapons, including 500–pound to 2200–pound general purpose bombs, sea mines, nuclear gravity bombs and other ordnance. It can carry up to 40,000 pounds of weapons. Fully loaded it weighs 336,500 pounds. Its operating range is approximately 6000 miles, and it can take off and land on any field capable of accommodating a Boeing 727 airliner. The B-2 has relatively low take–off and landing approach speeds. It operates with a fly–by–wire flight control system which gives it fairly conventional handling and flying qualities. Its pilots find it pleasant to fly and a much better performer than either the B-52 or B-1 bombers. This radical airplane is composed largely of carbon–fibre–epoxy composite materials and is currently the epitome of operational stealth technology.

The Spirit is based at Whiteman Air Force Base in

eastern Missouri. It is operated there by the 509th Bomb Wing, descended from the World War II 509th Composite Group whose B-29s took the first atomic bombs to Hiroshima and Nagasaki.

In its stealthy mission, the B-2 is meant to lead the attack in the first night of raids in any coming conflict. It is dedicated to hit the best–defended, most vital and significant enemy sites. It can strike such targets from its US base while operating independently and virtually on its own terms.

The tiny masked light in the bomb-aimer's compartment had to be switched off before take-off but until that time I made myself at home. I felt more secure here than anywhere else in the aircraft. There wasn't sufficient space in which to sit and so I lay, and my couch was the escape hatch. To my left was the bombsight computer box which was connected by two drives to the sighting head and it contained two Browning .303 machine-guns. To my right, and within reach of my hand, was the pre-selector box on which the order for releasing the bombs could be set and whether they were to fall singly or in salvo. Packed into the remainder of the compartment, and filling all the spare room, were sheaves of "window" — thin metallized strips of paper which, when fed into the slipstream of hundreds of bombers, blurred enemy ground radar screens. It was the bomb-aimer's task to push "window" through a narrow chute near his right thigh.
– from *The Eighth Passenger*
by Miles Tripp

FROM ITS BEGINNING in World War I, the true bomber was designed to carry and deliver bombs in level flight against specific targets at medium to long range. Combatants who were utilizing airships for this purpose soon discovered their vulnerability to both ground fire and air attack by the scout planes of the day. They quickly shifted to the use of two-seat craft like the BE 2e, operated from the summer of 1916 by the Royal Flying Corps. It arrived in time for the Battle of the Somme, but left much to be desired as a bomber. Cruising at little more than 60 mph at only a few thousand feet of altitude, this flimsy craft was also prey to ground fire and its marginal performance was seriously reduced through having to carry the added weight of bombs. When sent to attack a target, and carrying a maximum bomb load, the observer had to be left back at the base.

Probably the earliest recorded concept of aerial bombing comes from the Hindu epic poem, the *Mahabharata* of Krishna–Dwaipayana–Vyasa. In it is a description of the enemies of Krishna inducing demons to construct a winged chariot to be driven through the sky until it stood over Dwarakha, home of the followers of Krishna. From it missiles would be thrown down upon the city destroying everything on which they fell. In 1670 the Italian Jesuit Francesco Lana de Terzi designed an "aerial ship" which was to be borne aloft by four copper globes from which the air had been evacuated. He is said to have allowed, though, that "God might prevent its construction since such a device might descend on an enemy's fleet, kill their men and burn their ships by artificial fireworks and fire-balls. And this they may do not only to ships but to great buildings, castles and cities, with such severity that they which cast these things down from a height out of gun-shot, cannot on the other side be offended by those from below."

It was in 1793 that aeronautic inventor Joseph–Michel de Montgolfier proposed that his balloon might be used to drop two large bombs on the port of Toulon, France, which was then rebelling against the Republican government. It didn't happen. But in 1849, Austrians laying siege to Venice became the first combatants to drop bombs on their enemy. In fact, while the Germans, French and British dithered over the concept of aerial bombardment by balloon, the Austrians had already established several balloon battalions using the balloons of Montgolfier, which were capable of lifting 33 pounds of bombs and staying aloft for more than half an hour. The Austrians utilized trial balloons for testing the strength and direction of the wind before successfully flinging some of their bombs on Venice, whose residents' morale suffered more than their property.

Among the earliest proponents of aerial bombing from balloons was Henry Tracey Coxwell who, in the mid–1800s, wrote: "I have no doubt that it

THE WEAPONS

The effects of the German heavy bomber raids on London in 1918 were vastly over-rated by both sides. The British Handley–Page 1500 was designed to attack Berlin, and by the end of World War I it was a widely held belief that the future lay with the bomber. This theory was embraced in the 1920s, by authorities on both sides of the Channel, and in America, which claimed that the bomber would be a war-winning weapon that was unbeatable. "The bomber will always get through." The British Air Staff needed no convincing. It was their belief that: "The strategic air offensive is a means of direct attack on the enemy state with the object of depriving it of the means or will to continue the war. It may in itself be the instrument of victory, or it may be the means by which victory can be won by other forces. It differs from all previous kinds of armed attack in that it alone can be brought to bear immediately, directly and destructively against the heartland of the enemy."
– from *Yesterday's Gone*
by N. J. Crisp

Left: Robert Shaw and Richard Todd in a still photo from the 1954 Associated British Picture Corporation film *The Dam Busters*, the story of the May 1943 Ruhr dams raid by aircrews of No. 617 Squadron Lancasters flying from RAF Scampton in Lincolnshire, England.

Below: In 1915, a German reconnaissance crew drops a small bomb. Bottom: Fanciful armoured aerial pods on the cover of a 1915 issue of *Leslie's* magazine.

would be possible to drop, with tolerable nicety, a host of aerial vessels charged with agents calculated to produce stupefaction, if not fatal effects. If by this method our warriors could secure prisoners instead of increasing carnage, humanity would rejoice at so desirable a consummation by such ingenious means." Balloons then, however, had certain drawbacks. They could only carry a relatively light bomb load, were at the mercy of the winds and were difficult to manoeuvre, and their ordnance could not be delivered with accuracy. They were, in fact, really only a terror weapon for their time. This changed to some extent with the coming of the steerable rigid airships like the great Zeppelins at the beginning of the 20th century. By 1910, Zeppelins had become capable of carrying a substantial bomb load over a considerable distance and were quite manoeuvrable.

In 1903 the brothers Orville and Wilbur Wright demonstrated their heavier–than–air flying machine at Kittyhawk in North Carolina, and in 1911 a Wright biplane was tested as a potential bombing aircraft by the US Army. In that year the first actual use of airplanes to drop bombs took place in North Africa when an Italian expeditionary force utilized six Blériot aircraft to drop a total of four 10–kilogram hand grenade "bombs" on Turkish positions.

In Britain during 1912, the Royal Flying Corps was formed and before long it began to develop offensive plans for aerial warfare, including the attacking of troop concentrations, supply centres and ammunition dumps as well as facilities for communications. The Naval Wing of the RFC split off from the parent organisation in July 1914 and became the Royal Naval Air Service, which was then headed by the First Lord of the Admiralty, Winston S. Churchill. Churchill made it the mission of the RNAS to seek and destroy the

enemy, and took the lead in developing bombing and aerial torpedo operations, relying mainly on aircraft from private companies like Sopwith and Shorts rather than Government–sponsored planes from the Royal Aircraft Establishment, Farnborough. Prior to this, in 1913, Churchill had written about the German airships: "The Zeppelin should be attacked . . . by an aeroplane descending on it obliquely from above and discharging a series of bombs or fireballs, at rapid intervals, so that a string of them, more than a hundred yards in length, would be drawn like a whip-lash across the gas bag."

From the start of World War I, the idea of aerial bombing was still suspect in most quarters and few military men believed that aircraft at that stage could even be useful in a reconnaissance role, much less as bombers. The only possible threat they could perceive was that of being bombed by the Zeppelins, and even that was offset to an extent by the difficulties facing the airship crews in crossing and navigating the great distance to England and locating worthwhile targets. Among the warring nations there was, in fact, little if any real priority given then to the development of bomber aircraft. The British War Office, for example, was interested in only three types of aircraft:
1. a light single–seat scout;
2. a two–seat reconnaissance machine;
3. a heavier two–seat fighter.
While employed in a token bombing role through the occasional lobbing of grenades or "bomblets", all of these aircraft were relatively underpowered and incapable of lifting more than a tiny bomb load. Thus, when the war came the Royal Flying Corps was operating aircraft with no real aerial bombing capability.

Initially, airmen of the various warring nations tried out the aerial bombing concept by dropping grenades. Some filled and dropped gasoline canisters and, in an interesting approach to anti–personnel bombardment, the French tried the dropping of *fléchettes* (steel darts) on the German cavalry units.

In the first true bombing attack of the war, the Germans sent the Zeppelin Z.VI to drop thirteen bombs on a fort defending Liège. The fort was untouched but nine civilians were killed in the raid. Ground fire damaged the airship which crashed on its return to Cologne. Various nuisance raids by individual scout aircraft of both sides followed and, within a month of the war's opening shot, it was the Royal Naval Air Service that conducted the war's first real bombing offensive. RNAS Sopwith biplanes based in Antwerp were modified to carry crude bomb racks and on 22 September 1914 four of the planes took off to attack the Zeppelin sheds at Cologne and Düsseldorf. Navigation and weather problems caused the raid to fail, but another strike by the Sopwiths two weeks later yielded significant results when one of the pilots located the main Düsseldorf Zeppelin shed. He dropped two twenty–pound bombs on the shed and managed to set aflame the new Z.IX Zeppelin inside. The airship was destroyed, as were three additional Zeppelins during this period. Then, in November, three specially–equipped Avro 504s flew from a field near the French frontier to hit the Zeppelin works at Friedrichshafen. Through clever planning and execution, the Avros surprised the Germans and damaged a Zeppelin then under construction. They further damaged the airship works and the local gasworks was destroyed as well.

Now the minuscule bombing capability of existing aircraft, and the extreme vulnerability of the airships, led visionary planners of several nations to conclude that development of dedicated bomber aircraft was important, even essential. They further realized that they had to differentiate between bomber aircraft to be developed for tactical purposes and those meant for strategic attacks. Tactical requirements were evident by the end of 1914 when both sides in the conflict were firmly dug in and stalled from the Channel coast all across France. Targets such as ammunition and supply storage, communications centres and troop concentrations were ripe for attack and were hit by the reconnaissance planes of the day operating in a dual capacity as bombers. Between early March and late June of 1915, some 141 tactical bombing raids were launched by the Allies, mostly on German–occupied rail junctions, but only a few of these attacks were successful.

The Kaiser had ordered German airship raids on British military targets such as arsenals in January 1915. The attacks were to be flown by night as they had lost the Zeppelin Z.VI and two other airships to ground fire in the early days of the war. Their airships did, however, tend to drift off course and, with the blackout in England, they frequently bombed undefended villages in East Anglia rather than the military targets they had been sent to hit. Often the airship commanders didn't know where their bombs had fallen and were unable to differentiate between military targets and civilian sites. On 19 January 1915 King's Lynn and Yarmouth, both in the county of Norfolk, received bombs from two Zeppelins. Six people were killed when the airships dropped their loads of 110–pound high explosive bombs and 6.5–pound incendiaries. The British reaction was one of shock and outrage. By the summer months the relative inaccuracy of the raids had led to the Kaiser ending his ban on the bombing of British cities and concerted German airship attacks on London and the Tyneside areas began. More than fifty Zeppelin raids hit London. Across Britain reprisal raids were demanded and a programme was initiated to radically improve anti–aircraft defences. By the end of 1915 more than 700 Britons had been killed or injured in the Zeppelin raids. These raids continued into the summer of 1918, but with far less effect.

London, when you can see its skyline at all, seems peculiarly beautiful under the black–out. And you may read a bitter, sad defiance in its silent stone. But for most night of the month it is just a black nothingness, in which you move gingerly for fear you will meet something. You hear the sound of passing feet. And you begin to read them. I think I know some of them now – particularly that rush of hurrying footsteps in the early morning, after the 'All Clear' has gone. They are hurrying home.
– from *Bomber's Moon* by Negley Farson

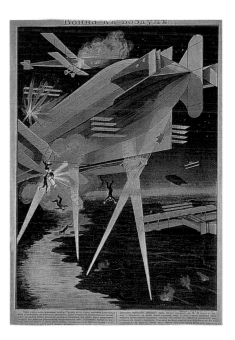

"Early in the spring of 1944 a Mosquito unlike any we had seen before flew into Oakington. It was a standard Mk IV modified to carry a 4000–lb bomb, the famous 'cookie'. To accommodate this large piece of ordnance the bomb bay had been strengthened and the bomb doors redesigned. The aircraft looked like a pregnant lady, because its belly was markedly rotund. Our CO announced that we were to fly the cookie–carrier as much as possible and the most experienced crews were detailed to take her on normal operations.

The night arrived when Bill Hickox and I were ordered to try our hand with this new machine on a target in the Ruhr. Take-off was not difficult, but quite definitely she was not a scalded cat. As soon as her tail came up I pushed the throttles quickly forward to the gate (plus nine pound boost, 3000 rpm) and then clenched my left hand over the gate catch releases and eased the throttles to the fully open position (plus twelve pounds boost, 3000 rpm).

In G-George this would have resulted in a glorious acceleration and a hop, skip and jump into the air. Not so with our pregnant lady; she waddled along and took most of the runway before she deigned to unstick. Moreover, the climb was a sedate affair and we took much longer to reach 25,000 feet than with our usual steed; and when we arrived there she took a long time to settle to a steady cruise. However, we eventually sorted ourselves out and headed resolutely for the Ruhr.

In the target area I felt distinctly nervous–there we *continued*

The best of the early British bombers was the Handley–Page 0/100 which, in 1917, equipped the first RFC strategic bombing unit. While only eighty of these aircraft were produced, it was an excellent bomber for the time, powered by two 250 hp Rolls–Royce V engines and capable of 100 mph. The 0/400 biplane had a range of 745 miles and carried a four–man crew armed with either four or five movable Lewis guns. It carried a 1984–pound bomb load.

Into the spring of 1917, the British and Germans traded raids and reprisals until, in May, a new and more sinister series of bombing attacks was begun by the Germans — the year–long Gotha offensive. The Gotha was a large, twin–Mercedes–powered heavy bomber made by the Gothaer Waggonfabrikwerk. It carried a crew of three, up to four machine–guns, and a 1300–pound bomb load. It was capable of 87 mph and had a ceiling of 21,300 feet and a range of 520 miles. Daylight Gotha raids on London and British port cities continued with devastating effect until September when British anti–aircraft guns got the better of them, and the Gothas were switched to night attacks. In that same month, a new and formidable four–engine German bomber, the "Giant", made its debut. With a crew of nine, it had virtually the same wingspan as the B-29 Superfortress of World War II. Together with the Gothas, the Giants dropped nearly 100 tons of bombs in 27 raids, killing about 800 Britons, mostly civilians, and injuring nearly 2000 more. Again, British defences improved significantly and the effectiveness of this major bombing campaign dropped off markedly.

Probably the most important result of this bombing offensive was the 1917 report by General Jan Christiaan Smuts, who had been authorized by the British Cabinet to investigate the effects of the German raids and British defence capabilities. His far–sighted recommendations included a radical overhaul of the British home defences; a doubling of the strength of the air forces; the creation and swift development of a large strategic bombing

force to bring the air war to the German homeland, and the immediate creation of an independent air service separate from both the Army and Navy. The report also stated: "The day may not be far off, when aerial operations with their devastation of enemy lands and destruction of industrial and populous centres on a vast scale may become the principal operations of war, to which the older forms of military and naval operations may become secondary and subservient." It was only at the end of the war in late 1918, that the Inter–Allied Strategic Bombing Force, composed of British, French, United States and Italian squadrons, was formed. More importantly, in April of that year, as a direct result of the Smuts report, the Royal Air Force was created.

During World War I, considerable advances were made in the development of aerial bombs. Great strides were made in design to improve their stability and predictability in flight, their fusing mechanisms and their destructive capacity.

In 1913 the British bomb–design pioneer F. Martin Hale developed a bomb for the RNAS, a 20–pound high–explosive type representing one of the first departures from older bomb shapes in an attempt to improve the weapon's stability in flight. The Hale, and the German Carbonit series of high–explosive bombs, were somewhat pear–shaped and had tail fins. Less accurate than the Hale, the Carbonits had a steel–tipped nose for improved penetration. They were made in a range of sizes from 4.5 kg to 50 kg.

An aerial bomb had to be transportable in safety; the bomber crew had to be able to jettison their bombs safely if necessary, and the bombs had to arm themselves as they were dropped, and detonate on impact. Thus, there was a major emphasis on bomb–fusing mechanism design in the war years.

Three types of explosive were required in the aerial bombs of World War I. Amatol, a relatively

were, with the bomb doors open and Bill droning away with his 'Left, left — right — steady' and I just knew that every gunner in the Ruhr could see the enormous bomb we were carrying and was determined to explode it and blow us to smithereens. I looked at the bomb jettison handle in front of me — no delicate lever this, it was a solid bar of metal which, if moved, would manually release the massive catch holding the 'cookie' and down the bomb would go. If the bomb doors had not been opened, that was hard luck — the 'cookie' would still drop away and take the bomb doors with it!

However, no such inglorious thing happened. Bill suddenly announced 'Bomb gone', and as he did so the Mossie shot up like a lift. There was no delicate porpoising, as with four 500–pounders; the altimeter moved instantly through 500 feet of altitude. I had never seen anything like this before. More importantly, as soon as I had closed the bomb doors our fat little lady became almost a normal Mosquito and accelerated to a fast cruising speed."
— J. R. Goodman, formerly with Nos. 37, 99, 139 and 627 Squadrons, RAF

Left: 500–pound bombs released over the railroad marshalling yards at Bekes–Csaba, Hungary, by heavy bombers of the 775th Bomb Squadron, 463rd Bomb Group (H), Fifteenth USAAF on 21 September 1944.

Below: A Fritz Erler poster, circa 1917, showing a German aerial gunner who is wounded but not defeated. Below right: A British DeHavilland BE2c observation plane crew displaying their bomb load.

insensitive type, was used as a main bursting charge until later in the war when it was largely replaced by TNT. An exploder was needed to detonate the bursting charge and an explosive called Tetryl was commonly used for this purpose. A fulmonate of mercury detonator was used to set off the exploder and required great care in handling as it was highly sensitive. Before the bomb was loaded into the aircraft, the detonator and exploder were fitted into it. On impact with the ground or the target, a striker pin hit the detonator causing the exploder to ignite and this then caused the bursting charge to explode.

A small propeller was used to arm the fusing mechanism of the Hale and Carbonit bombs. The tail—mounted propeller would unwind a spindle in the bomb when it was dropped, ultimately letting the striker contact the detonator on impact. The propeller had a guard clip attached to prevent premature arming, and was removed

before the bomb was released.

In time, bomb racks and release mechanisms were devised. Next to come along were bomb types with nose fuses and nose–mounted arming propellers such as the twenty–pound Cooper, which created an instantaneous explosion when the bomb impacted with the ground, scattering deadly fragments over a large area. Made with a light case, this bomb, along with the French *fléchette* dart canister, were among the first anti–personnel bombs to be developed. Tail–fused bombs, on the other hand, had a delayed action, from 1/20th of a second to up to fifteen seconds, and would bury themselves into the ground before exploding. Many bombs of British manufacture were designed to carry two fuses, one in the nose and another in the tail, as a fail-safe solution to the all–too–common problem of fuse mechanism failure.

Standardization of British bomb types came in

Below left: A US recruiting poster of World War I by Warren Keith, circa 1918. Below: The June 1937 issue of *Dare-Devil Aces* magazine.

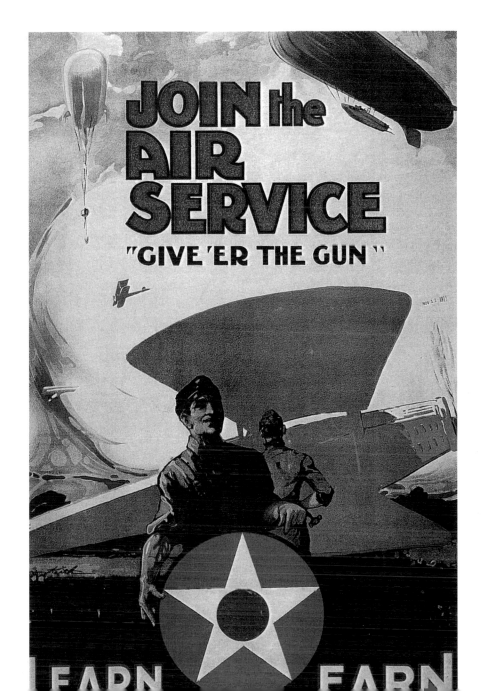

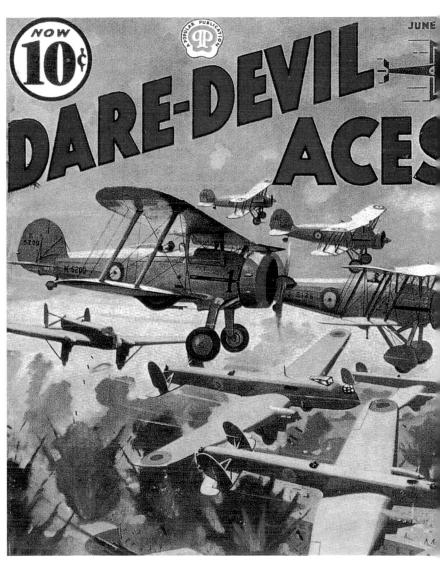

near the end of the war with four basic types then in use. Weights ranged from the old twenty–pound heavy–case Cooper, to the 3360–pound bomb that was developed to be carried by the Handley–Page V/1500 bomber.

Finally, the first true forerunner of the bombs of World War II was the German PuW. It had an aerodynamic torpedo–like shape and a high grade steel casing, as well as fin design quite similar to that of WWII bombs which caused the bomb to rotate as it fell, arming the fuses by centrifugal force. The PuW could be carried and dropped from a horizontal position in the bomb racks as well as in internal bomb bays, thus reducing drag and improving the performance of the aircraft.

The incendiary bomb was a concept developed primarily by the Germans during World War I. Earlier British incendiaries utilised a black powder or petrol filler. They were largely ineffective and were replaced late in the War by a phosphorus version. The French were also active in the

development of this type of weapon, but it was the Germans who pursued the refinement of the incendiary. Their early efforts were filled with an inflammable mix of kerosene, petrol and liquid tar, requiring last–minute insertion into the bombs before flight. A later variation using tar, thermite and benzol produced a 3000–degree C fire. In 1918 the Germans created an incendiary with a magnesium body that was itself the main burning material. It was intended fundamentally as an anti–personnel weapon.

Throughout the war it was mainly the British and

the Germans who made strides in bomber and bomb design and development. They both sought to perfect a combination of long–range heavy bomber aircraft and stable, accurate and effective bombs capable of generating terror and significant destruction on each other's cities.

Between World Wars I and II, some highly significant bombers were developed. This was the period when aircraft construction techniques gradually changed from conventional wood and fabric biplanes to stressed–alloy monoplanes. Large bomber types were multi–engined, many of them four–engined for greater safety and reliability.

In the 1930s the reborn German Air Staff was headed by General Max Wever, a staunch advocate of the strategic bombing concept. Wever planned and was building a sizeable strategic bomber force for Germany when, in 1936, he died in an accident and was replaced by General Albert Kesselring, who later was to command Luftwaffe units in the Battle of Britain and in North Africa. Kesselring favoured a purely tactical role for the German bomber, and immediately scrapped Wever's strategic force programme. Had it been allowed to continue to fruition, the course of World War II might have been quite different.

After 1937, the science of bomb development began to escalate. Britain pioneered a new range of weaponry in both armour–piercing and demolition bombs for fragmentation, blast or mining effect, and the RAF concentrated on a new programme including an improved class of pyrotechnic devices, flares, flame and smoke floats, as well as aerial mines and combustible magnesium incendiaries. In the early days of World War II, the principal "ordnance" being delivered by the RAF on enemy targets was incendiaries and leaflets. By the end of the first two years of the war, the British were employing more 250–pound and 500–pound general purpose bombs in their strikes than any

other bomb types. Their sizes were the most practical for the capabilities of all the then–standard RAF bomber aircraft.

German bombs available at the start of the war ranged from fifty–pound to 1100–pound types and were similar in fundamentals to those of the British, but a high incidence of failure soon led to the development and implementation of a new and more reliable electrically–fired fuse device. By spring 1940, the Germans were concentrating heavily on their parachute mine designs and it was these weapons which became their mainstay in attacks on British cities. Both the Germans and British went on to design and develop ranges of more sophisticated mines including magnetic, acoustic and influence types.

There followed the development of the radio–activated proximity fuse which allowed a bomb to be detonated at a prescribed altitude above the ground. The RAF then began experimenting with the so–called "light–case" concept in bomb design. Having discovered in practice during the first year of World War II that streamlining the shape and design characteristics of its bombs in order to minimise drag and prevent tumbling was, in fact, unnecessary, British scientists went to work on a new type of bomb. It was to be a 4000–pounder containing an explosive compound called RDX which offered both ease of manufacture and relative safety in handling it. The new LC bomb was actually a welded drum of thin gauge steel and the empty casing was filled with the molten RDX material. The highly powerful blast bomb that resulted was known by the Allies as the "blockbuster" and by the crews of RAF Bomber Command as the "cookie."

There was no more efficient and effective heavy bomber in World War II than the Avro Lancaster with its unobstructed bomb bay and its impressive load–carrying capability. As early as 1942 RAF Bomber Command was using its Lancasters to deliver both the 4000–pound "cookies" and an

The Town has opened to the sun. / Like a flat red lily with a million petals / She unfolds, she comes undone.
– from 'Bombardment' by D.H. Lawrence

8000–pound version of the same bomb, which was really two cookies bolted together for twice the effect. The immense bomb bay of the Lanc could accomodate even greater weapons, such as the triple–cookie unit known as the Tallboy, for use against special targets such as the 42,000–ton German battleship *Tirpitz*. The *Tirpitz* was sunk by Tallboy bombs of 617 Squadron off Tromsø Harbour in northern Norway on 12 November 1944, with the loss of more than 1400 German crew. The British had been determined to sink the *Tirpitz* since her commissioning in 1941 and had pursued her doggedly. The development of the Tallboy provided the RAF with the means for eliminating the great German warship.

To meet a requirement for a bomb of even more destructive force than Tallboy, the RAF turned to the innovative Vickers Aircraft Chief Engineer and designer Barnes Wallis, whose geodetic construction approach for the Wellington bomber had contributed hugely to the effectiveness of that aircraft. Wallis had also been asked to design a bomb for use by a new special task squadron, No. 617, against the Mohne, Eder and Sorpe dams of Germany's industrial Ruhr Valley. His solution to the problem of how to breach these enormous structures came in the form of a large drum–shaped device to be carried partially extended from the modified bomb bay of the Lancaster. Before release, the "dam buster" bomb was made to rotate on its mount at a high rate of speed by a motor within the fuselage of the Lanc. Wallis calculated that, to function properly, the spinning bomb must be released at a height of exactly sixty feet above the water of the reservoir behind such a dam. In theory, the spinning device would then bounce along the surface of the water to contact the wall of the dam and then sink towards the bottom and be detonated at a precise depth by a hydrostatic fuse. After much rehearsal it was felt that the squadron and the weapon, now called Upkeep, were ready, and the raid was carried out on the

night of 16–17 May 1943 by a small force of bombers, most of which managed to reach the target area and breach two of the three dams. Wing Commander Guy Gibson led the attack and for his effort was awarded the Victoria Cross, Britain's highest military distinction. Later in the war, Gibson was killed while flying as a Pathfinder for bombers attacking the Ruhr.

Now Wallis was asked to find a way of damaging targets such as the seemingly impenetrable German submarine pens along the Biscay Coast of France. These massive reinforced-concrete structures, with walls and roofs many feet thick, had proven utterly bomb–resistant in attacks by both the RAF and the American Eighth Air Force. The RAF's Sir Arthur "Bomber" Harris, in fact, believed that the effort expended attacking the sub pens was futile and that his force was better utilized in attacks on the shipyards where the U–boats were being built. Harris targeted the submarine construction facilities with considerable effect even though he felt that the requirement for such attacks diverted his force from its primary assignment, the all–out assault on German cities.

Wallis, meanwhile, felt that a possible solution for attacking the sub pens lay in a notion he had for what he called an "earthquake" bomb. It was to be a conventional high explosive device, but with a weight of 22,000 pounds. Streamlined, the bomb had canted tail fins to make it spin as it fell, and was made with a heavy case. Wallis intended that the bomb be dropped against great, solid structures like the pens. He expected it to go deep underground on impact and then be detonated, causing an earth tremor that would literally shake down the target structure. It worked well when employed against a target such as the enormous railway viaduct at Bielefeld, but, as visitors to France's Brittany coast will see, the great sub pens of Brest, Saint Nazaire, Lorient, La Pallice and Bordeaux remain today, largely unaffected by all Allied attempts to destroy them.

Left: A painting by Stuart Reid, *Bombing of the Wadi Fara, 20 September 1918*. Above: Wing Commander Guy Gibson, VC, who led No. 617 Squadron, RAF, on the Dams Raid of 16–17 May 1943. Overleaf: Page 92, USAAF airmen carry a bombsight to their AT-11 trainer at the San Angelo Army Air Field Bombardier School in January 1943. Page 93, an airman at Chanute Field, Illinois adjusts a top secret Norden bombsight, the standard bombardment sighting device employed in World War II by the US armed forces.

We opened the bomb–doors, fused the bombs, and Taffy took over. Right over the target at 2000 feet. It was a gift. The factory was working full blast, we could see it all like daylight. Even cars and lorries. I have never felt such a thrill, and not a gun to stop us. One long stick right across the whole works and we circled round watching results. Two fires straight away, and the incendiaries should start some more: they were burning in one of the sheds, but a stream of tracer started up behind us, so Pike said goodbye in his usual manner, and we left for home in high spirits. Ten hours twenty minutes when we landed. I did not even feel tired. Back at base they had bombed hell out of the aerodrome. I was thankful not to have been there.
— from *Bomber Pilot*
by Leonard Cheshire

The time after the briefing is not very pleasant. No one knows what to do. Some sit in the Mess, listening to the radio, and wishing they were far away from all this. A few play billiards.. But most of them just sit in chairs picking up papers and throwing them down, staring into space and waiting for the clock on the wall to show the time when they must go down to get on their flying clothes.
— from *Enemy Coast Ahead*
by Guy Gibson

Other bombing weapons and techniques resulting from this wartime development period included the Royal Navy Disney rocket bomb, a 4500–pound hard–case bomb with a rocket in the tail, thought to be useful against hardened targets like the sub pens. The rocket was ignited by a barometric fuse after the weapon had fallen freely from release altitude to 5000 feet. The rocket accelerated the bomb to a velocity of 2400 feet a second. The US Eighth Air Force made limited use of the bomb in the spring of 1945 with arguable results. Another development of the time was the fire weapon Napalm, a jellied petroleum mixture taking its name from the combination of naphtha and palm oil. The mix was carried mainly in 108–gallon US fighter fuel drop tanks with small igniter units. The Napalm "bombs" were first used against German strong–points on the French coast in 1945.

Yet another amazing bombing technique was the Aphrodite Project, in which an American bomber, usually a war–weary B-17, was completely filled with the high explosive Torpex, 20,000 pounds of it, and was flown to a point on the English coast. There the pilot bailed out and the aircraft continued to its target under radio direction guidance from a ground station. The intended targets were the German V–weapon sites in the Pas de Calais. One such sortie cost the life of the pilot, US Navy Lieutenant Joseph Kennedy, Jr, son of the former US Ambassador to Britain and elder brother of the post–war President. Kennedy and another crewman were killed when their Liberator drone prematurely exploded near Blythburgh, Suffolk on 12 August 1944. A similar radio–guided "aircraft drone bomb" programme of the Germans called Mistel involved a variety of fighter and bomber combinations in which the fighter was mounted on top of the bomber, which was guided toward its target by the fighter pilot who then released the "bomber–bomb" which was supposed to continue to its target under radio–control. The

effect of this effort was minimal.

Probably nothing contributed more to the success of the Eighth and the other American Air Forces' bombers than the Norden bombsight. As famous as the Andrews Sisters, Lucky Strike Green and Kilroy, the ultra–secret Norden was the standard high– and medium–altitude sight of the US bomber forces throughout the war. The device was, for the time, quite sophisticated. Its development was begun in 1928 by the Dutch–born inventor Carl L. Norden. Utilizing ground speed, drift, trail and bomb ballistics information fed into it by the bombardier, the instrument was able to compute a precise release point for the bomb load. The bombardier used a telescopic element on the Norden unit to establish and compensate for deflection and synchronize the sight. For the final moments of the bomb run, he "flew" the airplane through the Automatic Flight Control Equipment (AFCE) of the sight package, which was linked to the autopilot of the bomber. Thus he was able to make flight adjustments through the marvellous bombsight. It was the accuracy of the Norden sight that, in large part, gave the Americans confidence to persist with their daylight bombing philosophy in World War II.

The other principal aid to bombing accuracy in that war was radar. A range of radio navigation and radar systems was developed and deployed to bring improvements in accuracy of placement and in target marking by the Pathfinder aircraft. The British H2S and Oboe systems were key elements in the bombing campaigns of Bomber Command. The H2S was a radar set mounted in RAF bombers which provided a terrain image that enabled the aircraft to bomb more effectively at night and through heavy cloud cover. It was used for the first time in RAF attacks on Hamburg in July 1943. The Oboe system was a means by which the British bombers could be directed to their targets at night through the use of two radio beams being

Nov 17th 1916

Ostend again. Up at 4 a.m.
Usual hot cocoa gathering
round the Mess stove. Clear
and starlight but little moon
left. Caudrons away at 5.10. I
was again fourth Sopwith away
at 5.29. A mechanic hung onto
my wing tip after I had waved
'all clear' and as a
consequence I swung to
starboard badly and nearly
crashed but recovered and got
off nearly tail to wind. Three
miles off coast at Nieuport at
8,000. Batteries and
searchlights already active.
Planed down from 9,000 off
Ostend at 6.05 a.m., observing
many bombs bursting on and
around the target. Loosed off
my bombs over the objective
from 4,000 at 6.10.
Immediately picked up by
searchlights and, not dodging
quickly enough, was coned
and held by several and, dive,
dodge and turn as I would,
could not shake them off.
Several guns were quickly on
to me and for some two or
three minutes I had an
extremely lively time. The air
seemed full of bursting shells
and flaming onions and some
of the HE burst much too
close for comfort, the flash
and crash virtually
synchronizing. The guns
certainly had my range all
right! With full engine I
pushed the old Sopwith down
to 110 knots and streaked out
to sea, soon shaking off those
infernal searchlights. Well out
to sea, I again circled for
several minutes watching the
fun as later arrivals came
over—a great sight and vivid
red flashes from our bombs
around the docks area. All
aircraft safely back by 7.20 a.m.
— from *Bomber Pilot
1916–1918*
by C. P. O. Bartlett

transmitted from England. The beams intersected over the bomber's target and the aircraft's pilot simply flew along one beam until he crossed the other beam, indicating he had reached the bomb release point over his target.

With the final weeks of the war came the advent of the most significant and terrifying weapon yet devised. The bombs called atomic were the products of scientists of many nations and many disciplines. The story of these weapons is told in another chapter of this book, and it is perhaps enough to note now that the concept behind the first atom bombs revolved around a staggering release of energy which caused the surrounding air to be heated to an extremely high temperature, coupled with the emmission of high levels of radiation on a variety of wave lengths. The first two atomic bombs were known by their makers as Fat Man and Little Boy. Little Boy, the weapon delivered over Hiroshima, Japan on 6 August 1945 by the B-29 *Enola Gay*, piloted by Colonel Paul W. Tibbets, was a "gun–type" device. Within its casing lay a shaped element of Uranium U-235 which, when the bomb reached detonation altitude over its target, was "fired" into another U 235 shape, resulting in a nuclear explosion. The blast, heat and radiation release of Little Boy killed more than 80,000 people in Hiroshima. The second atomic bomb, Fat Man, killed 40,000 more Japanese at Nagasaki three days after the Hiroshima raid. These immensely powerful and destructive weapons which helped to bring World War II to an end were but relative firecrackers when compared to the force and fury of the nuclear and thermonuclear weapons to follow in the post–war years. Ultimately, several nations were to join the nuclear club, and the world arms race was on in earnest.

In the half century since the end of World War II, the world's nuclear arsenals have grown to the point where the estimated casualties in a major nuclear confrontation range from a few hundred

Death is a matter of mathematics. / It screeches down at you from dirty white nothingness / And your life is a question of velocity and altitude, With allowances for wind and the quick, relentless pull / Of gravity.

Or else it lies concealed / In that fleecy, peaceful puff of cloud ahead. / A streamlined, muttering vulture, waiting / To swoop upon you with a rush of steel. / And then your chances vary as the curves / Of your parabolas, your banks, your dives, / The scientific soundness of your choice / Of what to push or pull, and how, and when.

– from 'Death is a Matter of Mathematics'
by Barry Conrad Amiel

Left: A Japanese phosphorus bomb explodes beneath B-29s of the USAAF Twenty–First Bomber Command attacking an air depot at Kagamigahara, 30 miles north of Nagoya, the site of the major aircraft manufacturing plants of Kawasaki and Mitsubishi. The Japanese used phosphorus bombs fired from ground batteries or air–dropped in their attempts to break up the B–29 formations in early 1945.

million to upwards of 25 per cent of the Earth's population. The United States alone is believed to have the nuclear capability to obliterate all human life several times over. But in the time since the end of the war, the US and other world powers have continued the development of conventional bomb–type weapons and have produced them in the hundreds of millions. They range from demolition and high–explosive to incendiary, fire and chemical types, to depth charges and aerial mines, fragmentation, cluster, unguided aerial rockets and laser–guided "smart" bombs. In the Gulf War, the range of Paveway laser–guided bombs included high and low speed, penetrator and glide bomb types in 500–, 1000– and 2000–pound weights. In the precision–guided bombing system a target designator–supplied infra–red or daylight image appears on a screen in the attacking aircraft cockpit. The pilot or the Weapons Systems Officer then aligns the cross hairs on the target impact point and locks the Impact Point into the system. Now the infra–red sensor and its laser stay locked on the target IP. The laser–guided bomb or bombs are released in the vicinity of the target and, just seconds before impact, a pre–coded energy beam is fired by the designator at the targetting impact point. A seeker in the nose of the weapon picks up reflected laser energy which aims the missile at the precise Impact Point, "flying it" by means of movable fins on the weapon.

Typically in the Gulf, four RAF Tornados utilized three 1000–pound British LGBs each in a successful attack on an Iraqi bridge, whereas destroying a hardened aircraft shelter usually required only a single aircraft carrying two of the smart weapons. Tornado GR.Mk 1s flew more than 1600 sorties in the Gulf War, dropping more than 4200 conventional free–fall bombs and more than 950 LGBs. Coalition aircraft using mainly LGBs destroyed approximately 350 of Iraq's 594 hardened aircraft shelters in the war.

Additional airfield targets included fuel and ammunition storage facilities, command bunkers and runways. F-117A stealth fighter/bombers starred in their ultra–precise delivery of laser–guided weapons on Iraqi command and control facilities, bridges and other difficult targets, many in Baghdad itself.

In the late 1970s one estimate of the combined destructive power of just the conventional bombs arsenal of the US at that time was a capability to destroy ten per cent of the Earth's inhabitable surface and up to 35 per cent of its population. Weapons development continues world–wide at a pace at least as frenetic as that of the debate over the ethics and effectivity of bombing. The characteristics of the weapons are limited only by the imaginations of the designers and those who cause them to be developed. Aerial bombardment has been with us for most of the twentieth century and the concept and practice continues in its many forms into the new century.

To the left, clouds of black smoke were billowing up, but straight ahead, looking like tiny silver tuning–forks, a line of docks was moving rapidly towards the bombsight. There was no time to make any comment — and there would never be a better target — the docks had already reached the intersection of the bombsight graticule, so I pressed the release and said, "Bombs gone."
— from *The Eighth Passenger* by Miles Tripp

Left: An attack by B-24s on the German U-boat pens at La Pallice, France, 29 May 1943. Below: The relatively undamaged La Pallice pens, photographed in 1997.

IF THE CREWMEN of Eighth Bomber Command and RAF Bomber Command were a little paranoid in World War II, who could blame them? It would have seemed to them that practically everything was stacked against their survival. Any insurance actuary would have projected a very low probability for their completing their tours of duty.

If the flak didn't get you, the fighters would; and if not the fighters, the cold, anoxia, mechanical failure, outrageous weather, or battle fatigue. Even ordinary everyday fear could nail you.

flak, n. [German Flieger Abwehr Kanone (anti–aircraft cannon).]

"I could hear him yelling, 'I've been hit. I've been hit.' He was standing in the middle of the floor. He had his hands between his legs . . . he was jumping up and down and yelling, 'I've been hit.' "
– Larry Bird, formerly with the 493rd Bomb Group (H), Eighth USAAF

"It wasn't always the long trips that were the worst. Sometimes we got more flak near the English coast than we did over the target. That was the Royal Navy. It didn't matter what we did — shoot off the colours of the day and everything — the Navy always fired at us."
– Leonard Thompson, formerly with No. 550 Squadron, RAF

"Most of the time when you are over enemy territory you have a funny feeling, particularly when you can see flak, you know that it can hurt, but you look out there and it's fascinating because it comes up like a little armless dwarf. There's a round puff here and then there's usually two strings that come out of the bottom like legs, and this thing will appear out of nothing. You don't see any shell; you don't hear anything. You just see this little puff of smoke and then shortly after, it sounds like somebody is throwing gravel all over

the airplane. You're fascinated by it. You know it can hurt you very badly, but you're fascinated by it . . . you watch it. It's kind of like watching a snake."
–W.W. Ford, formerly with the 92nd Bomb Group (H), Eighth USAAF

"The flak was unpleasant, although one always felt we were unlikely to get a direct hit. On the run into the target it became more accurate, mainly because we had to fly straight and level for a few minutes for the bombsight to settle down and the bomb aimer to ensure that the cross hairs were on the target when he released the bombs. With a hundred or so aircraft making virtually the same run, the anti–aircraft gunners had an opportunity to get some steady shooting in."
– John Curtiss, formerly with Nos. 578 and 158 Squadrons, RAF

". . . Kept telling myself, just the way I told the men, that it was going to be a lot better to fly straight instead of zigging. We'd get through the area where they could shoot at us more rapidly, and the enemy would necessarily fire fewer rounds. All in all, we'd have a better chance of getting off with whole hides — people and airplanes alike."
– from *Mission With LeMay*
by General Curtis E. LeMay and MacKinlay Kantor

"Flak was ever–present, a fact of life, a thing to be endured. We encountered flak on all but a half dozen missions. We learned to live with it, but we never became used to it."
– Robert F. Cooper, formerly with the 385th Bomb Group (H), Eighth USAAF

"The noise is the soft flak. You can't hear it hit the airplane. I remember vividly on a raid . . . it wasn't Schweinfurt, it wasn't that rough on our crew, but it was terrible. We lost about half a dozen planes, and one of them was right in front of me in the formation, and it just absolutely exploded . . .

Left: B-17s of the 96th Bomb Group (H), flying from their base at Snetterton Heath, Norfolk, England to bomb a target in German–occupied Europe during World War II. Below: A very fortunate airman displays fragments stopped by the flak vest that he is wearing.

Nobody will ever know what it took to climb into a bomber and fly thousands of miles over enemy territory, through all the hazards of the weather and the enemy's defences, which brought the crews to the brink of mental and physical exhaustion.
– Marshal of the Royal Air Force Sir Arthur Harris

Now, he will spend a few sick years in institutes, / And do what things the rules consider wise, / And take whatever pity they may dole. / Tonight he noticed how the women's eyes / Passed from him to the strong men that were whole. How cold and late it is! Why don't they come / And put him into bed? Why don't they come?
– from 'Disabled'
by Wilfred Owen

just a big ball of debris and you could feel that debris hit your airplane, and that was a very unpleasant sensation."
– David Parry, formerly with the 390th Bomb Group, Eighth USAAF

"Flak is flak is flak, right? Wrong! Depending upon your mental state, the same flak that on one given mission might only make your mouth dry and your breathing laboured could, on another day, cause near–panic. Take for example our mission of 23 March 1945 to the marshalling yards at Gladbach, Germany. On that day each nearby burst of flak convinced me that the next one would tear our plane out from under us.

"From the moment the CQ flashed his light inside our tent and yelled 'Up'n at 'em!' that miserably cold dark morning, the die was cast. Not one of the six of us crewmen ventured a toe into the chilling damp air to pull the light cord and we all nodded off again. The second time the CQ poked his head inside our tent, he began bellowing like a banshee. We were late, very late.

"Normally, on wake–up call, my five crew mates would roll off their three–biscuit upper or lower bunks, pull their flight coveralls over their sack–warm long johns and head for the ablutions to wash up. Then we'd be off to the mess hall to bolt down breakfast before heading for the briefing room. It usually took me a minute or so longer because, from childhood, my mother had instilled in me the habit of sleeping in pyjamas. As soon as my feet hit the deck, I'd toss off my pyjamas, pull on my long johns, zip up my coveralls, pull on my shoes, and wash up. 23 March caused a fateful change in my routine. Fearful of missing the mission and facing court martial, sheer bedlam ensued in that cramped tent with the six of us cursing and grabbing for clothes. In that desperate moment, I made the decision to fly in my bright blue ski pyjamas. After all, how different were ski pyjamas from long johns? In practical terms, very

little; psychologically, tremendously.

"Initially I was quite satisfied. The blue pyjamas felt just as warm as long johns; but slight reservations cropped up when I undressed down to the pyjamas in the equipment room. Catcalls arose in the area of my locker, and smiles lit up otherwise grim faces. Quickly I concealed the bright blue object of derision under my heated flying suit and I began to think that I might have made a strategic error. The busy pre–flight routine kept me occupied and as our heavily–laden B-17 rose slowly from the runway, I prepared for the next six hours of duty. My .50 calibre machine gun was cocked and ready, and the radio receiver and transmitter were tuned to our Grafton Underwood frequency and the message pad and code of the day on my desk. My 'chute pack, flak vest, and steel helmet were at arm's length under my transmitter, while the cardboard box of chaff lay on the plywood floor under the chaff chute. I was ready.

"As First Lieutenant Bill Smisek jockeyed our Fortress into the squadron deputy group lead position in the formation, my mind returned to the blue pyjamas. I considered the fact the ski pyjamas did not have an open fly — bad news if nature called while airborne. Then a more ominous thought came: what if I had to bail out over enemy territory? Captured in blue pyjamas? The whole Wehrmacht would have hysterics. And then an even more devastating thought occured to me: how about the H nicely embossed in a corner of my dog tags? What a field day the Nazis would have with a decadent Army Air Corps Jewish Tech Sergeant in bright blue pyjamas! Panic set in. Obviously, this was the day we were destined to be shot down — and all because of my smart–ass snap decision back in the tent that morning. At that moment I would have gladly exchanged my clean blue pyjamas for a pair of cruddy, raunchy, odoriferous long johns.

"Each time the Fort bucked and rocked as the

102

pilots juggled the throttles and wheels, trying to maintain combat formation, I expected to hear the propellers of another Fort ripping through our wing or tail surface, sending us scurrying to an escape hatch — a not uncommon occurrence on bomb runs. On reaching the Initial Point, Lieutenant Smisek ordered me to begin throwing chaff. On this clear day, it was a useless effort, but at least it gave me something to do. I swivelled my seat around, grabbed the foot–long triangular cardboard package of aluminium foil strips and heaved it out of the chaff chute. With my two–piece flak vest tied snugly above each hip and my steel helmet pulled down over my goggles, I waited the recommended twenty–second interval and heaved out another batch of chaff. At 25,000 feet, with unlimited visibility, our squadron began its unwavering run in to the target while the enemy anti–aircraft batteries began tracking our progress. With the rhythmic concussions of ever–closer flak bursts causing our plane to bob and bounce, I thought, 'To hell with the 20–second interval,' and started chucking chaff out the chute as quickly as I could.

"Suddenly, a near burst sent pieces of shrapnel tearing through our bomber's thin skin. I was seeing bright blue and I was terrified. I had no doubt that the next burst would herald the start of my bright blue march through the streets of Gladbach. The countdown commenced and at 'bombs away' the Fort lurched abruptly upward as it shed its three tons of bombs. The lieutenant poured on the power and banked us quickly out of harm's way. I started to breathe again.

"Gladbach was not a deep–penetration raid, and we were soon over friendly territory. Behind us lay the ruined marshalling yards, and one of our unfortunate crews. The blue pyjamas? Yes, I wore them again, but they never saw the light of day outside our tent at Grafton Underwood."
— David C. Lustig, Jr., formerly with the 384th Bomb Group (H), Eighth USAAF

ar.mour n. A defensive covering, such as chain mail, worn to protect the body against weapons.

Like the medieval knights, the airmen who flew in bombers during World War II were well motivated to protect themselves in any way they could from occupational hazards. They feared flak more than enemy fighters, and many had rather crude items of personal "armour" made for them by obliging, sympathetic ground personnel.
Late in 1942, at the behest of the Chief Surgeon of the Eighth Air Force, Brigadier General Malcolm Grow, the Wilkinson Sword Company designed and produced a bullet–proof vest composed of overlapping 1 3/4" magnesium steel plates. The plate network was covered in heavy canvas and was called a "flak vest" or "flak suit". It was designed to be worn over the parachute harness. It could be removed in a hurry by the use of a pull cord, and it weighed twenty pounds. Production of this personal body armour began in October 1942 and was first worn on an Eighth Bomber Command mission by crews of the 91st Bomb Group (H) on 12 December. Eventually it was determined that, of the personnel wounded by flak shrapnel fragments while wearing the flak vest, two–thirds escaped significant injury.

an.ox.i.a, n. A pathological deficiency of oxygen.

Many bomber crewmen experienced severe problems from an insufficient supply of oxygen during their missions in World War II. A number of fatalities resulted from faulty or inadequate oxygen equipment in the early days of the British and US bombing offensives in the European Theatre of Operations.

"I knew nothing about the guns, but anything else was supposed to be my department. Oxygen, everything. One night we were over Mont Blanc, on our way to Munich through the back door. We'd

The weather reports were real inaccurate, so if they said you should break out of the clouds at fifteen hundred feet, it might actually be eighteen thousand feet — and I recall one time when it was.
— Ray Wild, formerly with the 92nd Bomb Group (H), Eighth USAAF

Left: Lloyd Stovall flew in B-17s as a radio operator/gunner with the 398th Bomb Group (H) at Nuthampstead, Hertfordshire, England in WWII. Below: A Lancaster bomb aimer at his crew station in May 1944.

gone over Italy and were coming back over Mt Blanc when Jeff, our pilot, started going a bit weird. Woozy, drunk almost. It was lack of oxygen. That's one of the signs. So, I whipped off his pipe. We had portable oxygen bottles strewn about and I put one on him and turned it on full. It took quite some time before it had any effect. He was still woozy and we were going to yank him out of his seat. I could fly the thing. I'd had some instruction and I'd flown it on air tests as the flight engineer was supposed to fly it in case of an emergency. All I could have done was fly it straight and level so everybody could bail out. Then Jeff came round and said, 'What the hell are you doing?' I said, 'You suffered from lack of oxygen, Jeff. Are you all right now?' I shook his disconnected oxygen tube and ice had collected in it."
– Jack Clift, formerly with No. 463 Squadron, RAAF

fire n. A rapid, persistent chemical change that releases heat and light and is accompanied by flame, especially the exothermic oxidation of a combustible substance.

Probably the airman's greatest fear is fire. More than any of his other worries — oxygen starvation, extreme cold, fatigue, frostbite, enemy fighters and flak — it was the horror of a fire in the aircraft that disturbed the sleep of bomber crewmen and went with them every time they flew.

"On 25 January 1945 we flew on a Fighter Affiliation training sortie with a Spitfire. After completing the training with the Spitfire we started our recovery to base when the port inner engine caught fire. We were unable to put the fire out or to feather the prop. It subsequently transpired that the oil pipe line to the feathering motor had cracked, spraying oil onto the hot engine.

"The fire quickly spread to the whole wing and the aircraft became very difficult to control. Our pilot ordered us to abandon the aircraft. In the Halifax the navigator's seat was over the foreward escape hatch so that I was quickly able to fold the seat, put on my parachute, jettison the hatch and jump out.

"We were very low, about 1500 feet, but the canopy deployed quickly and almost before I had time to look around and see the aircraft plunge into the ground I had landed heavily in a ploughed field.

"A farmer arrived on the scene promptly and took me to his nearby farmhouse where I was able to phone the base which was only a few miles away.

"When I arrived back at base I found to my great distress that only the wireless operator had survived and that my pilot and four of the crew had been killed. The bomb aimer was a stand-in as ours had laryngitis. He should have been second out but he was a young Canadian Sergeant who froze. The wireless operator sensibly decided to go next."
– John Curtiss, formerly with Nos. 578 and 158 Squadrons, RAF

"I was flying a B-52 night training mission out of Bergstrom Air Force Base, Austin, Texas. After the usual lengthy pre-flight, the crew boarded the airplane. We stowed our equipment and strapped ourselves in our ejection seats. We ran the checklists and, with all eight engines running, completed the taxi checklist and received clearance into the number one position for take-off. I aligned the bomber with the runway heading and set the brakes. I set the power, released the brakes and we started to roll.

"The co-pilot adjusted the engine pressure ratios evenly, and all engine instruments checked OK. A hundred things were going through my mind . . . acceleration, engine output, exhaust gas temperatures, what to do in case of an emergency, and many more. I was watching the runway marker boards as they flashed by, 1–2–3–4–5–6–7–8, 12,000 feet of runway with a 2000-foot over-run

On 28 October 1944 we had a somewhat different trip to Cologne. The pilot's escape hatch opened on take off and remained open. The flight engineer struggled to get it closed with no success and it broke off and disappeared. I knew it would be very cold with the large opening over my head, but I reasoned that none of the rest of the crew would be as cold as I was and if I could manage, they could. Fortunately, the auto pilot worked very well and I was able to sit on my hands to keep them from freezing. Normally, in the daytime you saw the flak as sudden puffs of black smoke appearing round about and at night you saw flashes as the flak exploded. On this trip, with the roof open over my head, I *heard* the flak exploding, which was a new experience. We dropped our bombs from 20,000 feet and set course for home. There was a great deal of fighter activity and anti-aircraft fire but we were unscathed. As soon as we were clear of the target area I descended to a lower altitude where it was warmer, and we had a comfortable trip home.
– Gordon Bennett, formerly with Nos. 429 and 434 Squadrons, RAF

Left: With its right inboard engine on fire, this B-17 of the 447th Bomb Group, based at Rattlesden, Suffolk, England, begins its final descent over Berlin on 3 June 1944.

TO OPEN THIS PACK TEAR DIAGONALLY FROM ANY
CORNER AS INDICATED BY ARROWS.

FIRST AID OUTFIT FOR AIR CREWS

... CONTENTS ...

AMPOULES SYRINGE (MORPHIA) ... 2.	FOR SEVERE PAIN
ANTI-BURN MITTENS .... 2.	FOR HAND BURNS
ANTI-BURN JELLY IN 1oz. TUBES ... 1.	FOR BURNS OTHER THAN
LARGE WOUND DRESSING .... 1.	
SAFETY PINS .... 1.	

NOTE:- SEE INSTRUCTIONS FOR USE ON EACH PACKET INSIDE.

FOR BURNS OTHER THAN
ON HANDS SPREAD ANTI-
BURN JELLY OVER BURN
AREA AND ALLOW TO DRY.

DO NOT USE ANTI-
BURN JELLY WITH
THE MITTENS

A M

PULL TO OPEN

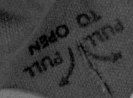
PULL TO OPEN

marker at 180 knots of airspeed as the airplane got light and began to fly. I climbed to 1000 feet and started my flaps–up profile, trying not to lose too much altitude. I climbed out to 37,000 feet on an easterly heading and then started a long navigation leg toward Albany, New York. We completed the take–off and climb check–list and settled down for the long, twelve–hour flight.

"At about the four–hour mark, I had to go downstairs to relieve myself. There was a fireplug urinal that you could stand at, and while doing this I decided to flip on the bomb bay lights and look in there. I was shocked to see a three–inch stream of jet fuel running on top of the alternator bay to the deck underneath, which had a four–inch lip. The fuel was pouring over the edge onto the tyres in the wheel well, and down into the bomb bay. I let junior go and snapped up as I studied the situation. I went over to where the navigator was sitting and told him what was happening. His eyes got as big as saucers and he said something about bailing out. I said, 'No, but plot me a course that will take me back to Bergstrom, avoiding any populated areas.' I went back up the ladder to my seat and told Tom, my co–pilot, about the situation in the bomb bay and asked him about the fuel state. He said that about 10,000 gallons or 60,000 pounds were missing. I didn't know then that the Marmon clamp, which held the three–inch fuel lines together at the top of the fuselage, had come apart and no amount of valve closing or cross–feeding would stop the flow of fuel.

"The alternator deck was located just below the four alternators which supplied electrical AC power to the aircraft, and was now full of JP5 fuel. The alternators were evidently vapour–proof as they did not create sparks that might have ignited the fuel fumes.

"Tom brought up the question of our ejecting, and I said, 'No, not yet.' I banked the airplane five degrees and headed back to Texas. I then called the SAC Command Post and told them about our problem. I said that I was not transferring fuel across the airplane and that I had more than 10,000 gallons of JP5 running out into the alternator bay. They asked about my intentions and I said I would continue the flight back to Bergstrom. They asked if we intended to eject, and they left that to my discretion.

"We arrived back in the Bergstrom area where it was still dark. We had returned there at 44,000 feet to conserve fuel, and we were still losing fuel at the same rate and had now lost some 20,000 gallons. We had a major leak.

"As the sky became lighter, I called our base. They knew what was going on as they had been monitoring the SAC Command frequency. I set us up in a holding pattern in the Bergstrom area and asked the radar operator to go take a look in the bomb bay. He said I would have to give him a direct order to do so, and I decided to go myself. I went back downstairs and saw to my dismay that the fuel was still pouring out of the three–inch pipe at the same rate. I then returned to my seat, strapped in with oxygen mask on and the bail–out bottle knob in a handy position, and advised everyone to get ready for a quick ejection. Some of the crew said that they wanted to eject, but I told them that there was nothing electrical that wasn't vapour–protected, and that it was safe. They reluctantly agreed. I then ordered the radar operator to open the bomb bay doors. At Bergstrom they had a telephoto camera aimed at us and we were in good range as we had now descended to 6000 feet, the minimum bail–out altitude. The bomb doors opened and all 20,000 gallons of fuel seemed to evaporate in an instant, but some of it covered the airplane. The engine exhaust then ignited it and there was a big flash, but we flew out of the flash in one piece.

"All of the fuel that had accumulated in the bomb bay was now gone, but there was a fuel stream coming out through the bomb bay doors, which

Left: A World War II FIRST AID OUTFIT FOR AIR CREW packet from an RAF Lancaster bomber. In the air war of the 1940s the most that airmen could hope to do for their wounded fellow crew members was to apply sulfa powder to minor open wounds, and inject ampules of morphine to lessen the pain of their injuries. Below: Army Air Force Flight Nurse, Second Lieutenant Martha Radspieler who served with the 388th bomb Group at Knettishall, Suffolk, England during World War II.

coming out through the bomb bay doors, which could certainly be lethal. We were now very low on fuel, having flown some seven hours, and we needed to land soon. I had Tom lower the flaps and they worked fine as the flap motors were sealed. Next came the landing gear. We had steel–impregnated tires, which meant that we could land on ice, snow, or a wet runway and have a good co–efficient of friction for stopping the plane. But all of the four forward tires were saturated with jet fuel and I expected them to lay a trough of fire when we touched down. I lowered the gear and again nothing happened, except for more streaming fuel. I flew the downwind leg to land to the north, turned base and final and approached the end of the runway at 145 knots indicated. We touched down at the 1000 foot marker. It was a smooth landing, but as soon as we touched, a streak of flame erupted from the tires and they began to burn the fuel that had soaked into them.

"I braked hard and had Tom pull the drag 'chute; we stopped in 7000 feet. I immediately cut the eight engines and rang the bell to evacuate the airplane. I was out of my harness and behind Tom as we jumped down the ladder and out of the bottom of the plane, where the fire was burning real well. We ran ahead of the airplane and off the left wing to our crew assembly point in case of a crash–landing.

"The crash crew arrived with their foam and hoses. They had to go into the bomb bay to squirt foam up into the alternator deck. It took them thirty minutes to get the fire under control and put out all of the smouldering tires. A crew bus picked us up and took us to the maintenance debriefing room. All the 'wheels' were there wanting to know what had happened. After cleaning up the foam, the maintenance inspectors looked at the Marmon clamps and saw what had happened. They wired SAC headquarters and Boeing in Seattle. All B-52s were promptly grounded until they had been inspected. A permanent fix was made and all of the

"We put a pressure bandage on Ralph's leg wound, but the temperature at our altitude really did more to stop the bleeding and the blood started to freeze around the wound. I took the morphine out of the first aid kit. The syrette looked like a small tube of toothpaste with a needle on the end. I warmed it up under my heated suit and aimed the needle at the muscle a few inches from the anterior hole in his thigh. At first I pushed kind of easy, but the darned thing didn't go in, so I shoved hard and it slid into his thigh. Then I squeezed the contents of the tube into him and in a few minutes Ralph drifted off to sleep."
– Roger Armstrong, formerly with the 91st Bomb Group (H) Eighth USAAF

Left: The result of a collision which occurred at the 100th Bomb Group (H) base, Thorpe Abbotts, Norfolk, England, 27 December 1943. The 100th suffered appalling operational losses and became known in the Eighth Air Force as the 'Bloody 100th.' By the end of the war the group had lost 200 heavy bombers and 86 per cent of its original air crews. In his fine book *A Wing And A Prayer*, former 100th Group navigator Harry Crosby wrote: "Did we deserve to be called the 'Bloody 100th'? Other outfits lost more planes and crews than we did. What marked us was that when we lost, we lost big."

forty–five from the head of his bed, walked down the line and shot all those lights out. We had it dark in there after that, for the rest of the night anyway."
– Lawrence Drew, formerly with the 384th Bomb Group (H), Eighth USAAF

"I remember that period of 40 hours in which I flew three ops. On 14 October 1944, Harmer [our pilot] was grounded with a cold. Flying Officer Lewis needed a bomb aimer so I went along with him to Duisburg in daylight. I had just gone to bed when I was dragged out to go to Duisburg again with Lewis. Take–off at 00.39 on 15 October. It was a bad trip. We could see the target burning 100 miles away, from our morning attack. There were nightfighters around and we were nearly coned by searchlights over the target. I began to appreciate the talents of my own crew. So I got back home, ate my bacon and eggs with sleepy eyes, and suddenly found that I was scheduled for another trip with Harmer and my own crew at 1800. I napped for a couple of hours in the mess, checked my bomb load, perspex, guns, circuits — check, check, check — dozed through the ops briefing and took off for Wilhelmshaven. On the way home I could hardly keep my eyes open, but I was with my own crew so it didn't really matter. At the interrogation, the squadron commander suddenly realized that I had been out on the last three. He was impressed. I was not — all I wanted was a bed. One more, to Essen, and my tour was over — 39 trips.
– Ken Roberts, formerly with No. 158 Squadron, RAF

weath.er n. The state of the atmosphere at a given time and place, with respect to variables such as temperature, moisture, wind velocity and barometric pressure. Adverse or destructive conditions such as high winds or heavy rain.

December 1940. The crews of RAF Bomber Command were operating in the worst European winter in living memory. The Hampdens,

FORWARD TO VICTORY

clamps were changed. For us it had been a rather hair–raising experience."
– Joseph Anastasia, former US Air Force B-52 pilot

fa.tigue n. Physical or mental weariness resulting from exertion.

"We would make runs in formation, on fictitious targets in England, get back to base, and make some instrument approaches and landings for hours — just touch the wheels down, give it the gun, go around, and come back for another. All the time there was something to do — work on your radio operator's speed, your engineer's know–how, there was always training to do. We carried a very high fatigue factor at that time. If I had five minutes in a chow line I could go to sleep standing up."
– Lawrence Drew, formerly with the 384th Bomb Group (H), Eighth USAAF

"The people playing poker in our Nissen hut had the lights on, and they would play all night. An officer said, 'C'mon fellas, have a heart — some guys have got to fly tomorrow.' They just said something back to him and went right on playing. So, he took a

Wellingtons and Whitleys they flew in were being subjected to ice that formed on their wings, in their turrets and hydraulic systems, instruments and radio equipment, causing catastrophic malfunctions. Perspex windscreens were opaqued bringing cockpit visibility down to zero. Airmen whose jobs required them to remove their leather gauntlets and lining gloves to attend to some essential task, risked severe frostbite. If they were unfortunate enough to touch bare skin to any metal surface in the aircraft while at the sub–zero temperatures of high altitude, their flesh would freeze instantly to that metal.

Flying missions at high altitude in the big, heavy Liberators, Lancasters, Fortresses and Halifaxes meant prolonged exposure to extreme cold and the hazards it could bring. Frostbite was a very real concern for the men who flew in the bombers of World War II. For the unfortunate airmen who experienced this injury, exposure to the bitter −20 to −50°F cold at operational altitudes could and did bring about the destruction of the skin and underlying tissues of the nose, ears, fingers and toes. To combat this natural enemy, specially designed flying clothing had to be worn. Often, it failed to provide the necessary levels of protection and led to additional problems for already overburdened aircrew. The General Electric F-1 "blue bunny suit" first utilized by the B-17 and B-24 gunners of the Eighth Air Force in the winter of 1942 – 43 had an inherent flaw. Its wiring tended to short out and the suit then failed. It happened so often that the majority of those using the F-1 elected to wear additional heavy fleece–lined leather flying clothing over the electric suit. In addition, gunners wore electrically–heated gloves and boots.

They were also provided with electric muffs for use on hands and feet should the gloves or boots fail. Instead of trusting the reliability of the various electrically–heated garments, many airmen chose

to wear a suit of thick pile sheepskin that included a B-6 jacket and A-5 trousers. This outfit was worn over heavy woollen underwear, usually long johns, two pairs of wool socks, sometimes a pair of felt electrically–heated moccasins, a shearling–lined helmet and standard A-6 boots. Pilots had the problem of keeping their hands warm while being unable to properly feel the cockpit controls through the heavy or heated flying gloves issued at the time. Many wore a thin silk glove under a relatively thin USAAF–issue A-10 goatskin winter flying glove, providing reasonable warmth and allowing enough sensitivity. With cockpit heating, pilots and co–pilots were often comfortable wearing their A-2 leather flying jackets.

As the war progressed, so too did the efficiency of garments developed for the Allied bomber air crews, and the overly bulky, cumbersome and awkward togs of the war's middle years gave way to ones of greater comfort and reliability.

"It was fairly cold in the Nissen hut and we never did have enough coal to heat it well. People were forever tossing CO_2 cartridges into our stove. You'd be backed up to it on a cold day, when all of a sudden it would just blow up and hot coals would fly all over the place and scare everybody."
– Lawrence Drew, formerly with the 384th Bomb Group (H), Eighth USAAF

"No bomber went off without a rear gunner. I went up in a Wellington, just an air test with a squadron leader up in Scotland near Lossiemouth, and I think he forgot about me. He said we were not going far. He just wanted to air–test it and he went up to about ten thousand feet. I hadn't got any gear on at all. Mae West and parachute. No flying gloves, nothing. Ended up nearly frostbitten on my fingers and hands. To this day they get white when it's cold. Hands are always cold in there. It was dreadfully cold in the tail of the Halifax. You had no heating. You had an electric

Colonel Cold strode up the Line (tabs of rime and spurs of ice); stiffened all that met his glare: horses, men, and lice.
– from 'Winter Warfare' · by Edgell Rickword

"I looked out the window and saw what looked like a very pretty and shiny flower bloom on our left wing. It was flak that had entered the bottom of the wing and came out through the top. We had self sealing fuel tanks and, luckily, it missed anything vital. That shiny flower fascinated me and didn't really seem dangerous."
– Roger Armstrong, formerly with the 91st Bomb Group (H) Eighth USAAF

27 December 1944 – we were woken up at 3 and got to briefing at 5. It was a good mission. Very little flak and only about 5 1/2 hours long. But the weather was bad on the ground, with a thick ground fog. We were number three to take off. The first plane went down the runway. A couple of seconds later seven men were dead. Their plane crashed on take–off. It sure was a horrible sight. The same thing happened that day at four other fields.
– Gerald D. Phillips, formerly with the 453rd Bomb Group (H) Eighth USAAF

Above left: Royal Air Force identification dog tags.

Below: Lieutenant–Colonel Joseph Anastasia, USAF (Ret) had an astonishing military flying career in which he flew as command pilot of several bomber aircraft including the B-29, B-45, B-36 and B-52, surviving some of the most dire experiences that airmen can have. Right: A wounded crew member of a 381st Bomb Group (H) B-17 is treated in the airplane immediately after it landed at Ridgewell, Essex, England after the raid of 20 February 1944.

suit. Sometimes they worked all right. Sometimes. But if you got a duff one, you wouldn't know it until you plugged in. I had four guns, .303 Brownings, and we had a removable slide in the turret, so we were completely open there, along with two panels at the side which we removed as well. At night, when you are looking out, looking and looking, the least little speck on that turret, after four hours of looking, that speck is a German fighter. You keep coming back to it and you convince yourself that it's a fighter. So you remove the panels to see better. Of course you have your goggles... up on your forehead. We never had them on over our eyes. You could see better without them. But, oh, the cold. I had both my eyes operated on while I was in the Air Force, for cysts from the cold."
– Fred Allen, formerly with No. 158 Squadron, RAF

fear n. A feeling of agitation and anxiety caused by the presence or imminence of danger.

"There is an old saying which goes something like this: 'Cowards die many deaths, but a brave man dies but one.' If this saying be true, then I am not only a coward myself, I am fighting this war with a lot of other cowards. A story in the Eighth Air Force tells about a group commander who read an advertisement in a magazine which asked the question, 'Who's afraid of the new Focke-Wulf?' This group commander cut out the advertisement, signed his name to it and pinned it on the bulletin board. After all of the pilots in the group had confessed their fear by signing, the page was mailed back to the US advertiser.

"We are all afraid and only liars or fools fail to admit it. There are a variety of possible deaths which face a member of a bomber crew and each man is free to choose his own pet fear. A tire could blow out or an engine could fail on take–off. The oxygen system or electric heating system might fail at high altitude. There is the fear of

explosion or mid–air collision while flying formation. In addition to these there is the ever–present possibility of being shot down by enemy fighters or anti–aircraft fire.

"In dealing with the enemy, there is a certain feeling of helplessness about the bomber business which I find to be very distasteful. Imagine, for a minute, that you are required to carry two five–gallon cans of gasoline down a dark alley. These cans weigh over thirty pounds each so your hands are full and you can't run very fast. As you pass a certain corner in this alley, you know that a number of thugs are waiting to club you as you pass. However, there is a policeman patrolling this beat (your fighter escort) and if he happens to be at the dangerous corners at the time you arrive, then everything will be OK, unless, of course, there are more thugs than the policeman can handle. Some of the thugs don't attack with clubs, but stand back (out of sight) and throw firecrackers at your cans of gasoline.

"The bomber pilot can't fight back, but must just sit there and take it. I believe this explains why there is such a difference between the bomber and fighter boys. The men in this latter group can match their skill against the enemy. He carries a club of his own with which to fight back. I do not find the light–hearted devil–may–care spirit on the bomber station which has been so often described in stories about pilots in the last war. Our men go about their grim business with sober determination. When we are alerted for a mission, the bar closes early and everyone goes to bed. To be sure, at our monthly parties if there is no mission the next day, the boys get pretty drunk. I do not discourage this as I feel it gives them a much–needed chance to blow off some steam.

"When a new crew arrives on the station I try to have a talk with the men during the first twenty–four hours after arrival. One of the points stressed is that we are all afraid. I tell them that the worst part of a mission is just before the

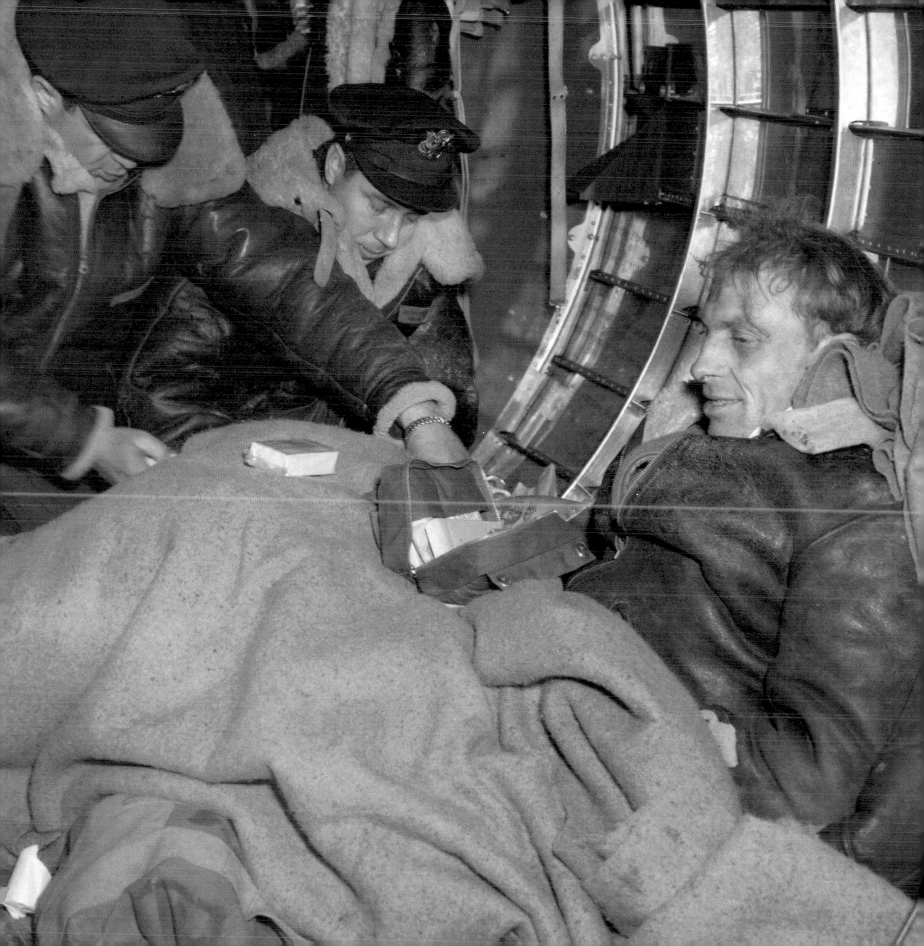

Below: Bill Graham was a Halifax pilot with No. 102 Squadron, 4 Group, RAF. He survived being struck by the whirling blade of a Wellington propeller. Above right: A wounded airman is treated beside his bomber at the Deopham Green air base of the 452nd Bomb Group (H) after a raid on 14 February 1944. Below right: The base hospital ward at the 388th Bomb Group (H) base, Knettishall, Suffolk, England during World War II.

take—off. If they can 'sweat it out' through this period, they will get through the rest all right. The flight surgeons are particularly helpful in spotting men who are showing signs of anxiety. If a crew goes through a particularly rough mission and is badly shot up, we try to send them to the 'flak house' (rest home) for a week. In fact all crews are sent to the 'flak house' for a rest at some time during their combat tour. Although I never find time to get to one of these rest homes myself, I am told that they are well run and very successful.

"Winston Churchill's personal physician, Lord Moran, wrote a book about courage in combat. I like his definition of courage: 'a moral quality . . . not a chance gift of nature like an aptitude for games. It is a cold choice between two alternatives, the fixed resolve not to quit; an act of renunciation which must be made not once but many times by the power of the will . . . Some men were able to see more clearly that there was no decent alternative to sticking it out and to see this not in a hot moment of impulse but steadily through many months of trial. They understood on what terms life was worthwhile.' "
– from the World War II letters of Major—General John M. Bennett, Jr., a Commander of the 100th Bomb Group (H), Eighth USAAF, to his father in Texas.

haz.ard n. A chance of being injured or harmed; danger.

"I arrived at No. 19 Operational Training Unit, RAF Kinloss in Scotland around 10 November, 1940 and was greeted with the news that nineteen aircrew had been killed during training in the previous week, which was rather daunting. The morning after our arrival, I was asked to escort a coffin to the railway station. There was only one casualty on our course — a trainee who went under the wing of a Whitley to pick up a practice bomb that had fallen off. He was struck by a

propeller and suffered brain damage. Generally, training was more or less incident—free."
– Alfred Stanley Tarry, formerly with No. 51 Squadron, RAF

In a similiar incident, coincidentally also at Kinloss, but in 1944, Halifax pilot Bill Graham, being tour—expired, had been posted to the Scottish base to instruct newly—trained pilots in the ways of heavy aircraft, in this instance the Wellington bomber. The procedure called for a new pilot and his crew to have an hour of instruction, then return to the base, park the aircraft at its dispersal and hand it over to the next trainee crew and instructor. Graham was to be that instructor on this occasion, and the Wellington had just arrived on its hardstand. The previous crew had departed and the crew Graham was to instruct had boarded the aircraft while Bill remained on the hardstand to do an outside pre—flight inspection of the machine.

It was the practice on such instruction flights for the previous crew to leave the engines of the bomber idling at about 1200 rpm when they passed the plane to the next crew. Engrossed in his walk—around inspection, Graham had the misfortune to stray into the spinning port propeller. "I thought the aircraft had fallen on me. It struck me, by the merest fraction of an inch, from the top of my temple to the tip of my nose. I staggered, fortunately, away from the propeller blades, blood streaming from the wound. I remember how my forage cap flew over the top of the kite. I never found it again and had to buy a new one later. The young WAAF driver who had ferried the crew and me out to dispersal then had to drive me to sick quarters, with my blood dripping all over as I tried to stop it with my gloved hand.

"The medical officer cleaned me up, put nine stitches in the wound and bound my head in bandages saying, 'That's it, Graham. You can buy me a pint in the Mess bar. Off you go.' "

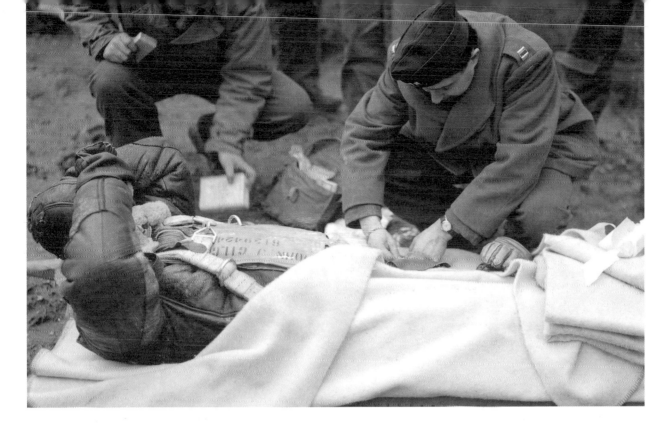

A former bombardier with the 92nd Bomb Group (H) at Podington, Northamptonshire in World War II, Sol Greenberg recalls that there was always a lot of flak over the target areas, and it was always extremely cold at their mission altitudes of 28,000 to 33,000 feet. "On the mission of 14 October 1943 we went to Schweinfurt to attack the ball–bearing plants there. We made it back to England, but the weather there was very bad and we were running out of fuel. Finally, we found an opening in the clouds, came down and crash–landed in southern England, destroying the B-17, but the entire crew walked away uninjured. We didn't have enough gas left to cause a fire."

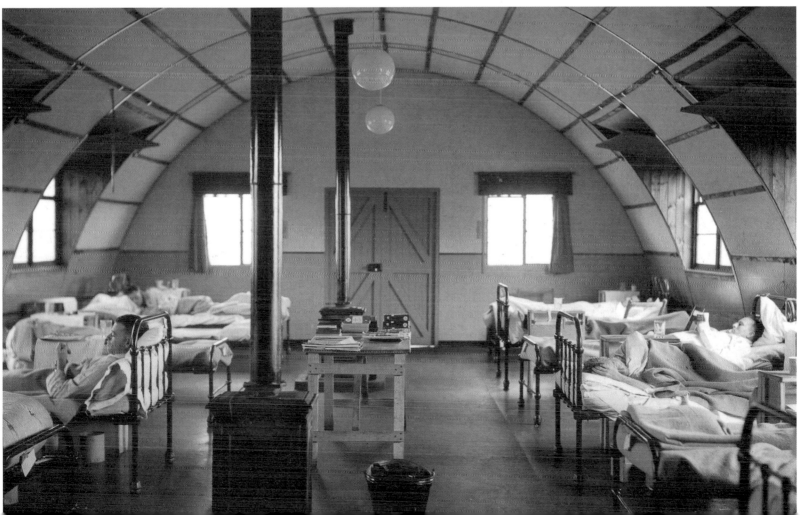

RECEPTION COMMITTEE

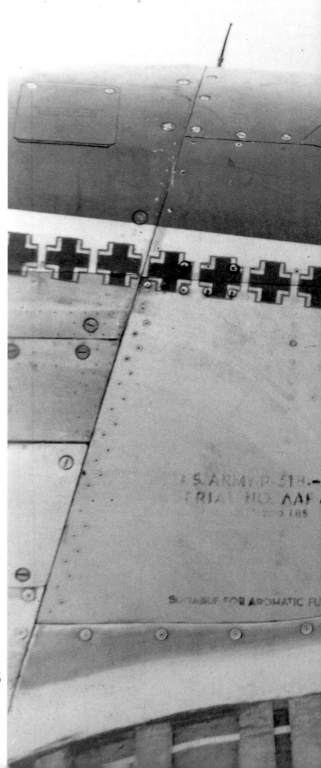

Right: Lieutenant Ralph K. "Kid" Hofer, a P-51 Mustang pilot with the 4th Fighter Group at Debden, Essex, England. On 2 July 1944, the 4th escorted bombers of the Fifteenth USAAF on a mission to Budapest, Hungary. Led to the target by Colonel Don Blakeslee, the Debden pilots ran into more than 75 Me 109s of the Luftwaffe's JG52. They were credited with 7.5 German fighters, but lost six of their own, including Lieutenant Hofer. Hofer was credited with 16.5 aerial victories and 14 enemy aircraft destroyed on the ground, sharing with Major John T. Godfrey the distinction of highest–scoring ace in the 4th. In World War II, fighter pilots of the various combatant nations provided their bomber adversaries a warm and (for the survivors) memorable aerial reception.

LIEUTENANT–COLONEL Beirne Lay, Jr, who later was to co–author *12 O'Clock High!*, one of the great books and screenplays about World War II, was co–pilot of an Eighth Air Force B-17 on the Regensburg raid of 17 August 1943. The target that day was the Messerschmitt factory where Me 109 fighters were assembled. It was a target of prime importance both to those who planned the missions flown by the Eighth, and to the young men of the crews who flew them. He remembers:

"The fear was unpleasant, but it was bearable. I knew that I was going to die, and so were a lot of others...

"A few minutes later we absorbed the first wave of a hailstorm of individual fighter attacks that were to engulf us clear to the target in such a blizzard of bullets and shells that a chronological account is difficult. It was 10.41, over Eupen, that I looked out the window after a minute's lull, and saw two whole squadrons, twelve Me 109s and eleven Fw 190s climbing parallel to us as though they were on a steep escalator. The first squadron had reached our level and was pulling ahead to turn into us. The second was not far behind. Several thousand feet below us were many more fighters, their noses cocked up in a maximum climb. Over the interphone came reports of an equal number of enemy aircraft deploying on the other side of the formation.

"For the first time I noticed an Me 110 sitting out of range on our level out to the right. He was to stay with us all the way to the target, apparently radioing our position and weak spots to fresh *Staffeln* waiting farther down the road.

"At the sight of all these fighters, I had the distinct feeling of being trapped — that the Hun had been tipped off or at least had guessed our destination and was set for us. We were already through the German fighter belt. Obviously, they had moved a lot of squadrons back in a fluid defence in depth, and they must have been saving

116

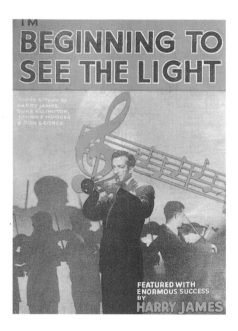

Bottom: A 1934 photo of future–Luftwaffe chief Hermann Göring enjoying the attentions of his pet lioness, Caesar.

up some outfits for the inner defence that we didn't know about. The life expectancy of our group seemed definitely limited, since it had already appeared that the fighters, instead of wasting fuel trying to overhaul the preceding groups, were glad to take a cut at us.

"Swinging their yellow noses around in a wide U-turn, the twelve–ship squadron of Me 109s came in from twelve to two o'clock in pairs. The main event was on. I fought an impulse to close my eyes, and overcame it.

"A shining silver rectangle of metal sailed past over our right wing. I recognized it as a main exit door. Seconds later, a black lump came hurtling through the formation, barely missing several propellers. It was a man, clasping his knees to his head, revolving like a diver in a triple somersault, shooting by us so close that I saw a piece of paper blow out of his leather jacket. He was evidently making a delayed jump, for I didn't see his parachute open.

"A B-17 turned gradually out of the formation to the right, maintaining altitude. In a split second it completely vanished in a brilliant explosion, from which the only remains were four balls of fire, the fuel tanks, which were quickly consumed as they fell earthward.

"I saw blue, red, yellow and aluminum–coloured fighters. Their tactics were running fairly true to form, with frontal attacks hitting the low squadron and rear attackers going for the lead and high squadrons. Some of the jerries shot at us with rockets, and an attempt at air–to–air bombing was made with little black time–fuse sticks, dropped from above, which exploded in small grey puffs off to one side of the formation. Several of the Fws did some nice deflection shooting on side attacks from 500 yards at the high group, then raked the low group on the breakaway at closer range with their noses cocked in a side–slip, to keep the formation in their sights longer in the turn. External fuel tanks were visible under the bellies

or wings of at least two squadrons, shedding uncomfortable light on the mystery of their ability to tail us so far from their bases.

"The manner of the assaults indicated that the pilots knew where we were going and were inspired with a fanatical determination to stop us before we got there. Many pressed attacks home to 250 yards or less, or bolted right through the formation wide open, firing long twenty–second bursts, often presenting point–blank targets on the breakaway. Some committed the fatal error of pulling up instead of going down and out. More experienced pilots came in on frontal attacks with a noticeably slower rate of closure, apparently throttled back, obtaining greater accuracy. But no tactics could halt the close–knit juggernauts of our Fortresses, nor save the single–seaters from paying a terrible price.

"Our airplane was endangered by various debris. Emergency hatches, exit doors, prematurely opened parachutes, bodies and assorted fragments of B-17s and Hun fighters breezed past us in the slipstream.

"I watched two fighters explode not far beneath, disappear in sheets of orange flame; B-17s dropping out in every stage of distress, from engines on fire to controls shot away; friendly and enemy parachutes floating down, and, on the green carpet far below us, funeral pyres of smoke from fallen fighters, marking our trail.

"On we flew through the cluttered wake of a desperate air battle where disintegrating aircraft were commonplace and the white dots of sixty parachutes in the air at one time were hardly worth a second look...

"I took the controls for a while. The first thing I saw when Murphy resumed flying was a B-17 turning slowly out to the right, its cockpit a mass of flames. The co-pilot crawled out of his window, held on with one hand, reached back for his parachute, buckled it on, let go and was whisked back into the horizontal stabilizer of the tail. I believe the impact killed him. His parachute didn't open.

"I looked forward and almost ducked as I watched the tail gunner of a B-17 ahead of us take a bead right on our windshield and cut loose with a stream of tracers that missed us by a few feet as he fired on a fighter attacking us from six o'clock low. I almost ducked again when our own top–turret gunner's twin muzzles pounded away a foot above my head in the full forward position, giving a realistic imitation of cannon shells exploding in the cockpit, while I gave a better imitation of a man jumping six inches out of his seat.

"Still no let–up. The fighters queued up like a bread line and let us have it. Each second of time had a cannon shell in it. The strain of being a clay duck in the wrong end of that aerial shooting gallery became almost intolerable. Our *Piccadilly Lily* shook steadily with the fire of its .50s, and the air inside was wispy with smoke. I checked the engine instruments for the thousandth time. Normal. No injured crew members yet...

"Near the initial point, at 11.50, one hour and a half after the first of at least 200 individual fighter attacks, the pressure eased off, although hostiles were still in the vicinity... Almost idly I watched a crippled B-17 pull over to the kerb and drop its wheels and open its bomb bay, jettisoning its bombs. Three Me 109s circled it closely, but held their fire while the crew bailed out. I remembered now that a little while back I had seen other Hun fighters hold their fire, even when being shot at by a B-17 from which the crew were bailing. But I doubt if sportsmanship had anything to do with it. They hoped to get a B-17 down fairly intact.

"And then our weary, battered column, short twenty–four bombers, but still holding the close formation that had brought the remainder through by sheer air discipline and gunnery, turned in to the target. I knew that our bombardiers were grim as death while they synchronized their sights on the great Me 109 shops lying below us in a curve

of the winding blue Danube, close to the outskirts of Regensburg. Our B-17 gave a slight lift and a red light went out on the instrument panel. Our bombs were away. We turned from the target toward the snow-capped Alps. I looked back and saw a beautiful sight — a rectangular pillar of smoke rising from the Me 109 plant. Only one burst was over and into the town. Even from this great height I could see that we had smeared the objective..."

"When a Fortress goes down it doesn't suddenly go into a violent manoeuvre. Everything seems to happen very slowly. The first thing you notice is a thin trail of smoke; usually from one of the engines. The ship then slowly turns out of the formation and starts losing altitude. At this point he's a dead duck for enemy fighters because he doesn't have the supporting fire power of the rest of the ships. Now its course may follow any number of general patterns of behaviour. The fire in one ship increases as the gasoline tanks in the wing begin to burn. Parachutes begin to blossom out as the crew abandons ship. As the wing becomes enveloped in flame, there is an explosion and there's practically nothing left but four orange balls of fire. These are the main gas tanks.

"Another ship burns hardly at all but goes into an ever–tightening turn until it spins. As it goes down twisting, the tail comes off and you may see three or four 'chutes as the gunners are thrown out. Because of centrifugal force the pilot and co–pilot don't usually get out. This ship slowly disintegrates as increasing speed tears it apart."
– from the World War II letters of Major General John M. Bennett, Jr, a Commander of the 100th Bomb Group (H), Eighth USAAF, to his father in Texas.

The favourite mount of Feldwebel Oscar Boesch was the Fw 190-A8. In it he downed eight four–engined heavy bombers, and ten Allied fighters.

Below: Former commander of the 384th Bomb Group (H), and co–author of the novel and screenplay *12 O'clock High!*, Colonel Beirne Lay, Jr. Bottom: Hauptmann Joachim Kirschner, who was credited with 188 enemy aircraft downed in World War II.

"On 8 May 1944, I was diving and firing at a B-24 formation when I ran out of ammunition midway through my firing pass. I decided to ram a B-24 and aimed at one of the bomber's ailerons. However, the turbulence was so severe that I missed. I found myself out in front of some B-24s, in a vertical dive. My Fw 190 was being shredded by many impacting shells. At 26,000 feet I bailed out and was lucky to get out because my aircraft was in a dive at full throttle, going more than 800 kph. I was also lucky because I did not hit the tail of my aircraft. Being machine–gunned in our 'chutes was always our concern when bailing out, and I fell 25,000 feet before opening my 'chute at 1000 feet above Goslar."
– Oscar Boesch, formerly with IV Gruppe, 3JG, German Air Force

No. 433 Squadron, RCAF pilot Ray Mountford

was flying a Halifax bomber near Bonn, Germany on the way back to England after attacking a target at Bochum in 1944. A German night fighter rose to meet the bomber, firing straight up into Ray's starboard inner engine and starting an uncontrollable fire. The crew's only option was to abandon the aircraft as quickly as they could. Ray gave the order and stayed at the controls of the crippled Halifax to keep the plane level while his crew bailed out. When at last he released his grip on the control column he was thrown violently out of the nearby hatch, hitting his head on the way out and lapsing into unconsciousness. Free falling, he revived just in time to pull the D–ring and deploy his parachute. After a hard landing he made a kind of tent arrangement of his parachute and paused to collect his thoughts and have a cigarette. It was midnight. Ray found that he had lost his flying boots and his socks in the descent.

He then noticed a light in a house near the field where he had fallen, and walked to the house in his bare feet. He knocked and a lady answered the door. He told her he was an "Englander" and she invited him into her home. There was a man in the house, and a teenage girl who could speak some English. The woman treated him kindly, bathing his feet. She then gave him a pair of slippers, and showed him a photo of her son, a German airman who had been lost over England. Shortly thereafter, the man left the house and quite soon the Gestapo arrived with drawn guns.

Ray spent the rest of the war in Stalag Luft III at Sagan, Silesia.

Horst Petzschler flew 297 combat sorties in Me 109s and Fw 190s. He is credited with 26 confirmed victories, including 22 Russian, one B-17, one B-24 and two P-51s. In his combat career he was shot down thirteen times, survived eleven crash landings and two bail–outs. Every time he was shot down, it was by flak . . . except once, on 28 May 1944, when a Mustang brought him down near Magdeburg.

"We students had barely flown four hours on the new Fw 190-A2 type fighter, with as yet no air–to–air shooting practice. We took off to do a job we had not yet been trained to do. Over the city of Paris we intercepted the shiny, silver B-17s at about 24,000 feet. Our instructor shot one of them out of the formation, and all seven of us students fired from all directions trying to shoot it down. We opened fire from 1000 yards away and, naturally, had no success. You had to go in closer to score hits. All of the other B-17s flew home to England. The one that had been hit flew south and crashed near Orléans. We counted ten parachutes. All the crew bailed out between Paris and Orléans. When we flew home and reported to Colonel Leppla, our school commander, he wanted to put us all in jail for our behaviour. 'Next time,' he told us, 'they will come with escort. You missed your great

chance.' We did. The next time they did come with escort, and we 'felt' it."
– Horst Petzschler, formerly with JG3 and JG51, German Air Force

"On 7 January 1944 at about 1.30 p.m., while coming back from our tenth bombing mission, to Ludwigshafen/Mannheim, Germany, we were attacked by Me 109 fighters. Our number two engine was hit and caught fire. When I checked the waist section I found that Staff Sergeants Sweet, Kudej and Stainker had all been killed. Second Lieutenants Smith and George had parachuted from the nose. Staff Sergeant Hite, First Lieutenant Walters, Second Lieutenant Bickley and I all bailed out of the bomb bay.

"We all landed in Brou, France. I came down on a farm where some children were working. As they approached me they seemed friendly. They hid me in their farmhouse until the French Underground was informed about me. I was told that two of my crew members, Lieutenants Smith and George, had been captured by the Germans, and they were looking for the rest of us. At 4.30 p.m. some members of the Underground arrived and gave me some civilian clothes. They took me to the home of Lucienne and Maurice Vouglement, and from there to a potato warehouse where I was hidden in a room with sacks of potatoes stacked around me.

"At around 10.30 p.m. the sacks of potatoes were removed and I was taken to a safe house where my pilot and co-pilot were waiting. We then began travelling from house to house with the Underground for two days. I stayed with the family of a Mr Milleroux, a chemist in Juvisy et Seine. Sergeant Hite was taken to Paris to stay with a French doctor. My pilot, Lieutenant Walters, and co–pilot, Lieutenant Bickley, stayed about two blocks from where I was, with a family named Lèvres. Then the Underground gathered the four of us together and told us that we would be

Above: RAF Battle of Britain pilots of No. 249 Squadron in a photo by Charles E. Brown. Above right: Captain Don S. Gentile (left) and Colonel Don Blakeslee, of the 4th Fighter Group at Debden, Essex, England, on 11 April 1944 when both men were awarded the Distinguished Service Cross by the Supreme Allied Commander, General Dwight D. Eisenhower.

escaping over the Pyrenees mountains. We travelled for fourteen hours on a German troop train to Toulouse, France where we were turned over to the Maquis resistance group. They were known for sabotaging railways and German troop trains. They informed us that we would have to wait until they had gathered a total of fourteen escapees because the German ski patrols operated in groups of six and it would be safer if we had at least a two–to–one advantage in numbers. They then armed us with hand grenades, pistols and machine guns. In addition to the four of us, there was a Belgian officer, an actress, an elderly English spy, and seven Jews from various countries.

"It took us four days and three nights to cross the mountains. We were told that when we reached Pau in Spain, we would be picked up by a Spanish patrol. In Pau, Sergeant Hite and I were taken by the Spanish to a remote prison for the

criminally insane. Lieutenants Walters and Bickley were detained by the Spanish Military Police for two weeks. After two days Sergeant Hite and I were handcuffed and marched seven miles to the railway station, and while we walked local citizens threw stones at us. From Pau we went by train to Zaragossa where we were put into solitary confinement. There were no windows and no beds. We slept on the floor and were given one meal a day, soup and bread.

"Because of ill will between Spain and the United States and Britain, Spain would not voluntarily notify the US or Britain that they were holding US or British airmen as prisoners. So, American and British military attachés made the rounds of Spanish prisons asking for their airmen and requesting their release. We were finally turned over to the British Military Attaché who brought us to Madrid where we were handed over to the US Military Attaché, and were then brought back

to England. We were taken to 1 Brook Street, London, to be identified and debriefed. Our entire evasion had taken about a month and a half. In London, Generals Eisenhower and Patton, and Field Marshal Montgomery, who were in town for a joint staff meeting, personally congratulated us for escaping."
– Louis DelGuidice, formerly with the 93rd Bomb Group (H), Eighth USAAF

Gordon Wright, a bomb aimer on Stirlings at RAF Mildenhall, was shot down while on an op to Kassel in west central Germany, 3 October 1943. On the way to the target that evening, Wright made his way back to relieve the wireless operator of the task of throwing out bundles of "window", the thin strips of silver foil paper dropped by Allied bombers to confuse German radar images. He began the job there on the floor of the Stirling just in front of the main spar.

After only a few minutes of ejecting the "window" Wright heard the rear gunner tell the pilot, "Go port." The gunner had spotted a German fighter closing quickly on their bomber and the pilot immediately began the diving manoeuvre to port. Just as he did so, the rear gunner began firing at the fighter and at almost the same instant the German opened fire on the Stirling, raking the big bomber with hits from tail to cockpit.

Intercom communication with both the rear gunner and the mid–upper gunner was lost then as the intercom system was damaged. The plane's hydraulics were also knocked out, and in a few moments a large fire broke out in the centre of the fuselage.

Though seriously wounded in the right hip, the wireless operator came forward at this point. The navigator had left his table to confer with the pilot about their position. He then returned to his table to try and recover his maps which were being blown around in the fuselage due to a large hole that had been blasted just above his position. Had

he been sitting there during the fighter attack he would almost certainly have been killed instantly. Now the dazed and injured wireless operator reached the navigator and asked him what they were going to do. Gordon Wright joined them by stepping carefully over the body of the flight engineer, who had been killed in the attack. The pilot, who was struggling to keep the crippled bomber stablized, then gave the order, "Abandon aircraft."

Wright responded quickly, grabbing the pilot's parachute from behind his seat and fastening it onto his skipper. He then followed the wireless operator to the front exit in the nose, followed by the navigator. When he reached the escape hatch he found it had slammed shut again. Now the Stirling, in its death throes, was entering a slow spiral, pinning the navigator alternately to the floor or the ceiling and frustrating his attempts to leave the plane. Finally, he managed to open the hatch again and, after contacting the pilot, bailed out. With the Stirling now down to less than three thousand feet, the pilot was able to switch on the "George" auto-pilot, leave his seat and make his way forward to the escape hatch only to find that once again it had slammed shut. The big bomber continued to spiral downward; the centre section and right wing were now burning furiously, and the 6000–pound load of incendiaries remained in the bomb bay. With the disabled hydraulic system, the crew had been unable to get rid of the bomb load as the bomb doors could not be opened.

The Stirling fell through a height of 1500 feet when the pilot at last got to the escape hatch and somehow re–opened it. He left the aircraft with no time to spare.

"On beginning my third operational tour in 1944, I took command of No. 138 (Special Duties) Squadron at Tempsford. Our task was to drop agents and supplies to Resistance groups in enemy–occupied countries of Europe. We usually

What was the greatest air battle of all time? Some historians would say it was the second Schweinfurt attack by the Eighth USAAF on 14 October 1943. On that day the Eighth lost 60 heavy bombers and their ten–man crews. In terms of sheer ferocity, and the length of time in which the bomber crews actually experienced the German flak and fighter defences, this raid was probably without parallel. But it is likely that most people who have studied war in the air would argue that the RAF Bomber Command raid of 30–31 March 1944 on Nuremberg takes the title. Of the 1009 bombers that took off to attack the German city, 95 were missing; ten crashed in England, and one was a write–off with extreme battle damage in the aftermath of the operation. The RAF loss rate was 13.6 per cent. According to historian and author Martin Middlebrook, "The damage caused by the bombs dropped was by comparison minimal. In Nuremberg one factory was half destroyed and three others suffered lesser damage. It is impossible to calculate the exact effect of this on Germany's war effort but clearly it was no more than a pinprick." In this attack, Bomber Command paid dearly for this failure; 545 airmen died and 152 became prisoners of war. Middlebrook: "In its aim this raid was typical of hundreds carried out during the war; in its execution it met almost all the difficulties and dangers which enemy defences and the weather could between them produce. These and a measure of bad luck combined to turn a routine operation into a tragedy."

operated during the moon period to have the best chance of locating the dropping zones. While these conditions assisted navigation, they also helped enemy fighters. We flew as low as possible to avoid detection. I recall one occasion on a sortie to Belgium when we were attacked by an Me 110. He came in fast, unseen by my rear gunner, and overshot. My upper gunner spotted him first off our starboard wing silhouetted against a full moon. We were higher than usual because of the terrain. I immediately descended, taking evasive action at the same time while the gunner opened fire. The enemy fighter dived and got below us where he could use his upward firing cannons. My bomb aimer took up position in the nose of the Halifax from where he opened fire while I continued to take evasive action. I kept decreasing height until my navigator warned me that we were lower than some of the hills ahead. The enemy pilot must have realized the danger as well, and with a parting burst broke away — probably like us — unscathed. We carried on to our dropping zones but found no reception. We later learned that there were enemy forces in the area and the Resistance had to abandon the DZ. On the return journey, we saw two of our aircraft shot down in flames near the place where we had been attacked. We learned subsequently that a Luftwaffe night-fighter training school was in operation near our route. Our attacker must have been a trainee as night fighter attacks were usually more conclusive. We had been lucky."
— Wilfred Burnett, formerly with Nos. 76, 49, 408, 138 and 148 Squadrons, RAF

Larry Henderson was an Electronic Warfare Officer in B-52s and flew two tours during the Vietnam war in 1969 and 1971. "My experiences with flak and triple A were very limited as we flew our combat missions at altitudes of 36,000 to 38,000 feet. We could see flak going off well below our aircraft, but it was never considered a threat.

The surface–to–air missiles, however, were quite different; they had no trouble reaching us. Normally, the B-52 was not flown into a SAM threat area, but this was not the case on the first three missions of my second tour in the Vietnam arena. Our first mission was to lead a flight of three bombers, together with Ironhand (Wild Weasel/defence suppression) F-105s to southern Laos in support of US Marine forces.

"As we began the bomb run, I detected SAM radars tracking our aircraft from our 11 o'clock position. Just as we released our weapons I picked up a signal that indicated missiles were airborne and being guided at us. I called over the radio for all aircraft to break left due to the threat, and within ten seconds two SAMs exploded high and to the right of our aircraft. No injuries were suffered. The Ironhand aircraft had been out of position and had not seen the missiles.

"During the debrief [it was clear that] no one outside of our three aircraft had seen the missiles and 7th Air Force Intelligence could not confirm the presence of the missiles on the ground. The actions were listed as 'unknown.' With typical military [logic] we were scheduled to lead the same mission the next day, at the same time, same altitude and same attack heading. Again, we were fired upon; this time by at least six missiles; again, with no damage. On the third day of flying the exact same mission and again being fired on by the SAMs, the 7th Air Force finally confirmed the presence of the [missile] threat and cancelled further missions in the area until the threat had been suppressed.

"We were known to the rest of crews as the 'Blytheville Missile Magnets' (as we had been part of the 97th Bomb Wing from Blytheville AFB, Arkansas). Actually, the B-52s were rarely under threat of attack until they were released to operate in North Vietnam, where they came under very heavy attack from all types of SAMs and enemy fighters."

He shall enlarge upon the danger of his adventure, but in my sleeve shall be heard the tinkling of silver laughter.

Above: Sergeant George Unwin flew Spitfires with No. 19 Squadron at Fowlmere, Cambridgeshire in 1940. Left: Lieutenant–Colonel Francis Gabreski of the 56th Fighter Group, Eighth USAAF downed 28 enemy aircraft making him the top–scoring American fighter ace in the European Theatre.

DEALING OUT PUNISHMENT

Not I, not I, but the wind that blows through me! / A fine wind is blowing the new direction of Time. / If only I let it bear me, carry me, if only it carry me! / If only I am sensitive, subtle, oh, delicate, a winged gift! / If only, most lovely of all, I yield myself and am borrowed / By the fine, fine wind that takes its course through the / chaos of the world
– from 'Song of a Man Who Has Come Through' by D. H. Lawrence

Right: In his introduction to the book *The History of Aircraft Nose Art, WWI to Today*, by Jeffrey L. Ethell and Clarence Simonsen, psychologist and former WWII B-17 navigator George R. Klare notes that military aircraft nose art has featured the following subjects. He reviewed 1000 examples of such artwork and determined that 55% were female figures, with about a quarter of them nude and most of the rest partially clothed. Four-legged animals, birds and insects made up almost 15% of the total. Another 30% involved cartoon characters, babies and children, death symbols, zodiacal signs, devils and gremlins.

MANY OF HER CREWS owe their lives to the strength and power of the Avro Lancaster bomber. One such crew was that of my late friend and former co–author, Squadron–Leader Jack Currie, DFC. From his fine book *Lancaster Target*:

"Hamburg had taken a terrible pounding while we were enjoying our first leave from Wickenby at the end of July. We returned in time to help deliver the final blow on Monday, 2 August. We started DV190 Baker Two's engines at 11.30 p.m., and took off twenty minutes later. We circled base on the climb, and emerged into a clear sky at about 9000 feet, setting course for Mablethorpe 25 minutes after midnight. An hour and ten minutes later we were thirty miles west of Heligoland and in trouble. One port engine was giving no power, the airspeed indicator had iced up, and the 19,000 feet of altitude that we had struggled to attain were steadily slipping away. Paths became more difficult to find between the towering thunderclouds that had built up over the North Sea, and whenever the turbulent masses closed about us Baker Two took on more ice and fell another couple of hundred feet.

"Johnny Walker left the cabin and crawled aft. The Command's new tactic to confuse the enemy radar was the use of 'window', thin strips of metal foil, and Walker's chilly task was to drop them through the flare chute in the dark and shaking fuselage. Fairbairn left his radio compartment to assist, remarking as he went, with his usual regard for accuracy, that ice on the aerials had increased their diameter from three–sixteenths of an inch to one and a half inches, and was still growing.

"We plunged on south–east for thirty minutes, as hail beat harshly on the canopy, and mauve light flickered about the aerials and front guns. Vivid stabs of lightning opened sudden gorges in the sky, then swirling vapour wrapped us round again. I felt the ice begin to grip the aircraft, now losing height more rapidly. I spoke to the navigator.

126

Above: Just as British and American armourers often personalised the ordnance they loaded on bombers, so too did their German counterparts. Right above: Crewmen of a Heinkel He 111 bomber en route to a target in England during the Battle of Britain. Right below: Twin–engined WWII Dornier Do–17 "Flying Pencil" bombers also on a mission to a British target.

" 'Where are we, Jimmy?'
'Should be about twenty miles south of the target, but I haven't had a fix for some time. Can you see any flares?'
'Can't see anything but cumulo–nimbus.'
"The bombs fell into the storm from 14,000 feet. Baker Two leaped at their release and settled into a slow and lurching climb. At 18,000 feet we broke into a shaft of clear air as lightning played among the anvil–headed clouds. Then the guns found us, and the aircraft shook and rattled as the shells burst close. As I turned to miss them, the cloud enveloped us again, and now its icy grip became like iron. Within seconds, the thirty–ton bomber was a toy for the storm to play with, the wheel locked, immobile as a rock. Baker Two was out of my control.

"I could see nothing through the window, nothing but a blue, infernal glow. I heard no engines, only roaring wind and savage thunder–claps. For the first time in the air, I felt impotence and, with that, a sudden prick of panic. There was nothing I could do — and yet surely I must do something. I held the wheel, watched the instruments, and waited for a clue to action. The instruments belied each other: no airspeed, but climbing fast.

"I felt the stall. The harness straps were pressing hard on my shoulders, my legs were light, loose objects fell about the cabin. Was I hanging in my harness upside–down, or was the aircraft falling faster than my weight? I tried to reject the evidence of the whirling gyro–controlled instruments and to believe the others, which showed nose down, a spin to port, and mounting speed. The ASI had left its ice–bound stop, and was swinging round the dial a second time.

" 'Pilot to crew, prepare to abandon aircraft — prepare to abandon.'
"I tried to judge the rate of our descent, and chose 8000 feet as the height where I must tell the crew to jump. They had to get the hatches open, and push themselves into the roaring slipstream, and still leave time for me to follow, before we fell too low to give the silken canopies time to open.

"I don't know whether Baker Two or I recovered from the spin, but now there was only the tearing rush of wind, and the steady movement clockwise of the ASI. The needle made a second circuit of the dial, and verged upon the limit of its travel at 400 miles per hour. If the pitot head were free of ice, so might be the elevators; I pulled back on the wheel with all my strength, as the altimeter read 10,000 feet. At 9000 feet, the wheel jerked violently in my hands, still I pulled and slowly felt my weight increase, and press into the seat, as the diving angle decreased. Briefly, we emerged below the cloud base, and shot up into it again as I struggled with the wheel.

"At last, I found a level attitude at 8000 feet, and brought the ASI back into the realm of reason. But there was something badly wrong: the wheel, although answering my back and forward pressures to climb or dive, wagged loosely left and right without response from either aileron to bank or turn. I wondered if the control cables had snapped — that might have been the violent tremor of the wheel. I pushed the rudders alternately, and Baker Two yawed gently in reply.

" 'Ok, I've got some control now. Let's have an intercom check — rear gunner?'
No reply from Charlie Lanham.
'Mid–upper?'
'Mid–upper OK, skipper.'
'Engineer?'
No answer from Johnny Walker.
'Wireless operator?'
'Wireless operator strength nine.'
'Any idea what's happened to Johnny?'
'Last time I saw him, we were both floating up and down the fuselage like a brace of pheasants on the glorious twelfth.'
'OK, Charlie, go back and see of you can find him. And check the rear-gunner, too.'

The rain slanted under the wing on a raw northeast wind. Of Cambridgeshire we had only an impression screened through the deluge—somber flatness, and mud; mud oozing up over the edge of the asphalt circle where we were parked; mud in the tread of the jeep, which rolled away on twin tracks of ocher, leaving us marooned; a vast plain, or lake, of mud stretching off toward a cluster of barely
visible buildings.
– from *The War Lover*
by John Hersey

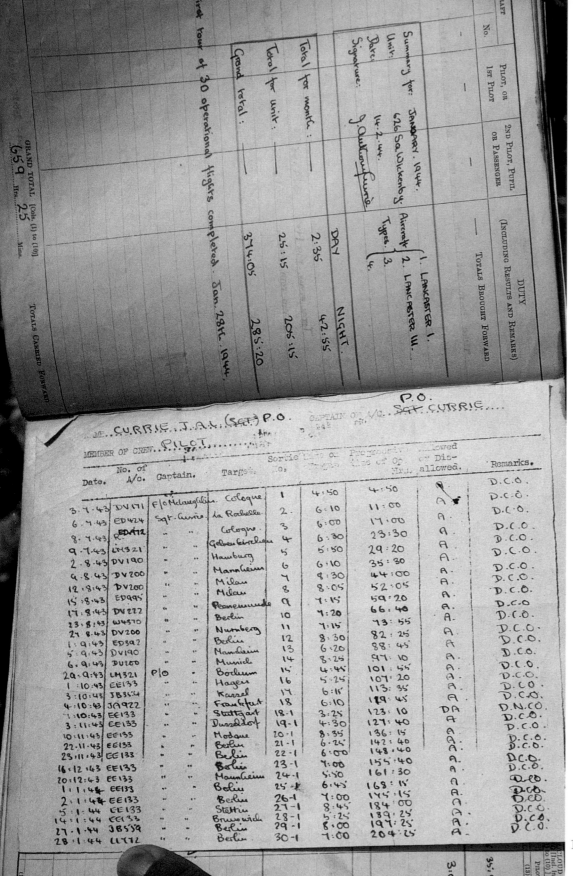

'Wireless op going off intercom.'

"Fairbairn's microphone clicked off, and I continued with the roll–call.

'Navigator?'

'Navigator loud and clear.'

'Bomb aimer?'

'Bomb aimer OK, skip.'

"Cassidy could hardly wait for the bomb-aimer to reply before he called.

'What course are you on?'

I spun the compass dial.

'210 magnetic.'

'You're heading straight for Bremen. Turn on to 330.'

'330. I'll try.'

'Mid–upper to skipper. A bloody great piece of your starboard wing's missing—did you know? Jesus . . . the port wing's the same!'

'Thanks, George.'

"So that was it. Both ailerons had been torn off in that screaming, spinning dive. I pushed the starboard rudder, and Baker Two veered right for a few degrees, wings level, then swung back as I released the pressure on the rudder. I tried again, held the pressure on, and pulled the wheel back slightly. A slow, slithering turn developed. Halfway round, I remembered the rotary potential of the engines — the port outer, free of ice, was running smoothly. Playing with the throttle, I let the Merlin bring the port wing up, and Baker Two settled into a steady, balanced turn.

"A familiar 'puff-puff' in my earphones indicated that Fairbairn was checking his microphone before venturing an utterance.

'Wireless op here, Jack. I can't find any sign of Johnny, I'm afraid. The main door's open — he might have fallen out. Or jumped. There's a terrible mess down here — "window" all over the place. The rear gunner's in his turret.'

"Myring chimed in from the nose compartment.

'I'll have a look for the engineer, skip. I want to go to the Elsan, anyway.'

'Go ahead, Larry. Better get back to your set, Charlie. Pilot to rear gunner?'

'Rear gunner, Jack.'

'Where were you?'

'I got out to find my 'chute. I sat down on the doorstep while you were bringing her down...'

"I liked that; she was bringing me down. Lanham continued:

'The whole kite was covered in St Elmo's Fire — ice all over the wings — really a marvelous sight.'

'I'm glad you enjoyed it. Did you see anything of the engineer?'

'You can't see anything in the fuselage. There's 'window' and stuff everywhere. Shall I...'

Protheroe interrupted.

'Mid–upper to skipper.'

'Go ahead, George.'

'I thought the rear gunner ought to know — I shan't be able to fire my guns. The interrupter gear's gone unserviceable. I think something broke off in the spin. Shall I get out and look for Johnny?'

'No leave that to Larry. Stay in the turret and keep your eyes peeled.'

'Wireless op here, Jack. I've been checking the external aerials, and there aren't any. I guess they blew off.'

'Bad luck.'

"I flew on, holding Baker Two just below the cloud–base, at 8000 feet. When Myring called from the fuselage, he was panting, and I could hear the sound of the slipstream behind his voice.

'I've found the engineer, skip. Buried in bloody "window." He's out cold — I think he's banged his nut.'

'Is he on oxygen?'

'Yep. That's why I don't want to take his helmet off to look at his head. I'm going to put him on the rest bed. I'll be off intercom for a few minutes.'

'Right.'

"We crossed the coast near Bremerhaven at ten minutes to three. Ten minutes later, a searchlight waved towards us from the right, groped closer, and swept the starboard wing. Two more lights from straight below joined the first, and crept along its beam to find us. The flashing stars of flak began to twinkle round us, and I played what evasive games I could with engines, rudders and elevators. I looked for clouds, but they had disappeared. I spoke to Jimmy.

'We're in some defences, nav.'

'Ah, good–oh, Jack, that'll be Heligoland. I've been waiting for a fix. Let me know when it's right underneath, will you?'

'Oh, sure.'

"But now, miraculously, the flak dwindled, and the last two searchlight beams climbed higher up the ladder of the first. I looked up, and there on the port beam, 5000 feet above us, cruised another Lancaster, majestic, straight and level. The searchlights settled on her, the twinkling flak shells clustered, but she passed on oblivious, like Oberon's imperial votaress.

'Mid–upper here, skipper. What d'you think of that bugger at ten o'clock high? They must all be asleep!'

"I was glad when another drift of cloud hid the sacrifice from my view. The feeling came that Baker Two and we were leading charmed lives that August night, and it was with a degree of confident abandon that, five minutes later, I threw her into steep corkscrew turns to evade a prowling fighter.

"At 3.30 we turned west-south-west, with 400 miles to go for Mablethorpe. I began to consider how I might make a landing. I had heard no precedent for a Lancaster landing without aileron control, but in my present mood I couldn't think it impracticable, not that night. Larry shattered my euphoria when he returned from nursing Johnny. Crouching beside me, his eyes squinting with alarm, he growled:

'Cripes, Jack, we're bloody short of petrol. These tanks are damn near empty — we'll never make the coast.'

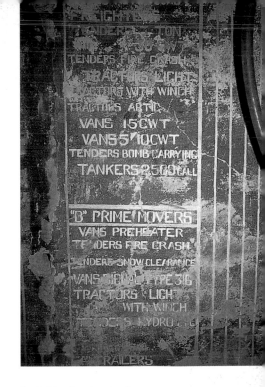

Left: The log book of Lancaster pilot Jack Currie. Above: Wartime signing in a garage at Snaith, a former RAF bomber station in Yorkshire. Below: The memorial at RAF Wickenby, Lincolnshire.

Everyone who was in London during the Blitz wants to describe it, wants to solidify, if only for himself, something of that terrible time.

"It's the glass," says one man, "the sound in the morning of the broken glass being swept up, the vicious, flat tinkle. That is the thing I remember more than anything else, that constant sound of broken glass being swept up on the pavements. My dog broke a window the other day and my wife swept up the glass and a cold shiver went over me. It was a moment before I could trace the reason for it."
– from *Once There Was A War*
by John Steinbeck

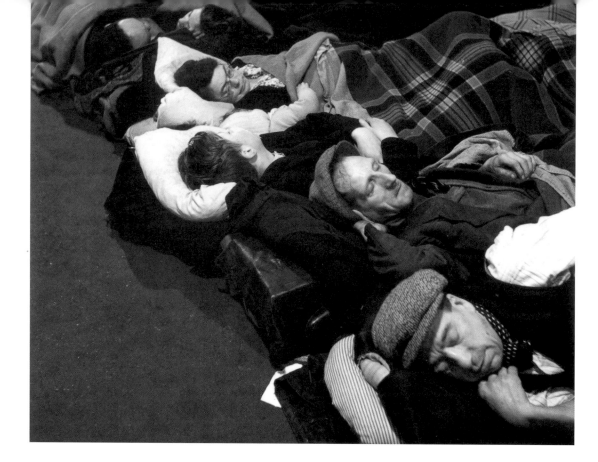

'They should be half full. How's Johnny?'

'He's conscious, but I reckon he's got concussion.'

'Pilot to engineer. I need you here to check the fuel. Go and give him a hand, will you, Larry?'

"Walker reached the cabin, white–faced and pale–lipped, but with enough sense to get the true readings from the fuel gauges. Charlie Lanham cackled from the rear turret, 'Duff gen, Myring!'

"Larry crept down into the nose, muttering. Walker was slumped against the starboard cabin window, fumbling at the intercom switch on his mask. I leaned over to turn it off for him, and looked into his eyes. They seemed unfocused, and his face was drained of blood. I told him to go back to the rest bed, but he didn't move, and the wireless operator had to take him aft. When Fairbairn reported that he had made the engineer comfortable, and checked that he was breathing oxygen, Lanham's voice came through my headphones:

'Pilot from rear gunner. Do you reckon we're clear of fighters?'

'I don't know. I should think so. Why?'

'I'll come up and take Johnny's place. Give you a hand.'

"It crossed my mind that he might be feeling lonely in the cold extremity of Baker Two's tail–end, or that he had decided that I could use some close moral support. Either way, it would be good to have him by my side.

'OK, rear–gunner, you're clear to leave the turret.'

"Lanham appeared in the cabin a few minutes later, and perched on the engineer's bench seat. Crawling up the fuselage in his heavy suit had brought him out in a sweat. He wiped the back of his gauntlet across his face, then folded his arms and stared ahead into the darkness. His gravely alert expression was exactly suited to the situation, but it made me want to make him laugh. I nudged him with my elbow, and waggled the useless control wheel loosely with my fingertips. I spun it round from left to right, and back again, grinning

at Lanham. He looked worried for a moment, staring at the wheel and back at me, then I saw the gleam of his teeth as he laughed. There wasn't really much to laugh about, but the atmosphere was getting too serious; it needed some of the gravity taken out of it. Lanham settled himself more comfortably, and passed me a pellet of chewing gum. He stayed beside me for an·hour or so while Baker Two flew on westward, sometimes side–slipping a little when I picked up a wandering wing too harshly with the rudders, but on the whole making good her course.

"High above the Lincolnshire coast I brought the speed back, put the wheels down, and tried a rate–one ninety–degree turn to port. I couldn't get any flap down — presumably another system had fractured there — and that meant that I must make a long downwind leg, a shallow approach, and add ten mph to the landing speed. I practised it at 4000 feet, and brought Baker Two to the point of the stall. The rudder control was good, but I couldn't manipulate the throttles fast enough to keep the wings level. It would have to be a very straight approach.

'Pilot to crew. The landing may be a bit difficult. You'd better bail out.'

"There was silence for a few seconds, then Lanham called:

'What are you going to do, Jack?'

'I'm going to put her down at base. But I might make a balls of it.'

'You won't. This is your lucky night. I'm staying on board.'

"I warned them again, but nobody would go. We reached Wickenby five minutes later than the time on our flight plan, and the circuit was clear. I flew parallel with the runway, flashing dash – dot– dot– dot dot– dot– dash– dash– dash on the downward identification light. A green Very cartridge puffed up from the caravan. I made an accurate approach, but half a mile from touchdown I began to doubt the wisdom of my decision to land her. The way

Above: John Turnbull was a WWII RCAF Halifax pilot with Nos. 419 and 424 Squadrons. He also flew Wellingtons and Lancasters. Turnbull was the youngest of three brothers who served as Bomber Command aircrew. Above left: Exhausted Britons try to sleep in the shelter of the London underground during the Blitz of 1940–41. Far left: An English child photographed in a bomb–damaged site during the Blitz. Left: Many British children were evacuated to safer country locations when London and other UK cities were being bombed by the Luftwaffe.

Top: Crew of the Halifax *Friday The 13th* and above: her rear gunner, Fred Allen. Right: A plaque that marks the Cheltenham, England birthplace of Marshal of the Royal Air Force and chief of RAF Bomber Command, Sir Arthur T. Harris.

THE CHELTENHAM CIVIC SOCIETY

MARSHAL OF THE R.A.F

SIR ARTHUR T. HARRIS
BT. G.C.B., O.B.E., A.F.C., LL.D.
CHIEF OF BOMBER COMMAND
DURING THE 2ND WORLD WAR
BORN HERE 13TH APRIL 1892

THE R.A.F. ASSOCIATION CHELTENHAM BRANCH

Above far left: A damaged runway light at RAF Langar, a WWII bomber station in England. Above centre: The wartime parachute building at RAF Marston Moor in Yorkshire. Above left: Gooseneck flares which had been used to light the runway at RAF Elvington, Yorkshire in WWII. Below centre: The control tower at RAF Tholthorpe in Yorkshire, home to Nos. 420, 425, 431 and 434 Royal Canadian Air Force Squadrons in WWII.

LET LIGHT PERPETUAL SHINE UPON THEM

SQUADRON
405 405
ESCADRILLE
DUCIMUS

THIS WINDOW COMMEMORATES THE EIGHT HUNDRED AND ONE AIRMEN OF 405 SQUADRON ROYAL CANADIAN AIRFORCE WHO GAVE THEIR LIVES ~ 1941-1945

Battle of Britain 1940

4d

Battle of Britain 1940

4d

Left: A memorial window in the church at Great Gransden, Cambridgeshire, to the airmen of No. 405 RCAF Squadron, who lost their lives in World War II while on flying operations from the nearby air base.

Below: A Fifteenth USAAF B-24 Liberator crossing its target on 6 September 1944, Nyiregyhaza, Hungary.

the wings were dipping, left to right and back to the left, was much worse than it seemed at 4000 feet. However, there was a rhythm in their rolling movement, and, picking the instant in mid-roll when the wings were level, I banged the main wheels down on the runway and held them there. Baker Two pulled up, squealing, in the last few feet of concrete. It was twenty–seven minutes past five.

"The muscles of my legs were tired from the unusual exercise of kicking Baker Two's rudders for three hours, and it was some time before I could stand without support. The crew were less boisterous than usual, oddly gentle as they helped

me to get into the crew bus, and had Walker taken to the sick-bay. When we reached the briefing room, the Station Commander strolled towards me as I took a mug of cocoa from the padre's serving hatch.

'Not one of your better landings, Currie.'

'No, sir. If I'd known you were watching I'd have tried harder.'

"He smiled and started to turn away, but Myring stopped him.

'The skipper was in difficulties, sir. He did bloody well to get it down at all.'

'Oh? What difficulties were you in, Currie?'

'I hadn't any aileron control, sir. And no flaps.'

'Why didn't you have aileron control?'

"Mentally, I cursed Larry's intervention. I had hoped to report the incident in my own time to the debriefing officer, with a cigarette to smoke and my feet under the table, and let it go through the normal channels. Now here was the Station Commander staring at me imperiously, one eyebrow raised. The Squadron Commander was at his elbow, and other officers were edging closer. I hadn't had time to sip my cocoa.

'I'm afraid they broke off, sir.'

'Broke off. Are you serious, Currie?'

'Yes, sir. We got in a spin, in some cumulo–nimbus near the target.'

'I see.'

"He looked at me quizzically for a moment, then beckoned to the Squadron Commander and walked out to his car. I turned to the crew.

'I don't think he believed me.'

'He'll get a shock when he sees the kite, then.'

"That was the first of several inspections to be undergone by Baker Two, as expert and lay examiners looked at her damaged surface areas, sprung rivets and gaping wings. Meanwhile, I called at the sick bay to see the damaged Walker, who gave a pallid smile of recognition. The MO said he had concussion, confirming Myring's diagnosis, and that he would be moved to hospital in a few hours' time. I trudged back to the hut.

"I felt slightly aggrieved when I was required to report to the Squadron Commander a few hours later, while the rest of the crew slumbered on. Woody gave me a chair in his office, and he sat at his desk making notes while I told him what had happened to Baker Two. When I had finished, he looked up with a smile.

'Well, I think it was a magnificent show. Has it shaken you up a bit?'

'No, I don't think so, sir. We're all fine, except for the engineer. He's gone into Rauceby.'

'Would you like to take a few days leave?'

"I considered the kindly suggestion. We had returned from our last leave on Friday night, and this was Tuesday. The state of our finances varied from poor to very poor. Even Fairbairn's fabulous wealth could be measured in terms of shillings, and I decided that more time off would only be an embarrassment.

'No, thank you, sir. I think we'd better get on with the tour.'

His smile almost became a grin.

'Had enough leave for a while, hm?'

'That's right, sir.'

"I was pleasantly surprised by the reactions of my colleagues on the squadron, some humorous, all generous. It was good to realize that each could emerge from his own embattled world to remark and applaud another's fortune. But, putting personal thoughts aside, the raid had not been a success. Nature, more terrible and more effective than all man-made defences, had thrown her arms around the city and its ravaged streets and protected it from further horrors. Twenty–five of us had taken off from Wickenby; four thought that they had bombed the target, eight had bombed on ETA, not altogether certain where they were, six had been unable to reach Hamburg and had bombed some other town, three had jettisoned the bomb load in the sea, three had given up the sortie, and one did not return."

Robert M. Owen is the Official Historian of 617 Squadron Association. "On the night of 16–17 May 1943 a force of Lancasters of Bomber Command executed what has been described as the greatest feat of arms ever carried out by the Royal Air Force. Under the leadership of Wing Commander Guy Gibson, nineteen crews of No. 617 Squadron, a specially formed unit of experienced crews, attacked the major dams of western Germany using a unique 'bouncing bomb' designed by engineering genius Barnes Wallis. After flying in bright moonlight at tree–top height

Within the great irregular five–mile loop of the single–laned perimeter track there lay a triangle of concrete landing strips, each one a mile long, and except for the outer ring of mud on which we traveled the whole area was a great meadow, and even at the beginning of March a vivid, hopeful green carpeted the ground. To our north, near where our ship had been spotted, we could see a forest of bare-limbed trees, and what seemed to be a cultivated park, and a visible shoulder of a country house, where Wing was set up "like a bunch of God-damn noblemen," the Colonel told us, communicating to us in a flash the hatred of the combat unit for the next higher echelon. Ahead of us, south of the runways, was our objective, a camouflaged box-like building *continued*

Above: Eighth Air Force gunners use the time between a mission briefing and take–off to clean and assemble their .50 calibre machine guns.

Right: Nissen huts on the WWII 92nd Bomb Group (H) base at Podington, Northamptonshire, England, in 1988. Below: The derelict control tower and a runway at the 401st Bomb Group (H) base, Deenethorpe, Northamptonshire, England, photographed in 1965.

with a glass windowed penthouse on it and, atop that, a dark cubic water tank, on which an enormous number, 79, was painted in figures that must have been eight feet high. Several Nissen huts lay like old discarded beer cans around the control tower, and beyond the tower crouched a row of factory-like buildings which housed, the Colonel said, repair facilities and armament shops and the service organization.

The view from a distance of all these ominous low-lying buildings, which, like the Colonel, looked tired and experienced, filled me with a kind of tension — an eagerness to know what combat would be like, and a desire to acquit myself decently, yet also an apprehension, a wondering about unknown dangers, altogether a vague sadness of which I could not have named the cause.
— from *The War Lover* by John Hersey

Top: All that remains in 1999 of a runway, now grass, at Nuthampstead, WWII home of the 398th Bomb Group (H), Eighth USAAF. Left: The ground floor stairwell of the 401st Bomb Group (H), Eighth USAAF control tower at Deenethorpe, destroyed in spring 1999.

Right: Officers and enlisted men of the 303rd Bomb Group (H) at Molesworth, Cambridgeshire, England, anxiously awaiting the return of their group from the bombing mission of 28 September 1944 to Magdeburg/Rothensee, Germany. Below: Safely back at Bassingbourn after their 25 June 1943 mission, the crew of *Our Gang* is being interrogated after the raid.

to the targets, the attack was pressed home from precisely 60 feet with tremendous fortitude and skill in the face of formidable resistance. The Mohne and Eder dams were breached and a third, the Sorpe, damaged. There was a high price to pay. Eight of the Lancasters failed to return, 53 men died and three miraculously escaped from their doomed aircraft to survive as prisoners of war. In the flooded valleys, 1294 people were drowned, including many foreign forced labourers.

"The intention was to deprive the Ruhr Valley of vital water supplies required for industrial production, whilst the floods would cause additional destruction and disruption throughout the region. The success of the operation, illustrated by photographs of the breached dams and flooded countryside, was publicised immediately throughout the Allied countries. Leaflets were dropped over occupied countries demonstrating the effectiveness of Bomber Command. The purpose of this exploitation was to magnify the effects of the attack to boost morale, a factor which has been used by some post—war revisionists to question the cost and value of the operation. Nevertheless, the cumulative effects, which extended far beyond those of the physical damage caused, refute those who seek to question its value and effectiveness.

"Operation 'Chastise' as it was known, demonstrated graphically the courage, airmanship and technical ability of Bomber Command. A small force of aircraft could penetrate into the very heart of Germany and inflict a disproportionate amount of damage on the enemy. Crews were now able to navigate accurately at night to locate and successfully attack a small target despite strong defences and the additional hazards of flying at extremely low level. The aircraft could be controlled by their leader, using radio to allow tactical flexibility and more effective use of resources — a technique which would be developed into the role of Master Bomber.

"The effects cannot be counted only in the loss of industrial output: agricultural land and livestock for vital food production were severely affected, communications disrupted and property damaged. In order to repair the dams before the winter rains, to maintain essential services and carry out other restoration, the Germans were forced to divert thousands of workers, and equipment, from other tasks vital to the war effort, including the construction of the Atlantic Wall defences. Fearing repeat attacks vast numbers of weapons were withheld from the Eastern Front, along with their crews, to defend other dams and similar targets against an enemy who in the event did not come.

"The psychological effect of these realizations upon the German leadership, civil and military morale should not be underestimated. Added to this, the destruction of the dams, previously considered to be such substantial targets as to be almost invulnerable, suggested to the Germans that there could be few places secure from the might of the RAF.

"Thirty—four of the surviving members of No. 617 Squadron were awarded decorations for their part in the operation, their leader receiving the Victoria Cross. Reinforced with other experienced crews, the Squadron was retained as a specialist bombing unit. They and their successors, under the inspired leadership of Leonard Cheshire, James 'Willie' Tait and Johnny Fauquier, would build on the reputation established by the Squadron's initial operation. Pioneering new techniques leading to greater precision and lower casualties, they used new, larger weapons such as the 12,000lb Tallboy and 22,000lb Grand Slam (again developed by the fertile mind of Barnes Wallis) denying the enemy the use of large V—weapon sites, U-boat pens, the battleship *Tirpitz* and rail communications vital for ammunition and troop movements. As the catalyst for such developments the Dams Raid also should be recognized. Such is the true legacy of this one operation."

On 8 October 1943 two crew members of a 381st Bomb Group (H) 8USAAF B-17 experienced the nearest thing to a miracle. The target that day was Bremen in northern Germany and flak and fighters cost the bomber two of its four engines shortly after leaving the aiming point. The pilots were unable to keep up with the other B-17s of their group, and before long they had drifted behind the rest of the formation and were alone. From that moment German fighters mounted a continuous attack on the stricken bomber. After twenty minutes of being shot at, the B-17 had endured all it could and began its final dive. Very soon the aircraft broke in half near the waist. Two of the crew, waist gunner Matt Berk and tail gunner Wade McCook, were trapped in the tail section. Berk was badly injured and unconscious, but McCook was in relatively good shape. Still, he could barely cling to the insides of the tail section as it spiralled earthward from nearly 22,000 feet above the German countryside. Incredibly, the tail of the bomber fell to earth from that great height and both Berk and McCook survived the descent and impact, McCook with only slight cuts and bruises. German troops arrived shortly to take the Americans into custody and, believing Berk to be dead, McCook was later astonished to learn that his crewmate had regained consciousness in a German hospital and was recovering from his injuries. He was later repatriated to the United States in a prisoner exhange. Both men survived the war. Berk eventually became a crash investigator with the US Federal Aviation Agency. Wade McCook later re—enlisted in the Air Force and was assigned as a crew chief in Korea. He was killed in the mid—air collision of two B-29s.

"AND NOW, COMING TO YOU FROM the famous Café Rouge in the Hotel Pennsylvania . . . from Frank Dailey's Meadowbrook . . . from the College Inn in Chicago . . . from the Glen Island Casino just off the Shore Road in New Rochelle, New York . . . Chesterfield cigarettes brings you the music of Glenn Miller and his orchestra."

The King of Swing Benny Goodman, Artie Shaw, Woody Herman, Tommy Dorsey, Carroll Gibbons, Charlie Barnet, Jack Hylton, Ray Noble, Glenn Miller . . . they generated the musical sounds that were a part of you if you were a member of the armed forces in World War II. Maybe "Moonlight Serenade" was *your song*, you and your girl's, when you went to war. You heard it a lot on the AEF network in your Nissen hut at Podington, Rackheath or Grafton–Underwood, at Scampton or Woodhall Spa, in France and Italy and throughout the ETO. You heard it live when Major Miller's Army Air Force Band played a concert in one of the big hangars on your field. You may even have heard it when the radio operator in your B-17 or B-24 found it on the BBC and your pilot let him play it over the airplane's intercom for the whole crew to hear. It was the music of your time. It still is.

"The sound of thousands of GIs reacting with an ear–splitting, almost hysterical happy yell after each number. That's for us, brother!"

"We didn't come here to set any fashions in music. We merely came to bring a much-needed touch of home to some lads who have been here a couple of years. These lads are doing a hell of a job — they have been starved for real, live American music."

It was in the summer of 1944 that Major Alton Glenn Miller, US Army Air Force, wrote those words from England. On 30 September 1942 the band leader and trombone player from Clarinda, Iowa disbanded the high–flying orchestra he had formed in the late '30s . . . the band that had introduced the famous "Miller sound" (a single clarinet leading four saxophones, backed by a brilliant brass section) at the Glen Island Casino in 1939. He applied for a commission, received his captaincy in October 1942 and went to work creating a great new band for the Air Force. To that end he requested that he be signalled about the entry of every musician into the US armed forces, grabbing the best of them for his band, including pianist Mel Powell, clarinetist Michael "Peanuts" Hucko, drummer Ray McKinley and more than twenty string musicians from the finest American symphony orchestras. By May 1943 the band's personnel was complete and they proceeded to play Army posts around the US. For an Army used to the stirring marches of John Philip Sousa, the sounds of the new Miller band would take some getting used to. Miller brought his civilian arranger Jerry Gray into his unit and Gray, together with Ray McKinley, began writing charts for march tunes that would swing. The cadets loved marching to "St. Louis Blues" and "Blues in the Night", but senior commanders were less impressed. One major complained: "Our men marched to the regular marches in the last war. They didn't need any of that jazzy music, and they did pretty well, too, didn't they?" Captain Miller replied: "Just let me ask you one question, Major. Are you still flying the same planes you flew in the last war?" The new arrangements survived.

On 5 June 1943 the band, including the new string section, began a series of live, weekly, coast–to–coast radio broadcasts called *I Sustain The Wings*, featuring such singers as Tony Martin, Bob Carroll and Johnny Desmond, along with actors including Broderick Crawford playing sketches aimed at recruiting men into the Air Force. All during the highly successful year–long run of the show, Captain Miller campaigned to get the Air Force to send him and the band overseas and,

finally, the permission was granted. The Glenn Miller Army Air Force Band embarked for England on the *Queen Elizabeth*, now designated NY8245.

Miller's close friend, executive officer and band manager, Lieutenant Don Haynes, kept a diary during the band's stay in England and later in France.

28 JUNE 1944: "What a sight that was when we went out on deck and saw LAND for the first time in 5 1/2 days, and a green, like we had never seen before. At 11.30 I was paged over the ship's PA system to report to the Captain's cabin. I knocked on the door and was told to come in. As I stepped over the threshold there stood the ship's captain, and beside him, wearing a grin ten miles wide . . . another Captain . . . Captain Glenn Miller. What a welcome sight he was, though he looked tired, as a result (I later learned) of sleeping in underground bomb shelters in London for the past week. It was a real treat to see him. Glenn had flown up to Gourock, Scotland late yesterday and boarded the first tender out to NY8245. We went down to the band's quarters and what a session of back slapping ensued. Glenn said the Nazi buzz bombs were being dumped into London all day long and all night as well . . ."

When the Miller band arrived in London, it was billeted in a large house at 25 Sloane Court in Chelsea, an area that the musicians referred to as "Buzz Bomb Alley" because of the frequent alerts and crashes of the V–1 flying bombs being sent over by the Germans from France who may have been trying to hit bridges and the Battersea Power Station. To the men of the band, the continuing arrival of the buzz bombs meant spending sleepless nights in the deep underground shelters and bringing their precious band instruments with them.

Prior to the band's arrival, Miller had taken a two–room suite at the Mount Royal Hotel off Oxford

GLENN MILLER

Left: Major Glenn Miller, USAAF, the American band leader whose wartime musicians entertained thousands of airmen in England and Europe. Below: Marion Hutton, a lead singer with the Miller band in the war years.

Below: Mail Call for men of the 91st Bomb Group (H), Eighth USAAF, at their Bassingbourn base in Cambridgeshire, England during WWII. When Major Glenn Miller's Army Air Force band played a concert at High Wycombe on 29 July 1944, General Jimmy Doolittle greeted him: "Next to a letter from home, your organization is the greatest morale builder in the ETO." Right: A 353rd Fighter Group airman and his date dance to swing music at a Red Cross party on his English base, 4 July 1945.

Street. He had spent five nights in London before going to Gourock to meet the band members and, rather than trying to sleep in the hotel and having to run to a shelter every time an air raid alert was sounded, he elected to sleep on a cot in the deep cellar of the British Broadcasting Corporation building. He told the boys in the band that they could set their watches by the first alert of the night as the Germans invariably sent the first V–1 over to London at 23.45.

Miller and Haynes protested to the BBC and in a few hours accommodation was found for the boys at the American Red Cross Enlisted Men's Club 52 miles north of London in the town of Bedford, where buzz bombs were not raining down each evening. On 2 July the band boarded coaches for Bedford and their new quarters.

3 JULY 1944: "Glenn and I spent a very restful night at the ARC Officer's Club, our first night in

Bedford. Right after breakfast we headed over to the EM's barracks . . . most of them were still in the sack, enjoying the first good night's sleep in over a week. Left Sgt Sanderson a call for twelve o'clock (noon) to get the boys in fatigue uniforms and over to the Pottery Factory which we are to transform into a broadcasting studio . . . They reported there on schedule and began the work of cleaning the place up . . . Glenn and I had procured several hundred burlap sacks, and the boys started fashioning a ceiling of burlap by tying the sacks together. . . It was quite primitive but it did deaden the echo . . . by the end of the week we would have some semblance of a studio . . . British engineers would be there from London to put in the wiring on Wednesday . . . the boys named the studio '8-H' after the big studio in Radio City, New York."

9 JULY 1944: "First broadcast over the AEF Network and the BBC out of our improvised 8-H studio . . . In a matter of twenty-four hours GLENN MILLER'S AMERICAN BAND OF THE SUPREME ALLIED COMMAND was the talk of the British Isles . . . newspapers heralded its greatness, musicians in London found out where we were stationed, and as petrol was a very scarce item, they took the train from London to Bedford to see and hear the band rehearse, or to watch a broadcast from 8-H . . . We soon learned that British bandleaders were refusing to precede or follow us on the BBC . . . that they suffered by comparison with this star–studded outfit from the USA . . ."

13 JULY 1944: "All went well until today — we adhered to our schedule of thirteen broadcasts weekly and Glenn had told me to arrange for personal appearances at nearby air bases, when I received a call from Maurice Gorham of the BBC that Glenn and I were to come in for an important meeting at Broadcasting House (BBC studios in London) tomorrow morning . . . eleven o'clock sharp!

14 JULY 1944: "At eleven o'clock sharp we walked into Mr Gorham's office and, after being introduced to five other gentlemen from the BBC, we sat down, the door was closed and Mr Gorham spoke. 'Captain Miller and Leftenant [sic] Haynes, you are to be commended for the marvellous aggregation of musicians you have brought here to the British Isles, and for the simply marvellous programmes you have been doing the past week over the combined AEF and BBC stations. However, we have encountered complaints from our listeners' (and as he spoke he turned in his chair toward the wall, and with a pointer described a circle on a map, which started to the north of London several hundred miles, and went down to Plymouth and Southampton on the south coast), 'that the BBC transmitter, being located just outside London, sent its signal in all directions but stronger to the north.' He continued by saying, 'In this circle which I am describing, the listener's signal becomes weaker [farther out] and during the soft passages, they think we're off the air . . . so, we must insist that you keep your volume constant!' I looked at Glenn and he met my glance with a disbelieving look. A few seconds elapsed, and Glenn said, 'Mr Gorham, I don't believe I understood your explanation correctly. Would you mind repeating what you have just said?' Gorham, wearing a walrus–type mustache and tending to muffle his words, repeated what he had said, and with the pointer described again what he called the 'outer fringe' and again said, 'We must insist therefore, that you keep the volume constant!' Well, I knew all hell was going to break loose but quick, as Glenn's face was already flushed. I knew he was angry to the core and, though he was trying his best to restrain himself, he rose from his chair, walked over directly in front of Mr Gorham's desk and, looking directly at Mr Gorham, said, 'I can hardly believe what you have just said,' and raising his voice perceptibly, he continued, 'I have spent many thousands of dollars to achieve contrasts in sound. Much of my music is soft for a definite purpose. I'm sorry. I cannot alter my arrangements to accommodate the BBC. I have a solution [though]. Our mission over here is to broadcast over the AEF network, *not* over the BBC, therefore, you can do us and yourselves a favour by cancelling all future broadcasts over the BBC!' Glenn turned to me and said, 'Haynsie, let's get out of here', and we did just that.

"We were to hear reverberations of this meeting in the weeks following. One of our missions in the British Isles was to foster better Anglo–American relations, and here within two weeks we had wound up in a disagreement with the BBC. Needless to mention that our broadcasts were no longer fed to the BBC, but were confined to the AEF network. This made the British bandleaders happy because they didn't have to precede or follow us for their remote broadcasts over the BBC. Our being cancelled off the BBC caused an uproar among the British listeners, and letters by the thousands began pouring into the BBC and the London newspapers from all over Great Britain. Newspaper editorials appeared condemning the BBC for denying the people of Britain the famous Glenn Miller and his American Band of the Supreme Allied Command. In parts of England, people were able to tune in on the AEF network, but the BBC, as soon as they heard this was being done, put their engineers to work 'shielding' and pin–pointing the AEF network to the camps and front–line spots it was intended to reach, making it almost impossible for the British populace to tune in our broadcasts. We were not popular with the die–hards at the BBC, one of whom said of us, and in fact of all Americans stationed in the British Isles, 'You're overpaid, you're over–fed, you're over–sexed, and you're over here!'

"Glenn and I returned to Bedford in the early afternoon as we had scheduled an appearance at Thurleigh air base seven miles from Bedford for late this afternoon. Over 5000 pilots, crew members,

In World War II the Eagle pub in Cambridge was a popular spot with both RAF and American aircrew. Many of them used to smoke their names and units on the ceiling and, when the pub was renovated in 1993, the owners elected to preserve their piece of wartime history and their particular link with the past.

DEDICATED BY THE GLENN MILLER SOCIETY
TO THE EVERLASTING MEMORY OF
MAJOR ALTON GLENN MILLER
1904 'THE MOONLIGHT SERENADER' 1944
DIRECTOR OF THE AMERICAN BAND OF THE ALLIED EXPEDITIONARY FORCES
FOR HIS OUTSTANDING CONTRIBUTION TO POPULAR MUSIC
RECALLING HIS CONCERTS TO THE ALLIED FORCES AT THIS HALL
DURING 1944 THIS COMMEMORATIVE PLAQUE WAS UNVEILED AT A
TRIBUTE CONCERT BY THE MILLION AIRS ORCHESTRA AT THE CORN
EXCHANGE BEDFORD ON FEBRUARY 25 1976

and ground maintenance personnel crowded into a hangar, and Glenn and the band put on an hour–and–a–half show that had them screaming and applauding from the first strains of 'Moonlight Serenade', to the finish . . . This, then, was the first of several hundred appearances we were to make at air bases all over England and Ireland, in addition to several broadcasts daily for our men stationed all over the ETO."

23 JULY 1944: "The Queen of England was to make an inspection tour of the Red Cross installations in Bedford today . . . After lunch I returned to the ARC Officer's Club to complete some reports for SHAEF, and no sooner had I entered the lobby when Mrs Bowes–Lyon rushed up to me and asked if I had met the Queen . . . 'Was I supposed to meet the Queen?' was my answer, and she assured me that I most certainly should . . . so, with that she took me by the arm, through a doorway which led into the dining room . . . there stood the Queen with her entourage. She turned and smiled as Mrs Bowes-Lyon (her sister) introduced me by saying, 'Your Majesty, I would like you to meet Leftenant [sic] Haynes, the Executive Officer of the Glenn Miller American Band of the Supreme Allied Command.' The Queen extended her right hand warmly, and smiling all the while said, 'Leftenant [sic] Haynes, let me commend you, Captain Miller, and the members of your fine organization for the wonderful morale work you are doing . . . the Princesses Elizabeth and Margaret Rose are avid fans of the Glenn Miller Band and listen to your nightly broadcasts over the wireless regularly'. . . still shaking my hand, gently, and smiling sweetly (I was very impressed with her sincerity) . . . I thanked her with all the graciousness I could muster, and as the *Stars & Stripes* photographers' flash bulbs were popping from both sides and behind me, I told her that I would convey her gracious compliments to Captain Miller and the men in the band. She released my hand, and with a

slight bowing of my head, I backed into the crowd of officers who had gathered around us . . . still awed by the graciousness of this motherly–type woman, the Queen of England . . . a most charming and sincere person dressed entirely in grey, even to grey stockings, gloves and hat which matched her tailored grey suit. The Army photographers caught up with me a few minutes later and wanted to know what the Queen and I were talking about. They made their notes [and] promised that they would send me a set of the photos taken 'cause I wanted so badly to send [them] to my mother in Cleveland, Ohio."

29 JULY 1944: "Took the entire unit to Pinetree near High Wycombe by bus . . . Glenn and I went in a jeep. This was the headquarters of the 8th Air Force and USTAFF. . . the nerve–centre of the bombing raids being planned here . . . General Jimmy Doolittle's headquarters. Played a concert outside, late afternoon to the entire complement of this base. More brass here than I've yet seen! Band was set up on 'crash trucks' for elevation. Many of the British General Staff in attendance. After the concert, which was received most enthusiastically by several thousand, General Doolittle climbed up on the crash truck, shook Captain Miller by the hand and then over the microphone to the assembled crowd, said, 'NEXT TO A LETTER FROM HOME, CAPTAIN MILLER, YOUR ORGANIZATION IS THE GREATEST MORALE BUILDER IN THE ETO.' "

2 AUGUST 1944: "Over to Kimbolton, another B-17 base this afternoon for an outside concert to 4500 . . . same reaction as always . . . these guys are so hungry for entertainment and they love this band . . . at every appearance, it never fails, a dozen or more GIs come up to Glenn and the boys, and say, 'The last time I heard the band play was at Hershey Park, Pennsylvania, or Glen Island Casino, or the Palladium in Hollywood, or Pacific Square in San Diego, or Cedar Rapids, Iowa, etc. etc."

6 AUGUST 1944: "This base [Boxted] is the home of Colonel [Hub] Zemke and his 'Wolf Pack', the roughest fighter group in the ETO with more 'kills' to their credit than any fighter group over here . . . played to 2500 in the largest hangar on the base, then to a terrific dinner in the Officer's Club, followed by a half hour of combat films in the base theatre (with beer on the side). Colonel Dave Shilling, executive officer of this group, and one of the most feared fighter pilots of the war, flew us back to Twinwood in a four–passenger Fairchild while the band returned in Liberator bombers."

16 AUGUST 1944: "The band had been transported via trucks, and we met them at Bentley Priory. We set the band up on the huge veranda overlooking a lawn in front of a beautiful mansion, originally built by Lord Nelson for Lady Hamilton, which is now being used as a hospital for the injured being brought over from the battle fronts in France. Those who could not be brought out on the lawn were hanging out of the windows. The band was playing their first tune, 'In The Mood', when a buzz bomb made its appearance. The band kept playing (but much softer) as Glenn wanted to be sure he could hear if the motor cut out, but it didn't, and in less than thirty seconds [the buzz bomb] was out of sight."

17 AUGUST 1944: "Broadcasts from 8-H, and Captain Alton G. Miller received his Majority today, so at the conclusion of the last broadcast we gave MAJOR Miller a promotion party that lasted until the 'wee hours."

23 AUGUST 1944: "We played in a hangar at Podington, a B-17 base, at three o'clock in the afternoon . . . 5000 eager GI's crowded into the hangar and devoured every beat. Six B-17s from Framlingham picked us up at 4.30 [and] flew us to their base [where] they were celebrating their 100th mission over Germany. After a very good dinner in the Combat

"Scunthorpe was unknown to me, but it was the town most patronized by the Elsham men. There one could get drunk at the 'Crosby', or see a floor show and get drunk at the 'Oswald', or dance and get drunk at the 'Berkley'. And in the event of missing the bus back, it was always possible to stay the night at Irish Maggie's and return to camp by train in the morning. In my memory Scunthorpe is blacked out and wet, for only in poor weather did we escape to it. So often did I find my way about it in darkness, that its streets and buildings became places built in my imagination, rather than the streets and buildings of actuality."
— from *No Moon Tonight* by Don Charlwood

TAKING OFF!

Left: Memorials to Glenn Miller at the Bedford Corn Exchange, a hall where the Miller Army Air Force band played in 1944.

Mess we played for a dance in a hangar that had been cleaned out and decorated with straw, hay, trees and everything else they could lay their hands on. English girls were permitted on the base, and some brought their mothers, to get a good meal. Forty kegs of beer were brought in, as well as 10,000 doughnuts, and there was plenty of 'hard stuff' in evidence, from the private stock of the men who had been saving up for this party. After the dance, the CO gave a party for the band at the Officer's Club where fourteen quarts of Scotch were set up on the tables when we walked in. Quite a party!"

27 AUGUST 1944: "We had used the Royal Air Force Beaufighter base, Twinwood Farm, just outside of Bedford, so much that Glenn thought it would be advisable to play a concert for them on a Sunday afternoon, so today was the day. We played to a most enthusiastic audience of British pilots and crews of this base, numbering in excess of a thousand."

11 SEPTEMBER 1944: "We went to Leicester where we played to 4000 Airborne Troops who had been restricted to their base for four days awaiting word to take off and parachute into an enemy stronghold. They were brought into DeMontfort Hall, under guard — not allowed to talk with anyone. They were a tense group, but the band had 'em screaming for more, and Glenn did about an hour–and–a–half for them instead of the usual hour show... and did they love it, every note! (We later learned that this group took their 'jump' the following day with great success.) The C.O. of this base wrote SHAEF HDQRTRS one of the most complimentary letters I have ever read, to the effect that there just wasn't anything in the ETO to compare with [the] Glenn Miller AAF Band, and what a marvellous job they did to relax his 4000 paratroopers the night before they jumped back of the German lines."

A short life and a merry one my buck! / We used to say we'd hate to live dead –old,– Yet now . . . I'd willingly be puffy, bald, / And patriotic. Buffers catch from boys At least the jokes hurled at them. I suppose / Little I'd ever teach a son, but hitting, / Shooting, war, hunting, all the arts of hurting.
Well, that's what I learnt– that, and making money.
– from 'A Terre'
by Wilfred Owen

On London fell a clearer light; Caressing pencils of the sun Defined the distances, the white / Houses transfigured one by one, The 'long, unlovely street' impearled. O what a sky has walked the world!
– from 'Summer in England, 1914'
by Alice Meynell

Left: Visiting Piccadilly Circus, crew members of the B-24, *Shoot Luke*, relax on their leave in London in April 1943.

149

Right: The Foxy Theatre at Grafton Underwood, home of the 384th Bomb Group (H), Eighth USAAF, in Northamptonshire, England in 1944. Below: Second Lieutenant John Moeller and Staff Sergeant Robert Elroy arranging their social life at an American air base in WWII England. Below right: A beer break on an American bomber station in England during the war.

15 SEPTEMBER 1944: "Left for Bury St Edmunds at 1.30 via trucks, arriving at Rougham, a B-17 base celebrating their 200th Mission Party. The cold, damp climate finally laid Glenn low. He was running a temperature when we left and his sinuses were giving him a fit with terrible headaches. This was the first appearance of the band in the ETO that he'd missed, but he was in no shape to subject himself to something more serious. Dinah Shore and a USO unit was here to appear with the band for this celebration party. Sgt Jerry Gray directed the band and all went fine with a rip–roaring show the end result."

15 OCTOBER 1944: "Glenn has welded this outfit into a well–oiled machine . . . five saxophonists who play and phrase and breathe like one; four trombonists and four trumpets which can play the sweetest muted passages you'd ever want to hear, and can turn about and blast the roof and walls off any ordinary edifice; four rhythm [players] with an outstanding man in each chair, such as Sgt Ray McKinley on drums, Sgt Mel Powell on piano, Sgt 'Trigger' Alpert, the gum–chewing bass player (we 'traded' ten musicians to get him from an Army Ground Unit in Fort Benjamin Harrison near Indianapolis), Sergeant Carmen Mastren on guitar; and twenty-one strings headed by Sergeant George Ockner, first violin; plus Sergeant Johnny Desmond, the featured vocalist; and the Crew Chiefs, the singing quartet, whose renditions of the old Miller favourites, plus tunes like 'The Trolley Song', 'Have Yuh Got Any Gum Chum?', 'Holiday for Strings', 'Poinciana', and many others help, as Glenn said: 'bring a hunk of home to the guys who were sluggin' it out for all of us.' This then, plus a staff of arrangers consisting of Sergeants Jerry Gray and Norman Leyden, and Corporal Perry Burgett, and copyists headed by Sergeant Jimmy Jackson, and instrument repair men Corporals Vito Pascucci and Julie Zifferblatt, and announcers Corporal Paul Dubov and Sergeant Broderick Crawford . . . this is the outfit that Glenn has moulded into what might be likened to a well–oiled machine, and with his know–how, impeccable taste, and his knack of scoring arrangements, then editing same, thereby separating the 'wheat' from the 'chaff', all adds up to an unbeatable musical organization, the like of which has never been assembled."

4 NOVEMBER 1944: "Driving in from the Officer's Club to the ARC Club, Glenn was in a very pensive mood, and talked like I had never heard him express himself before. 'Don,' he said, 'I have a strong feeling that I'll never see Helen and Stevie again . . . I know that sounds odd, but I've had that feeling for some time now. You know, the Miller luck has been phenomenal for the last five years, and I don't want to be around when it changes.' "

On 15 November Major Miller was summoned to Paris for a meeting with General Barker of SHAEF to talk about a proposal to bring the band to Paris to entertain front-line troops on leave in the area, and hospital patients there.

18 NOVEMBER 1944: "Glenn returned from Paris and Versailles. On the way back to Bedford [he] outlined [the] proposed movement to Paris for a six-week period on or about 15 December. We gave the proposal to the band and told them it was up to them to make the decision in that it meant we would have to record six weeks of programmes (102 shows) in addition to keeping up the regular schedule. They unanimously favoured doing just that . . . to get to Paris!"

13 DECEMBER 1944: "I had intended going to Paris ahead of the band by a day or two, but Glenn decided he'd go and I would take the band, so the orders I had were cancelled and I had orders cut for Glenn to go in my place today. Weather was very bad and he was unable to get off for Paris

Dressing is a long and complicated business. The men strip to the skin. Next to their skins they put on long light woollen underwear. Over that they slip on what looks like long light-blue-colored underwear, but these are the heated suits. They come low on the ankles and far down on the wrists, and from the waists of these suits protrude electric plugs. The suit, between two layers of fabric, is threaded with electric wires which will carry heat when the plug is connected to the heat outlet on the ship. Over the heated suit goes the brown cover-all. Last come thick, fleece-lined heated boots and gloves which also have plugs for the heat unit. Next goes on the Mae West, the orange rubber life preserver, which can be inflated in a moment. Then comes the parachute with its heavy canvas straps over the shoulders and between the legs. And last the helmet with the throat speaker and the earphones attached. Plugged in to the intercommunications system, the man can now communicate with the rest of the crew no matter what noise is going on about him. During the process the men have got bigger and bigger as layer on layer of equipment is put on. They walk stiffly, like artifical men. The lean waist gunner is now a little chubby.

They dress very carefully, for an exposed place or a disconnected suit can cause a bad frostbite at 30,000 feet. It is dreadfully cold up there.
– from *Once There Was A War* by John Steinbeck

Below: Not the easiest task, keeping a fire going in the small coal stove of a Nissen hut on an American air base in WWII England.

"Podington was a great big farm; it was pretty much like the plains of Texas. When the weather was bad anywhere in England, this place had fog. The officer's barracks were Nissen huts, about twenty feet wide and thirty feet long, and separated into rooms with two men to a room. I roomed with my co-pilot. There was a small, open fireplace. We slept with our socks and long johns on. Typically, they woke us up at one or two in the morning on the day of a mission. We would have breakfast and go to briefing. Take–off was about three hours later, and most of the time we took off in fog. The rendezvous a few hours after that over England at, maybe, 25,000 feet, with somebody shooting two colours of flares which you formed on. Somebody else was firing two other colours of flares to form the groups, and then other for the division line."
— Ray Wild, formerly with the 92nd Bomb Group (H),Eighth USAAF

today, but was scheduled to go tomorrow, so, I packed my bag, told Glenn I'd see him in Paris Saturday [and] gave him the various people to call to alert them for our arrival, such as the Transportation Officer at Seine Base; the owner-manager of the Hotel des Olympiades (where the band was to be billeted), and I left for Bedford about four o'clock. The fog was now so thick that the conductors of the big double–decker buses were walking three feet in front of the buses with a torch [flashlight] pointed back toward the bus driver, so that he wouldn't run up over the kerbing, or smash into another vehicle. I'd seen fog before, but nothing like this. It took me four hours to get to Bedford — ordinarily only an hour and fifteen minute trip."

14 DECEMBER 1944: "Had lunch with Colonel Norman Baessell at the Officer's Club and he said he was going to Paris tomorrow and would I like to join him. Told him I was taking the band over on Saturday and that Glenn was leaving today if the weather cleared. The Colonel said nothing was flying out of the UK today because of the bad weather, so suggested that we call Glenn in London, and have him fly over to Paris tomorrow with him and Flying Officer John R. S. Morgan. We called Glenn, and sure enough he was grounded and had little hope of getting out tomorrow as there had been no SHAEF SHUTTLE to Paris for the past five days and he was outranked even if flying weather prevailed tomorrow. He welcomed the Colonel's invitation and asked me to drive in and get him. Left for London right after lunch, arriving at the Mount Royal at four o'clock. Glenn was all packed and ready, so back to Bedford in

time for dinner with Colonel Baessell at the Officer's Club.

"After a few hands of poker with the Colonel, Major Koch, and Warrant Officer Earlywine, Glenn and I left for the ARC Officer's Club to get a good night's sleep, as the Colonel would be calling early (as soon as he got weather clearance). Glenn and I sat in front of the fireplace at the Club until 3.30 a.m. He was in a talking mood, and though he had said earlier that he wanted to get a good night's sleep, he seemed restless and not at all tired, so we sat and talked, and planned. We talked about the post–war band . . . taxes . . . etc, and came to the conclusion that we'd work not more than six months a year. The other six months we'd play golf, buy a trailer and go up into the Northwest and do some salmon fishing on the Columbia River, raise oranges at 'Tuxedo Junction' (Glenn's ranch in Monrovia, California), do an occasional recording date, and the balance of the time, we'd just loaf, and, of course, devote some time to our families. We even discussed who would be in the post–war band, and our first engagement after getting out of uniform. [It was] to be the Paramount Theatre, New York City, for six weeks with an option for two more, at $15,000 weekly, which was more money than had ever been paid for a band. So, these were the plans we discussed into the early hours of this cold and rainy 14 December 1944. We both took a hot shower and went to bed."

15 DECEMBER 1944: "I was awakened by a phone call from Colonel Baessell at 9 a.m. The weather was still bad, couldn't get clearance this a.m., but it showed signs of clearing by early afternoon, so he suggested that Glenn and I come out to the Club for lunch and bring Glenn's luggage, 'cause if the weather cleared they'd go to Paris this afternoon. After breakfast we read the morning papers and loafed around the lounge for a couple of hours. We went to the EM's billet and found everything in readiness for our move to Paris on the morrow. Then out to Eighth Air Force Headquarters and the Officer's Club. Colonel Baessell was packing his bag when we entered his room. The Colonel said he had just talked with Flying Officer Morgan at Station 595 and Morgan said the weather was improving and he'd know shortly after noon whether or not he'd get clearance for the flight to Paris.

"While at lunch the Colonel was called to the phone. He returned, smiling, and said that Morgan had just received clearance and would pick them up at Twinwood within the hour. Major Bill Koch and Warrant Officer Earlywine strolled out to the staff car with the Colonel, Glenn and myself, and after a few slaps on the back and a warning to look out for those mademoiselles on the Rue de la Paix, Glenn and the Colonel closed the door and I drove to General Goodrich's chateau, which was in the general direction of Twinwood Farm, as the Colonel wished to see the bed–ridden General for any last–minute instructions (General Goodrich was being returned to the States, having suffered a severe heart ailment, and Colonel Baessell was to arrange for his trip by ship on his return from Paris Sunday).

"Glenn and I sat in the staff car while the Colonel ran in to the General's chateau, and it started to rain again. Dark clouds, the low–hanging variety, were now much in evidence, and Glenn expressed doubt that Flying Officer Morgan would even be able to find Twinwood Farm to pick them up. The Colonel came running out after not more than ten minutes with the General, and said the General was much improved. Ten minutes later we drove up to the Flight Control Tower at Twinwood Farm, shut off the motor and sat in the car awaiting the arrival of Flying Officer Morgan. The hard rain had now levelled off to a steady drizzle and, looking skyward, the ceiling was not more than two hundred feet.

"Colonel Baessell went to the tower and returned a few minutes later with news that Morgan had

At the Admin block Colonel Whelan turned us over to the Ground Exec, a captain named Blair, who smelled of Vaseline hair tonic, and after checking our orders he drove us south of the flying line, where the land sloped upward into wooded groves in which, widely dispersed and well hidden, were the living quarters of the men. The enlisted men lived in prefab Nissen huts, officers in slightly more elaborate hutments with single and double rooms. Here, too, were sick quarters, the motor pool, the officers' club, the Red Cross Aero Club for the men, two officers' messes, a shed for movies, and the big enlisted men's mess.

It began to rain again as we drove.
– from *The War Lover*
by John Hersey

His fingers wake, and flutter up the bed. / His eyes come open with a pull of will, Helped by the yellow may– flowers by his head. / A blind– cord drawls across the window-sill... How smooth the floor of the ward is! what a rug! / And who's that talking, somewhere out of sight? / Why are they laughing? What's inside that jug? 'Nurse! Doctor!'
'Yes; all right, all right.'
– from 'Conscious'
by Wilfred Owen

Gather ye rosebuds while ye may, Old Time is still a–flying: / And this same flower that smiles today, To–morrow will be dying.
– Robert Herrick

Right: Milton Earnest Hall, wartime headquarters of the Eighth Air Force Service Command. Milton Earnest is located a few miles from both the Bedford billet of the Miller band personnel, and the Twinwood Farm airfield frequently used by the band during their stay in England.

my sweet old etcetera / aunt
lucy during the recent / war
could and what is more did
tell you just
what everybody was fighting
for, my sister / isabel created
hundreds(and hundreds) of
socks not to mention shirts
fleaproof earwarmers etcetera
wristers etcetera, my
mother hoped that / i would die
etcetera / bravely of course my
father used / to become hoarse
talking about how it was / a
privilege and if only he / could
meanwhile my / self etcetera lay
quietly in the deep mud et
cetera
(dreaming,
et
 cetera, of
Your smile
eyes knees and of your
Etcetera)
—'my sweet old etcetera'
by E. E. Cummings

taken off from Station 595 55 minutes earlier and was due at Twinwood at any moment. Glenn, visibly nervous, couldn't sit in the staff car any longer, opened the door and got out, peered skyward, and as a result his glasses became blurred from the drizzle. The Colonel and I joined Glenn on the concrete strip. It was cold, and walking over to the tower I took a look at the thermometer alongside the ladder, and it registered 34 degrees. Glenn said, 'Morgan will never find this field . . . even the birds are grounded today.' Then we heard the steady drone of an airplane motor. The engine noise was getting louder now and it sounded as though the plane was directly over the field and not too high, though we couldn't see it on account of the poor visibility and low ceiling of the cloud layer which couldn't have been more than two hundred feet. Now the motor noise was diminishing as it apparently was now past the field and heading south. 'What'd I tell you, Colonel, in this muck he can't even find the field. He's missed it', said

Glenn. 'Don't bet on it, Glenn', said the Colonel, 'Morgan's a helluva pilot — he flew thirty–two missions in B-24s and he's used to weather like this. My money says he'll be on this airstrip within ten minutes.' A couple of minutes later the plane came through the overcast directly over the centre of the field, circled once and came down into the wind which was blowing from west to east. We climbed back into the staff car and drove out to the end of the airstrip and Morgan taxied back down the strip and turned around alongside the car. Leaving the motor running he opened the door of the small [plane] and greeted us with a wave, 'Hi', and said, 'Sorry I'm late. Ran into some heavy squalls, but the weather is supposed to be clearing over the continent.' I shook hands with Morgan as I tossed Glenn's B-4 bag through the open cabin door. Glenn and the Colonel climbed aboard. The Colonel seated himself in the co–pilot's seat and Glenn sat in a bucket seat directly back of the Colonel facing the side of the ship. Morgan climbed into the pilot's seat, and as they all fastened their seat belts I waved a goodbye. 'Happy landings and good luck. I'll see you in Paris tomorrow,' I said, and Glenn replied, 'Thanks, Haynesie, we may need it!' I closed the door, secured the catch and stepped back from the plane to get away from the prop wash, as Morgan waved and revved–up the motor. He released the brakes and they started down the runway gaining speed and were soon airborne. In less than a minute they climbed into the overcast and out of sight. I got back into the staff car and drove back to Bedford and the ARC Officer's Club. It was 1.45 p.m. when they took off. They should arrive at Orly Field, Paris in two–and–a–half to three hours."

16 DECEMBER 1944 "Up at 0545 and after a fast breakfast we boarded the bus for Bovingdon Aerodrome arriving there two hours later. Still raining and plenty damp and cold. All planes grounded. We returned to Bedford."

17 DECEMBER 1944 "Up at 0600, into the buses and arrived at Bovingdon at 0830. Same deal as yesterday, and Flight Control Officer told me there hadn't been a plane take off for the continent in the past six days. Shortly before noon we boarded the buses back to Bedford, but not until I was able to arrange for the three C-47s to pick us up at Twinwood Farm IF the weather cleared tomorrow."

18 DECEMBER 1944 "At 10.00 a.m., loaded the buses and out to Twinwood Farm. As we drove onto the field three C-47s were circling for a landing. Beautiful day with sun pecking in and out of the clouds, and no rain! First nice day in a week. Loaded the equipment and men onto the planes and we took off for Paris at 11.25 a.m. Fifty minutes later we passed over the white cliffs of Dover and out over the English Channel, passing over the French coast at 12.50 p.m. Landed at Orly

Field at 1.45 p.m. Though a coded message had been sent by Bovingdon Flight Control that we were en route and to have transportation at the field, there was none when I checked in at the Transportation Desk. Checked Friday's arrivals and found that Glenn's plane had not landed there. The information I had learned at Bovingdon that no planes had cleared out of there all last week had me a bit concerned. I called the Transportation Officer at Seine Base Section and found that Glenn had not contacted him re confirming the arrangements I had made for the buses meeting us at Orly. Called Major May and General Barker at SHAEF in Versailles, and they hadn't seen Glenn or heard from him, and didn't know he was coming over a day ahead of our scheduled arrival, but knew that bad weather had grounded *all* flights out of the United Kingdom the past week.

Haynes then secured a staff car at Seine Base and drove directly to SHAEF Headquarters, arriving there shortly after 6.00 p.m.

"General Barker and Major May had been busy since I had talked with them from Orly Field, calling bases on the continent as well as bases on the English coast. They found one rather startling fact. A single motor ship had been charted out of the UK from a southerly point headed over the Channel in the general direction of Paris, but was not reported as flying over the French coast. They had also learned that no anti-aircraft guns had been fired from any coastal point between the hours of 1400 and 1800.

"General Barker placed a call to General Goodrich at my suggestion, as I felt certain Colonel Baessell would have contacted General Goodrich had he encountered any trouble, as the Colonel was due back on Sunday (yesterday). While we were talking and exploring the possibilities of what might have happened, the cross–Channel call to General Goodrich came through. General Barker motioned for me to pick up

Most people will agree with me when I say the worst part of any bombing raid is the start. I, for my part, hate the feeling of standing around in the crew rooms, waiting to get into the vans that will take you out to your aircraft. It's a horrible business. Your stomach feels as though it wants to hit your backbone. You can't stand still. You laugh at small jokes, loudly, stupidly. You smoke far too many cigarettes, usually only half–way through, then throw them away. Sometimes you feel sick and want to go to the lavatory. The smallest incidents annoy you and you flare up on the slightest provocation. When someone forgets his parachute you call him names that you would never use in the ordinary way. All this because you're frightened, scared stiff. I know — because I've done all those things.

Then comes the take–off. A thrilling sight to the layman. Exactly at the right time they taxi out, led by the Squadron Commander in his own aircraft with a gaudy design painted on the nose. They come out one after another, like a long string of ducks, and line up on the runway waiting to take off. There is a cheery wave of good–byes from the well–wishers on the first flare. Then the pilot slams his window shut and pushes open the throttles. The ground underneath the well–wishers shivers and shakes, sending a funny feeling up their spine, and the Lancasters lumber off one after another down the mile–long flare–path. And off they go into the dusk.
— from *Enemy Coast Ahead* by Guy Gibson

The late Dame Kathleen Raven, former Chief Nursing Officer of the United Kingdom, was a young ward sister at Saint Bartholomew's Hospital in London during World War II. There she learned to deal with sorrow and death during the Blitz on the city and became adept at managing heartbroken and grieving relatives. In one night 7000 Londoners were killed and a further 9000 were injured. The hospital itself was hit and a bomb blast that shattered all of the windows blew nurse Raven across the ward. "We were all so busy looking after the casualties that we did not have time to think about ourselves." For two years during the war, she slept on an air mattress on the first floor of the ward block. Diminutive, highly dedicated and determined, Raven was affectionately referred to by the doctors at Saint Bart's as the Pocket Battleship.

Above: Major Miller and the band are introduced to an eager and appreciative GI audience at a hangar concert on an American bomber station in England.

the telephone on Major May's desk. After Barker had inquired as to Goodrich's condition, he asked if Colonel Baessell was there, and with that Goodrich let out a blast to the effect that Baessell flew to Paris on Friday and was due back yesterday, and the so—and—so hadn't returned and he hadn't heard from him. Barker then brought Goodrich up to date on what was going on and told him I was on the extension, so I augmented what Barker had already told him. He was furious when I told him they had flown a C-64, which he said had no de-icing equipment, and as icing conditions were prevalent (34 degrees at Twinwood Farm and over the Channel it was eight to ten degrees colder). Goodrich expressed great disappointment with Flying Officer Morgan (his personal pilot) for flying a C-64 over the Channel in that kind of weather. General Goodrich said he'd have a search instituted as of daybreak tomorrow, but that it appeared to him they had iced up and gone into the Channel! The General had quietened down considerably now and talked very seriously. He knew how close Glenn and I were, and he assured me that he'd leave no stone

unturned to find out what had happened, that there was a possibility they had been forced down in some remote spot and had not been able to get to a communications centre to report their whereabouts. General Barker hung up the phone and turning to me said, 'It looks very bad, Lieutenant — I'm afraid Major Miller has had it!' "

19 DECEMBER 1944 "Called Major May several times during the morning. Nothing new. Four full days have elapsed since I saw them off at Twinwood Farm and not a trace of that plane since it went out over the English coast headed south for the coast of France. The narrow corridor from the coast of England to the French coast was ninety miles, all over water (German-held positions along the French coast prevented going the short route — the route the Channel swimmers take.)"

20 DECEMBER 1944 "Called Major May at SHAEF first thing, but he has received no word that would give us any encouragement, and said he and General Barker have all but given up any hopes of finding

Miller, Baessell and Morgan alive, *if* they are found at all. Said that we might as well prepare ourselves for the worst and that if no trace is found or reported today, he must turn in a Casualty Report tomorrow morning, which means that Helen Miller will receive a telegram tomorrow afternoon from the War Department that her husband is 'Missing in Flight as of 15 December 1944.' There is no way I can get word to Polly in New York City to get out to Tenafly to be with Helen, and my only hope is that she's already there. Polly and all the wives and families of the fellows in the band will naturally assume that if Glenn is missing, we all are too, as our many letters have told them of how we have been flying all over the ETO playing at the US air bases. What a Christmas present! Hopefully, the newspapers will carry the complete story and report that the personnel of the Glenn Miller Air Force Band landed safely in Paris, but not Major Miller who had flown to Paris three days earlier.

"Major May assured me that the newspapers would not be given the release until after Mrs Miller receives the wire from the War Department.

"Called Major May at six o'clock, but he's had no word, just the same 'no trace, no findings.' Talked him into deferring Casualty Report one more day."

21 DECEMBER 1944 "Went out to SHAEF early this a.m. Conference with Major May and General Barker. They've given up and said it all simmers down to three possibilities:
1. Flying blind, they might have strayed over enemy territory and were either shot down or forced down and are captives.
2. Crashed in remote spot and not yet found.
3. Went down in the Channel, and if so there'll never be any trace of the plane or occupants. 'Those are the cold facts', said General Barker, 'we might as well face them, and the Casualty Report *must* be released first thing in the morning.' He asked me why I had been so insistent that the Casualty Report be held up another day, and when

I told him I felt Major Miller might still show up, that the Miller luck had been so infallible the past five years that I just couldn't believe it could take such an abrupt turn, he put his arm around me and said, 'You thought a lot of the guy, didn't you, Lieutenant?' His question required no answer, and if it had I doubt if I could have uttered a word, the lump in my throat was king–size."

28 DECEMBER 1944 "Spent the entire day at SHAEF getting reports completed and making depositions on Glenn's departure from Twinwood Farm, in detail. Took mail to the billet and when Sgt Sanderson sorted it out he found a delayed cable for me from Helen Miller. She reported everyone at home OK and felt confident Glenn would show up. Here we were concerned about her and she sends a cable to bolster *our* morale."

29 DECEMBER 1944 "Ran into Lt Col Traistor and Col Early from Milton Earnest, Baessell's home base in England. They confirmed that there had been no trace of the C-64 piloted by F/O Morgan and carrying Col Baessell and Major Miller."

30 DECEMBER 1944 Out to SHAEF to turn in list of Glenn's personal effects."

5 JANUARY 1945 "Played Grand Hotel at eight o'clock, and a Captain told me he had heard over the radio that Glenn's body and wreckage of plane had been found on French-Normandy coast. Checked this out but nothing to it. This was the first of many rumours."

31 JANUARY 1945 "Bill Hearst said there were plenty of rumours about Glenn being seen in a German prison camp, but so far nothing they could really bank on as authentic, but they were checking them out and would let me know if anything came

Young Eagles of America, well done! When Freedom called you could not stay at home. You took a Fort and flew toward the sun: You took a map and marked Berlin and Rome.

And now, like Nemesis, but more precise, / In open day you drop your deadly rain: Seattle sees that Prussia pays the price, / And Munich takes her punishment from Maine.

And well done you who fight with nut and tool, / Who fondly tend the monsters in their nest, / And, night and day, obey the one big rule – 'Whatever bears the boys must be the best.'

The Spitfires guard the Fortress oversea, / Typhoon and Thunderbolt divide the kill: / Let statesmen doubt and scribblers disagree – / Your lads and ours fly on together still.

– 'Young Eagles'
by A. P. Herbert

Right: Remains of the wartime buildings at Twinwood Farm RAF airfield as they appear in 1999.
Below: The control tower at Twinwood, the field from which Major Miller, Colonel Baessell and Flying Officer Morgan took off for Paris on 15 December 1944.

of these rumours."

23 APRIL 1945 "The weather has improved from what has been a cold, damp winter, and though the tune 'April in Paris' is hardly known here, it is most descriptive of the colourful time of year this really is here in this beautiful city . . . toward the middle of the month we played many hospitals [that] we have been unable to play because of the lack of a large enough room to accommodate enough patients to make it worthwhile . . . we now played these hospitals by setting up on the lawns as the weather was almost like mid-summer."

7 MAY 1945 "Out to SHAEF where I learned that the war had ended at 0241 this morning with the signing of the Peace Treaty at Rheims . . . not to be announced until tomorrow (top secret)."

8 MAY 1945 "VE Day! . . . Paris really celebrated . . . we played the official VE Day Ceremonies at the Palais de Chaillot this afternoon, and another at the Grand Hotel at eight p.m. . . . went up on the roof after the show and watched the French celebrating below in the Place dé l'Opera . . . and Paris celebrated for five days . . . couldn't get our laundry out of the shops as they just closed up and celebrated."

11 AUGUST 1945 "Dropped anchor off Staten Island 7.30 p.m. At 6.30 the morning of 12 August we pulled up anchor and steamed slowly past the Statue of Liberty and up the Hudson River, a beautiful sight. Docked at Pier 84. Called Polly and requisitioned a staff car and driver. Stopped off to see her at our apartment for an hour. Then out to Tenafly to see Helen. Should have mentioned the reception we got coming up the Hudson River . . . tenders and harbor boats blowing their whistles, with signs WELCOME HOME GLENN MILLER AAF BAND and WELL DONE MILLER BAND WELCOME HOME. It was good to be home again, but we had returned minus one . . . Major Glenn Miller."

Rain at last which provides a welcome rest, but it is a pity that show can't come off. The enemy and our side were teed up for it and it would have been a thrilling spectacle if 60 of our fighters could have fallen upon the 'Red Baron' and all his crowd, but we of course might not have succeeded in drawing them into our territory and could have suffered heavy casualties in the attempt. Anyway there it is and we have a day off, thanks to the weather. After lunch the CO, Jobling and I drove into Amiens [where] we explored the cathedral, one of the finest I've seen with its enormous lofty nave and magnificent west front. The chancel is reputed to be the finest in Europe and there is much lovely stained glass. Amiens has excellent shops and we found a nice tea place in the arcade.
– from *Bomber Pilot 1916–1918* by C. P. O. Bartlett

THE FOLLOWING DOCUMENT was published on 26 July 1945 by the governments of the United States, Great Britain and China.

1. We, the President of the United States, the President of the National Government of the Republic of China, and the Prime Minister of Great Britain, representing the hundreds of millions of our countrymen, have conferred and agree that Japan shall be given an opportunity to end the war.
2. The prodigious land, sea, and air forces of the United States, the British Empire, and China, many times reinforced by their armies and air fleets from the West, are poised to strike the final blows upon Japan. This military power is sustained and inspired by the determination of all the Allied nations to prosecute the war against Japan until she ceases to resist.
3. The result of the futile and senseless German resistance to the might of the aroused free peoples of the world stands forth in awful clarity as an example to the people of Japan. The might that now converges on Japan is immeasurably greater than that which, when applied to the resisting Nazis, necessarily laid waste the lands, industry, and the method of life of the whole German people. The full application of our military power, backed by our resolve, will mean the inevitable and complete destruction of the Japanese forces, and just as inevitably the utter devastation of the Japanese homeland.
4. The time has come for Japan to decide whether she will continue to be controlled by those self—willed militaristic advisers, whose unintelligent calculations have brought the Empire of Japan to the threshold of annihilation, or whether she will follow the path of reason.
5. The following are our terms. We shall not deviate from them. There are no alternatives. We shall brook no delay.
6. There must be eliminated for all time the authority and influence of those who have

THE BOMB

"The war situation has developed, not necessarily to Japan's advantage."
— Emperor Hirohito announcing the Japanese surrender after the dropping of the two atomic bombs, August 1945

Ah! then and there was hurrying to and fro, / And gathering tears, and tremblings of distress, / And checks all pale, which but an hour ago Blush'd at the praise of their own lovliness; / And there were sudden partings, such as press The life from out young hearts, and choking sighs / Which ne'er might be repeated, who could guess / If ever more should meet those mutual eyes, Since upon night so sweet such awful morn could rise?
— from *Childe Harold's Pilgrimage, Canto III* by George Gordon, Lord Byron

Left: Hiroshima, as it appeared on the day after the atomic bomb attack of 6 August 1945. It was one of only a few Japanese cities that had been relatively undamaged by the B-29 fire bomb raids earlier in 1945 and, as such, was selected as one of the primary targets for the first combat use of the new nuclear weapon.

Below: J. Robert Oppenheimer, the US physicist who headed the atomic bomb laboratory at Los Alamos, New Mexico in World War II, and Major–General Leslie R. Groves, a US Army engineering officer in charge of the Manhattan Project, to develop the atomic bomb for the United States. Groves championed Oppenheimer for the Los Alamos position.

deceived and misled the people of Japan into embarking on world conquest, for we insist that a new order of peace, security, and justice will be impossible until irresponsible militarism is driven from the world.

7. Until such a new order is established and until there is convincing proof that Japan's war–making power is destroyed points in Japanese territory will be occupied to secure the achievement of the basic objectives we are here setting forth.

8. The terms of the Cairo declaration shall be carried out, and Japanese sovereignty shall be limited to the islands of Honshu, Hokkaido, Kyushu, Shikoku, and such minor islands as we determine.

9. The Japanese military forces after being completely disarmed shall be permitted to return to their homes, with the opportunity of leading peaceful and productive lives.

10. We do not intend that the Japanese shall be enslaved as a race nor destroyed as a nation, but stern justice will be meted out to all war criminals, including those who have visited cruelties upon our prisoners. The Japanese Government shall remove all obstacles to the revival and strengthening of democratic tendencies among the Japanese people. Freedom of speech, of religion, and of thought, as well as respect for fundamental human rights, shall be established.

11. Japan shall be permitted to maintain such industries as will sustain her economy and allow the exaction of just reparations in kind, but not those industries which would enable her to re–arm for war. To this end access to, as distinguished from control of, raw materials shall be permitted. Eventual Japanese participation in world trade relations shall be permitted.

12. The occupying forces of the Allies shall be withdrawn from Japan as soon as these objectives have been accomplished, and there has been established, in accordance with the freely expressed will of the Japanese people, a peacefully inclined and responsible Government.

13. We call upon the Government of Japan to proclaim now the unconditional surrender of all the Japanese armed forces, and to provide proper and adequate assurances of their good faith in such action. The alternative for Japan is complete and utter destruction.

The military men ruling Japan in the summer of 1945 rejected the Allied terms of surrender and President Harry S. Truman ordered the US Army Air Force to proceed with plans for the delivery of two atomic bombs . . . One would go to Hiroshima and the other to Nagasaki.

It was in the afternoon of 17 July 1945 that US Secretary of War, Henry Stimson, brought a paper to Prime Minister Winston Churchill, which bore the phrase, "Babies satisfactorily born." Stimson explained to Churchill that it was confirmation of a successful American effort to detonate an experimental atomic weapon at the Trinity Site north of Alamagordo, New Mexico. A day later, Stimson returned with a detailed briefing for the Prime Minister. He explained that the weapon, or its equivalent, had been exploded on the top of a 100–foot pylon in the desert. All civilian scientists and all military personnel had been moved a distance of ten miles from the blast location and were positioned behind concrete shields. What they witnessed was a massive, rapidly expanding fireball and a great column of flame and smoke rising from the centre of what had become in an instant a one–mile circle of absolute devastation. Churchill concluded that here, at last, was at least the possibility of a speedy end to World War II.

In the immediate aftermath of Stimson's visit, the Prime Minister and President Truman conferred on the Allies' conduct of the War's final phase. In their most horrific vision of events to come, the two leaders anticipated a continuing, desperate resistance by the Japanese. Until the advent of the Bomb, they had foreseen no viable alternative to a great assault on the Japanese homeland. It would require a gigantic, relentless progression of bombing attacks coupled with an invasion by millions of American and British personnel. Upwards of 1 1/2 million Allied casualties were expected in what would almost certainly be history's biggest and bloodiest battle.

According to Winston Churchill, the decision whether or not to use the atomic bomb to compel the Japanese surrender, was never an issue in his discussions with the President. They were agreed. "To avert a vast, indefinite butchery, to bring the war to an end, to give peace to the world, to lay healing hands upon its tortured peoples by a manifestation of overwhelming power at the cost of a few explosions, seemed, after all our toils and perils, a miracle of deliverance." Indeed, the leaders saw in the new weapon a way to actually save many lives, of friend and foe alike, and they talked of the terrible responsibilities they bore for the unlimited letting of American and British blood should the planned assault have to be carried out.

It was at this point that the decision was taken to send Japan the ultimatum calling for an immediate unconditional surrender of her armed forces.

"Boys, if you ever pray, pray for me now. I don't know whether you fellows ever had a load of hay fall on you, but when they told me yesterday what had happened, I felt like the moon, the stars, and all the planets had fallen on me."
– Harry S. Truman, the day after President Franklin Roosevelt's death.

"It is a profound and necessary truth that the deep things in science are not found because they are useful; they are found because it was possible to find them."
– J. Robert Oppenheimer, Director of the Los Alamos Laboratory, New Mexico, in the Manhattan Project to design and develop the first atomic bomb.

Robert Oppenheimer was born on 22 April 1904, to Julius and Ella Oppenheimer. His father had come to America from Hanau, Germany in 1898 and had prospered importing lining fabrics for men's suits. The family lived in New York City. Young Robert had become interested in science (geology) while on a visit with his grandfather in Hanau. There he was helped and encouraged to begin a collection of minerals. He pursued his scientific interests with fervour and, at the age of twelve, was invited to lecture to the New York Mineralogical Club.

In 1922 he entered Harvard University, majoring in chemistry and taking all the additional courses he could manage. Six feet tall and slight of build, he would never in his life weigh more than 125 pounds. He graduated *summa cum laude* in three years. "Harvard was", he said, "the most exciting time I've ever had in my life. I really had a chance to learn. I loved it. I almost came alive." After Harvard, he spent a year working in New Mexico, and from there he went to England, to Cambridge where, for perhaps the first time in his scientific education, he encountered his own limitations. For him, chemistry had become a brick wall. He was struggling with the work one day when he met the Danish theoretical physicist Niels Bohr. It was this meeting which caused him to change course and follow Bohr's example.

Offered positions at Harvard, the California Institute of Technology, and the University of California at Berkeley, Oppenheimer accepted the Berkeley and Caltech jobs and shared his time between them. His journey through the realm of theoretical physics would ultimately lead to his selection to direct the activities of the new lab where the American effort to design and develop an atomic bomb was to be undertaken. He was nominated by US Army General Leslie Richard Groves, director of the Manhattan Project, established to produce the atomic bomb for the United States. Groves had met Oppenheimer at

An ancient saga tells us how
In the beginning the First Cow
(For nothing living yet had birth
But elemental cow on earth)
Began to lick cold stones and mud: / Under her warm tongue flesh and blood /Blossomed, a miracle to believe; / And so was Adam born, and Eve. / Here now is chaos once again, Primeval mud, cold stones and rain. / Here flesh decays and blood drips red, / And the Cow's dead, the old Cow's dead.
– 'Dead Cow Farm'
by Robert Graves

With cheerful semblance and sweet majesty; / That every wretch, pining and pale before, Beholding him, plucks comfort from his looks. / A largess universal, like the sun, /His liberal eye doth give to every one, Thawing cold fear. Then, mean and gentle all, / Behold, as may unworthiness define, A little touch of Harry in the night. And so our scene must to the battle fly;
– from *Henry V (Act 4. Prologue)*
by William Shakespeare

Pushing up through smoke from a world half–darkened by overhanging cloud – / the shroud that mushroomed out and struck the dome of the sky, / the angry flames – black, red, blue – / dance into the air, merge, / scatter glittering sparks, / already tower over the whole city.
– from *Flames*
by Toge Sankichi

Above right: Italian–born nuclear physicist Enrico Fermi, who won the Nobel Prize for physics in 1938 for his work on artificial radioactivity caused by neutron bombardment. Fermi was Jewish and fled Europe to escape the Nazis in the late 1930s. He was instrumental in the early Manhattan Project research, including the design, construction and testing of the first man–made nuclear reactor, Chicago Pile Number One at the University of Chicago in November 1942. Right: Harry S. Truman, who succeeded Franklin D. Roosevelt as US President in April 1945. Truman is believed to have made the decision on 1 June 1945 to use the atomic bomb against Japan in order to force a surrender and end World War II.

Berkeley during an inspection tour in October 1942 and was impressed by the scientist's interest in developing a fast–neutron laboratory. Groves had become convinced of the necessity for a central lab which would be entirely dedicated to the development of the bomb. Then he learned of Oppenheimer's background (a former fiancée, wife, brother and sister–in–law who had all been members of the Communist Party at one time) and was disturbed by it. He had not yet taken over the control of Manhattan Project security from Army counter–intelligence, which refused to clear Oppenheimer for the role proposed by Groves. Then the Military Policy Committee balked at Groves's choice of Oppenheimer, who had other problems, including never having directed a large organization, not being distinguished by the award of a Nobel Prize, and being proposed for the role of directing a lab devoted primarily to engineering and experiment, when he was, after all, a theorist. Still, Groves wanted him for the job, believing him to be "a genius" and the best man available. The General asked each member of the Committee to propose someone who would be a better choice than Oppenheimer. A few weeks passed and it was clear that no better choice would emerge. Groves then took Oppenheimer to Washington to meet Vannevar Bush, head of the Office of Scientific Research and Development. Bush approved Groves's choice of Oppenheimer for the post and they set out to find a site for the new bomb–design lab that Oppenheimer would run.

General Groves wanted a site with room for at least 265 people, that was at least 200 miles from an international border, and west of the Mississippi River. It had to have some existing facilities and the terrain had to lend itself to adequate fencing and guarded security. The site finally chosen was the Los Alamos Ranch School for boys in New Mexico.

With a site selected, Robert Oppenheimer began a search for the scientists he would need to populate his new lab. He recalled: "The prospect of coming

to Los Alamos aroused great misgivings. It was to be a military post; men were asked to sign up more or less for the duration; restrictions on travel and on the freedom of families to move about would be severe. The notion of disappearing into the New Mexico desert for an indeterminate period and under quasi—military auspices disturbed a good many scientists, and the families of many more. But there was another side to it. Almost everyone realized that this was a great undertaking. Almost everyone knew that if it were completed successfully and rapidly enough, it might determine the outcome of the war. Almost everyone knew that it was an unparalleled opportunity to bring to bear the basic knowledge and art of science for the benefit of his country. Almost everyone knew that this job, if it were achieved, would be a part of history. This sense of excitement, of devotion and of patriotism in the end prevailed. Most of those with whom I talked came to Los Alamos." There was, however, significant resistance from many in the scientific community to the prospect of joining the Army in order to be a part of this great, potentially war winning project. Oppenheimer took the view that "although the execution of the security and secrecy measures should be in the hands of the military . . . the decision as to what measures should be applied must be in the hands of the Laboratory. I believe it is the only way to assure the co—operation and the unimpaired morale of the scientists."

A compromise was reached when General Groves agreed to allow the Laboratory to have civilian administration and a civilian staff until the time of the large—scale trials of the weapon, when anyone wishing to continue with the project would have to accept a commission. The Army would administer the surrounding community, and the Laboratory would be Oppenheimer's responsibility. He would report directly to Groves.

On 16 November 1942 the Columbia University physicist Enrico Fermi and his team began a day and night construction project in the west stands of Stagg Field at the University of Chicago. There, in a squash court, Fermi directed the initial assembly of something he had been planning since the previous May, a full—scale chain—reacting atomic pile. Control of the pile was clearly central to the success and safety of the project, and in this pioneering effort, no one really knew what would happen — how much risk was involved   when the neutron fission began in the pile. Fermi intended to control what was happening in the pile with the system of manual and automatic rods he had planned, but despite the staggering calculations done for the project, no one could guarantee that even slow—neutron fission generations, estimated to multiply in thousandths of a second, would not flash the pile to dangerous levels of heat and radiation in a wildly out—of—control scenario. The team was dealing with a large amount of potentially radioactive material in the pile and the prospect of excessive ionizing radiation was terrifying. Ultimately, though, Fermi concluded that the probability of acceptable control of the pile activity was sufficient and the decision was taken to build the first atomic chain—reacting pile, CP-1, there under the stands of the University of Chicago football stadium.

On the bitterly cold morning of 2 December, Fermi and company gathered at the pile in the squash court and began the agonizing, delicate procedure of withdrawing the cadmium rods from their creation. As the work progressed, the results were carefully checked and slide rule calculations were made again and again. The experiment went on through the morning and at 11.30 a safety rod was automatically released with a loud crash when its relay was activated by an ionization chamber because the intensity had exceeded the arbitrary level at which it had been set. Fermi calmly broke for lunch.

In the afternoon the team resumed the experiment where they had left off. By now 42 people were crowded into the squash court, most of them on the balcony. Fermi called for all but one of the cadmium

Dawn on the New Mexico desert is a very beautiful thing. We were up early and had breakfast at the Officer's club. I was assigned as the Bomb Commander and had to sign for the nuclear weapon on a statement of charges, $25,000,000 for one 42,500 pound, 41—foot long bomb. I was then driven to the cement bunker where the weapon was stored. The bunker was underground and had walls twenty feet thick and a long ramp going down into it.

There was a transporter that I had to use to move the weapon. It was full of hydraulics, cylinders, lines and wires, and had a 300 hp diesel engine. It would raise and lower the bomb, roll it from side to side and lift it into the bomb bay of the B-36. When I had been checked out on the transporter, I went to get my weapon, which had the equivalent of 18 megatons of explosives.

When I got the bomb loaded on the transporter, fastened and secured, a cover was dropped over it and I started off with it toward the airplane. I drove it under the back of the bomber and up under the forward bomb bay, where I was to load it. The aft bomb bay of the B-36 could accommodate another nuclear bomb of the same size, for a total bomb load of 85,000 pounds. But we were only loading one bomb this day.

After jockeying it around, I finally got the bomb into position and got it lifted up against the release mechanism. It was locked in and the four sway braces were fitted against the sides of the weapon. The transporter was then lowered and I drove it back to the bunker. I returned *continued* to the airplane and was cleared by the military police who made sure that I was, indeed, the airplane commander. We were now ready to fly back to Loring, our base in Maine, but with restrictions. Our flight path had to avoid populated areas and all cities en route, in case of an 'unscheduled drop.'

Murphy, our flight engineer who, prior to this mission, had suffered a severe injury to the fingers of his right hand while we were back at Loring, thought that he and his bandaged hand could make this flight with us as First Flight Engineer. So, after running through the pre-flight and start-engines checklists, and the taxi checklist, we were then number one for take–off and completed the take–off checklist. I started all four jet engines, setting them at 100 per cent thrust. I set number four throttle at 65 inches of manifold pressure, and the flight engineer followed on the other five reciprocating engines. We had all ten engines set at maximum power and I got clearance to roll. Off we went with the 42,500 pound nuclear bomb in the forward bay. We rolled and rolled. The field elevation there at Albuquerque was 5352 feet and, as we rolled past the airlines terminal, I was getting worried about the unsticking speed. Then I heard, 'Oh shit.' Murphy and his bandaged hand had not set the turbos at 10. The airplane would fly without turbos, but at that altitude we needed every bit of power we could get. The other engineer quickly turned them to Turbo Emergency 10, and went to 71 inches of manifold pressure, and the nose came
continued

rods to be removed from the pile, and continued making his calculations. Finally, he asked that the remaining rod be taken out twelve inches, along with the safety rod. In what was certainly one of history's most breathless moments, Fermi remarked: "This is going to do it. Now it will become self–sustaining." Herbert Anderson, an eyewitness: "At first you could hear the sound of the neutron counter, clickety–clack, clickety–clack. Then the clicks came more and more rapidly, and after a while they began to merge into a roar; the counter couldn't follow any more. That was the moment to switch to the chart recorder. But when the switch was made, everyone watched in the sudden silence the mounting deflection of the recorder's pen. It was an awesome silence. Everyone realized the significance of that switch: we were in the high intensity regime and the counters were unable to cope with the situation any more. Again and again, the scale of the recorder had to be changed to accommodate the neutron intensity which was increasing more and more rapidly. Suddenly Fermi raised his hand. 'The pile has gone critical,' he announced. No one present had any doubt about it. Everyone began to wonder why he didn't shut the pile off, but Fermi was still calm. He waited another minute, then another, and then when it seemed that the anxiety was too much to bear, he ordered ZIP [the safety rod] in!" The experiment had succeeded. Fermi and his team had achieved the controlled release of atomic energy.

High on the New Mexican mesa where the Manhattan Project lab was sited, Director Robert Oppenheimer had brought together about thirty of the one hundred scientists originally hired to work on the design and development of the bomb, for a series of introductory lectures to be given by Robert Serber, a Berkeley theoretician and former student of Oppenheimer's. He briefed the group on the achievements of the fast–fission research activity of the previous year. Many of

them now heard for the first time precisely what it was they were there to do. They were told that the object of the project was to produce a practical military weapon in the form of a bomb in which the energy is released by a fast neutron chain reaction in one or more of the materials known to show nuclear fission. Reducing their problem to its simplest form, then: designing and building a workable bomb, assembling a critical mass and firing the bomb. Their deadline: workable bombs ready when enough uranium and plutonium was ready. It was estimated they would have about two years to complete the job.

First came the Serber orientation lectures at Los Alamos. Then followed a conference to plan the work of the lab. After that, as more scientists, engineers, senior consultants and experts of the various required disciplines joined the project, it began to appear that General Groves's seemingly intuitive selection of Oppenheimer, the theorist, to head the work of the bomb–design team was most appropriate. Unlike the Fermi chain–reacting pile at Chicago, there could be no laboratory–scale bomb test. The bomb–making effort was to be a supreme challenge to Oppenheimer and the other theorists in the project, for nearly everything that the team would have to understand in the course of developing the weapon would need to be analysed theoretically. In a sense, they were having to shape a new science as they went, devising theory, technology and detailed experiments that would ultimately result in Little Boy and Fat Man, the bombs that would be delivered over Hiroshima and Nagasaki respectively. They did their jobs very well and at a few seconds before 05.30 a.m. of 16 July 1945 the first man–made nuclear explosion was detonated at the Trinity test site north of Alamagordo, New Mexico. The twelve–pound payload of plutonium released the energy of 18,500 tons of TNT, scoring a half–mile wide crater and sending a huge, fiery cloud from the desert floor to 38,000 feet in seven minutes. It worked. And it made Oppenheimer recall a line

Above: Little Boy, the type of uranium atomic bomb dropped on Hiroshima on 6 August 1945 by the crew of the B-29 *Enola Gay,* was 29 inches in diameter and 126 inches long. It weighed about 9700 pounds. Left: Fat Man was the plutonium bomb exploded over Nagasaki on 9 August and proved to be a more powerful and devastating weapon than the Hiroshima bomb. It was 60 inches in diameter and weighed about 10,000 pounds.

up, but we were out of runway and rolled off the end, just missing the steel fence.

The airplane began to settle into the valley and both Mulkey and I were pulling on the yokes as hard as we could. I had the plane trimmed way too much nose—up and was winding the trim tab as fast as I could, and still we settled into the valley, about 100 feet off the ground and down a slight incline sloping to the west. We were close to a shuddering stall and I was praying, when the bomber finally started to respond to the controls. We began to fly at about 185 mph and, very slowly, began to climb. I looked at Mulkey and he was as white as a sheet. I didn't feel so hot either. It's a good thing there was a valley there because we would have had a high—yield explosion if we hadn't got those turbos set.

We climbed and levelled out at 19,000 feet, north—east bound. We avoided all populated areas on our way to Loring. When we landed there, guards surrounded us and we left them with the airplane and went to debriefing and then home for twelve hours of rest.
— Joseph Anastasia, former US Air Force B-36 pilot

Right: US Army Air Force Colonel Paul Tibbets, Jr piloted the B-29 that dropped the atomic bomb on Hiroshima on 6 August 1945. He had flown one of the B-17s in the first USAAF attack on German—occupied Europe on 17 August 1942. Tibbets named the bomber that he flew on the Hiroshima raid *Enola Gay* after his mother.

from the *Bhagavadgita*: "I am become Death, the destroyer of worlds."

Through the spring of 1945 B-29 Superfortress bombers of Curtis LeMay's Twentieth Air Force had been fire–bombing upwards of 60 Japanese target cities with a fury and intensity surpassing even that of the Allied attacks on Germany. In early June Lieutenant–Colonel Paul W. Tibbets, Jr, who commanded the 509th Composite Group, the B-29 crews charged with delivery of the atomic bomb, or bombs if need be, arrived on Tinian in the western Pacific Marianas Islands. He met with LeMay and they discussed the progress of the specialized facilities being prepared on Tinian for the mission of the 509th. On 10 June the first combat crews of the group arrived on the island in new, specially modified lightweight B-29s, equipped with fuel–injection rather than carburetion, quick–action pneumatic bomb doors, fuel flow meters and reversible electric propellers. Many other modifications had been made to the planes so they could perform their secret task. The engineer in charge of their procurement later wrote: "The performance of those special B-29s was exceptional. They were without doubt the finest B-29s in the theatre."

By the middle of July much of the technical facilities for the bomb assembly and test activity had been established on the island base. Before that, the largest airport in the world had been built there, with six runways, each nearly two miles long. Literally hundreds of Superfortresses were in residence on the hardstands of the mammoth complex. Mid–July found the flight crews of the 509th practising navigation and bombing with standard general–purpose bombs.

On 2 July US Secretary of War Henry Stimson had summed up his assessment of Japan's current position: "Japan has no allies. Her navy is nearly destroyed and she is vulnerable to a surface and underwater blockade which can deprive her of sufficient food and supplies for her population. She is terribly vulnerable to our concentrated air attack upon her crowded cities, industrial and food resources. She has against her not only the Anglo–American forces but the rising forces of China and the ominous threat of Russia. We have inexhaustible and untouched industrial resources to bring to bear against her diminishing potential. We have great moral superiority through being the victim of her first sneak attack." Stimson felt there might be an alternative to an Allied invasion of Japan after all. He continued: "I believe Japan is susceptible to reason in such a crisis to a much greater extent than is indicated by our current press and other current comment. Japan is not a nation composed wholly of mad fanatics of an entirely different mentality from ours. On the contrary, she has within the past century shown herself to possess extremely intelligent people, capable in an unprecedentedly short time of adopting not only the complicated technique of Occidental civilization but to a substantial extent their culture and their political and social ideas. Her advance in these respects . . . has been one of the most astounding feats of national progress in history . . . It is therefore my conclusion that a carefully timed warning be given to Japan . . ."

Through 16 July top officials of the Truman administration had been considering the implications of Stimson's view, and of others high in the Government who disagreed with it. That evening Stimson, in Potsdam with the President for the summit meeting with Stalin, received the following message from Washington: OPERATED ON THIS MORNING. DIAGNOSIS NOT YET COMPLETE BUT RESULTS SEEM SATISFACTORY AND ALREADY EXCEED EXPECTATIONS. LOCAL PRESS RELEASE NECESSARY AS INTEREST EXPANDS GREAT DISTANCE. DR GROVES PLEASED. It confirmed for Stimson the success of the first test

A dark bird falls from the sun.
It curves in a rush to the heart
of the vast / Flower:
the day has begun.
– 'Bombardment'
by D.H. Lawrence

Below: Rubble and structures damaged in the atomic attack on Hiroshima, 6 August 1945.

detonation at the Trinity Site.

General George C. Marshall later recalled the situation as he had perceived it: "We regarded the matter of dropping the bomb as exceedingly important. We had just gone through a bitter experience at Okinawa [the last major island campaign, when the Americans lost more than 12,500 men killed and missing and the Japanese more than 100,000 killed in 82 days of fighting]. This had been preceded by a number of similar experiences in other Pacific islands, north of Australia. The Japanese had demonstrated in each case they would not surrender and they would fight to the death . . . It was expected that resistance in Japan, with their home ties, would be even more severe. We had had the 100,000 people killed in Tokyo in one night of [conventional] bombs, and it had had seemingly no effect whatsoever. It destroyed the Japanese cities, yes, but their morale was not affected as far as we could tell, not at all. So it seemed quite necessary, if we could, to shock them into action . . . we had to end the war; we had to save American lives."

Secretary Stimson learned on 23 July that it might be possible to drop the first atomic bomb after 1 August, and certainly before 10 August. The initial target list, in order of preference, was Hiroshima, Kokura and Niigata. Nagasaki was added to the list several days later. The target selection was based on factors such as the condition of the city (damage assessment after the strike would be easier with a target that had been relatively untouched by prior bombing attacks), and weather (if one target city was obscured by cloud cover, another might be clear.)

Harry Truman recorded in his private diary: "We have discovered the most terrible bomb in the history of the world. It may be the fire destruction prophesied in the Euphrates Valley Era, after Noah and his fabulous Ark. Anyway, we 'think' we have found a way to cause a disintegration of the atom. An experiment in the New Mexican desert was startling — to put it mildly. . . This weapon is to be used against Japan between now and 10 August. I have told the Sec. of War, Mr Stimson, to use it so that military objectives and soldiers and sailors are the target and not women and children. Even if the Japs are savages, ruthless, merciless and fanatic, we as the leader of the world for the common welfare cannot drop this terrible bomb on the old Capital or the new. He & I are in accord. The target will be a purely military one and we will issue a warning statement asking the Japs to surrender and save lives. I'm sure they will not do that, but we will have given them the chance. It is certainly a good thing for the world that Hitler's crowd or Stalin's did not discover this atomic bomb. It seems to be the most terrible thing ever discovered, but it can be made the most useful."

On 25 July a directive drafted by General Groves was approved by General Marshall and Secretary Stimson who, presumably, showed it to Truman. The President's authorization of the directive is not recorded.

To General Carl Spaatz, CG, USASTAF:
1. The 509 Composite Group, 20th Air Force will deliver its first special bomb as soon as weather will permit visual bombing after about 3 August 1945 on one of the targets: Hiroshima, Kokura, Niigata and Nagasaki . . .
2. Additional bombs will be delivered on the above targets as soon as made ready by the project staff . . .
3. Dissemination of any and all information concerning the use of the weapon against Japan is reserved to the Secretary of War and the President of the United States . . .
4. The foregoing directive is issued to you by direction and with the approval of the Secretary of War and of the Chief of Staff, USA.

The Reverend Mr Tanimoto got up at five o'clock that morning. He was alone in the parsonage, because for some time his wife had been commuting with their year–old baby to spend nights with a friend in Ushida, a suburb to the north. Of all the important cities of Japan, only two, Kyoto and Hiroshima, had not been visited in strength by *B-San*, or Mr B, as the Japanese, with a mixture of respect and unhappy familiarity, called the B-29; and Mr Tanimoto, like all his neighbors and friends, was almost sick with anxiety. He had heard uncomfortably detailed accounts of mass raids on Kure, Iwakuni, Tokuyama, and other nearby towns; he was sure Hiroshima's turn would come soon. He had slept badly the night before, because there had been several air-raid warnings. Hiroshima had been getting such warnings almost every night for weeks, for at that time the B-29s were using Lake Biwa, northeast of Hiroshima, as a rendezvous point, and no matter what city the Americans planned to hit, the Superfortresses streamed in over the coast near Hiroshima. The frequency of the warnings and the continued abstinence of Mr B with respect to Hiroshima had made its citizens jittery; a rumor was going around that the Americans were saving something special for the city.
– *Hiroshima*
by John Hersey

Left: The explosion cloud of a US hydrogen bomb in a 1954 test. The photo was taken at an altitude of 12,000 feet, approximately fifty miles from the site of detonation. Two minutes after the blast the cloud had risen to more than 40,000 feet.

Japan rejected the Allied ultimatum. On 27 July, in an effort to minimize the loss of life, eleven Japanese cities were warned by leaflets that they would be subjected to intense air bombardment. The following day six of them were bombed. On 31 July an additional twelve cities received the leaflet warnings and on 1 August four more were attacked. A final warning was issued on 5 August. The crews of the seven B-29s that would fly the first mission, to deliver the bomb Little Boy, were briefed by Colonel Tibbets at 3 p.m. on 4 August. They were shown photographs of the target cities with the exception of Niigata, which was apparently excluded owing to unacceptable weather conditions. Three of the aircraft were assigned to fly ahead on the day of the attack, to assess cloud cover over Japan. Two other B-29s would accompany the bomber flown by Colonel Tibbets which would actually drop the atomic bomb. Their role was to observe and photograph the event. The seventh bomber was a spare plane which would be available should Tibbets' B-29 develop a problem and be unable to make the trip. The Colonel's plane was called *Enola Gay*, for his mother.

In the final briefing the crews were told of the weapon they would be taking to Japan. The New Mexico test was described and they were forbidden to write about or discuss the mission even among themselves. Tibbets told them that he was personally honoured, and was sure they were, to have been chosen to take part in this raid which would shorten the war by at least six months. That afternoon the first combat–ready atomic bomb was prepared for loading into the bomb bay of the *Enola Gay*. One crew member is said to have described it as looking like "an elongated trash can with fins." It was 10 1/2 feet long, 29 inches in diameter and weighed 9700 pounds.

At 2.45 a.m. on 6 August Paul Tibbets released the brakes of the bomber and, using nearly all of the two–mile Tinian runway, the B-29 was airborne in

A second atomic bomb has been dropped on Japan, and as a result it is believed that a large part of Nagasaki, a city of 250,000 people, no longer exists. In Guam this afternoon, General Spaatz issued a brief announcement which said: "The second use of the atomic bomb occurred at noon, August 9, at Nagasaki. Crew members report good results No further details will be available until the mission returns." Press despatches from Guam add unofficially that preliminary reports indicate the bomb all but obliterated Nagasaki, which is an important port of traffic with Shanghai and has some industry and naval installations. Tokyo wireless is so far silent on the second atomic bomb attack. Three million leaflets telling the Japanese people to get out of the war of their own accord before the full fury of the atomic bomb was unleashed against them were dropped on Japan on Thursday by United States aeroplanes. The leaflets said: "We are in possession of the most destructive weapon ever designed. A single one of our atomic bombs equals the explosive power carried by 2,000 of our Super Fortresses. This is an awful fact for you to ponder. We have just begun to use this weapon. Before using this bomb again and again to destroy every resource which your military leaders have to prolong this useless war, we ask that you now petition your Emperor to end the war. Take steps now, or we shall resolutely employ this bomb promptly and forcefully."
– from *The Times* (London) 10 August 1945

Left: The aiming point for the Hiroshima bomb detonation was over the bridge, fourth from top in the centre.

We love peace, as we abhor pusillanimity; but not peace at any price. There is a peace more destructive of the manhood of living man than war is destructive of his material body. Chains are worse than bayonets.
– Douglas William Jerrold

just over a minute. He climbed slowly, to preserve fuel and because two crewmen had to complete assembly of the bomb in the unheated, unpressurized bomb bay.

Shortly before 6.00 a.m. the *Enola Gay* neared Iwo Jima and began climbing to 9300 feet where it rendezvoused with the two B-29 photo planes and continued on course to Japan.

At 7.30 am US Navy Captain William "Deke" Parsons, Scientific Officer for the mission and the man who would arm Little Boy, entered the bomb bay for the final time and Colonel Tibbets took the bomber on the long climb to the bombing altitude of 31,000 feet. Latest reports from the weather airplane over Japan indicated that the primary target city of Hiroshima was the best target, and Tibbets told the crew they would make the bomb run on that city.

The bomber reached 31,000 feet at 8.40 a.m. and the crew, except for the two pilots, put on flak suits and anti–glare goggles. There was no flak or fighters.

The target city was distinctively sited on a wide river delta and was divided by seven tributaries. The bomber approached the city over the Inland Sea on a nearly due west compass heading and at a ground speed of about 330 mph.

Major Thomas Ferebee, the bombardier and a veteran of 63 bombing missions in the European air war, was now flying the airplane through the Norden bombsight. His aiming point was the Aioi Bridge spanning the Ota River in the centre of the city. Headquarters of the Japanese Second Army was located near the bridge.

With her bomb doors open, the Superfortress passed over Hiroshima on course, on time and at the prescribed air speed and altitude. As she crossed the aiming point, Little Boy dropped from the bomb bay, dislodging the arming wires that would start its clocks.

Now relieved of the bomb's weight, Paul Tibbets banked the *Enola Gay* into an extreme fighter–like turn away from the coming blast. Forty–three seconds after the drop, Little Boy exploded 550 feet south–east of the aiming point and 1900 feet above the Shima Hospital. Tibbets recalled: "I threw off the automatic pilot and hauled *Enola Gay* into the turn. I pulled anti–glare goggles over my eyes. I couldn't see through them; I was blind. I threw them to the floor. A bright light filled the plane. The first shock wave hit us. We were eleven and a half miles slant range from the atomic explosion, but the whole airplane cracked and crinkled from the blast. I yelled 'Flak!' thinking a heavy gun battery had found us. The tail gunner had seen the first wave coming, a visible shimmer in the atmosphere, but he didn't know what it was until it hit. When the second wave came, he called out a warning. We turned back to look at Hiroshima. The city was hidden by that awful cloud . . . boiling up, mushrooming, terrible and incredibly tall. No one spoke for a moment; then everyone was talking.

"I remember Lewis pounding my shoulder saying, 'Look at that! Look at that! Look at that!' Tom Ferebee wondered about whether radioactivity would make us all sterile. Lewis said he could taste atomic fission. He said it tasted like lead."

174

"All the News That's Fit to Print"

The New York Times.

LATE CITY EDITION
Partly cloudy, less humid today. Cloudy and warm tomorrow.
Temperature Yesterday—Max., 72; Min., 66

Copyright, 1945, by The New York Times Company.

VOL. XCIV..No. 31,972.

NEW YORK, TUESDAY, AUGUST 7, 1945.

THREE CENTS NEW YORK CITY

FIRST ATOMIC BOMB DROPPED ON JAPAN; MISSILE IS EQUAL TO 20,000 TONS OF TNT; TRUMAN WARNS FOE OF A 'RAIN OF RUIN'

Jet Plane Explosion Kills Major Bong, Top U.S. Ace

Flier Who Downed 40 Japanese Craft, Sent Home to Be 'Safe,' Was Flying New 'Shooting Star' as a Test Pilot

KYUSHU CITY RAZED

Kenney's Planes Blast Tarumizu in Record Blow From Okinawa

ROCKET SITE IS SEEN

125 B-29's Hit Japan's Toyokawa Naval Arsenal in Demolition Strike

REPORT BY BRITAIN

'By God's Mercy' We Beat Nazis to Bomb, Churchill Says

ROOSEVELT AID CITED

Raiders Wrecked Norse Laboratory in Race for Key to Victory

Steel Tower 'Vaporized' In Trial of Mighty Bomb

Scientists Awe-Struck as Blinding Flash Lighted New Mexico Desert and Great Cloud Bore 40,000 Feet Into Sky

NEW AGE USHERED

Day of Atomic Energy Hailed by President, Revealing Weapon

HIROSHIMA IS TARGET

'Impenetrable' Cloud of Dust Hides City After Single Bomb Strikes

MORRIS IS ACCUSED OF 'TAKING A WALK'

CHINESE WIN MORE OF 'INVASION COAST'

ATOM BOMBS MADE IN 3 HIDDEN 'CITIES'

TRAINS CANCELED IN STRICKEN AREA

Turks Talk War if Russia Presses; Prefer Vain Battle to Surrender

War News Summarized

Reich Exile Emerges as Heroine In Denial to Nazis of Atom's Secret

---

Early that day, August 7th, the Japanese radio broadcast for the first time a succinct announcement that very few, if any, of the people most concerned with its content, the survivors in Hiroshima, happened to hear: "Hiroshima suffered considerable damage as the result of an attack by a few B-29s. It is believed that a new type of bomb was used. The details are being investigated." Nor is it probable that any of the survivors happened to be tuned in on a short-wave re-broadcast of an extraordinary announcement by the President of the United States, which identified the new bomb as atomic: "That bomb had more power than twenty thousand tons of TNT. It had more than two thousand times the blast power of the British Grand Slam, which is the largest bomb ever yet used in the history of warfare." Those victims who were able to worry at all about what had happened thought of it and discussed it in more primitive, childish terms — gasoline sprinkled from an airplane, maybe, or some combustible gas, or a big cluster of incendiaries, or the work of parachutists; but, even if they had known the truth, most of them were too busy or too weary or too badly hurt to care that they were the objects of the first great experiment in the use of atomic power, which (as the voices on the short wave shouted) no country except the United States, with its industrial know-how, its willingness to throw two billion gold dollars into an important wartime gamble, could possibly have developed.

— from *Hiroshima*
by John Hersey

IT BEGAN with Operation *Knicker*, a British response to the stranglehold that Red Army forces put on the British, American and French sectors of West Berlin from the middle of 1947. In April 1948 the Royal Air Force sent sixteen C-47 Dakotas to the airfield at Wunstorf in the heart of the British sector to bring supplies to their garrison. They brought in 65 (US) tons of urgently needed goods daily.

The Russians had put Berlin under siege. Relations had not been good between Russia and the Western powers in Berlin — the United States, Britain and France — for some time. Germany, since the end of World War II, had been under their combined military occupation and was divided into four zones. Berlin lay more than 100 miles deep in the Soviet Zone and was split into four sectors.

At the end of the war, the Russians had claimed they lacked sufficient transport to carry supplies to Berlin, and asked the Western Allies to assume responsibility for providing three quarters of the food and fuel needed by the three western sectors of the city. At the same time the Russians allowed access to their sector via only a single road, one railway line and a few canals. The Western Allies wanted and needed Soviet co–operation to keep Germany running, and didn't make much of a fuss about the limited access. They believed there was a "gentleman's agreement" among the four powers and that all would pull together. Clearly, the Russians had a separate agenda for Germany and never intended to relax their restricted access.

From the end of the war Russia's Josef Stalin pursued the domination of western Europe, exploiting the countries that were most weakened by economic depression, hunger and devastation from that conflict. His brand of Communism thrived amid the ruins of these suffering states. In an effort to help rebuild the various economies of Europe in June 1947, US Secretary of State George Marshall offered them enormous financial aid. The nations of western Europe gratefully accepted; the Soviet Union, on behalf of her satellites, flatly refused the assistance. The Russians, meanwhile, were systematically plundering their Zone and shipping everything of value, every vital resource, back to the Soviet Union. By the spring of 1948 the "working relationship" between the Western Allies and the Soviets was in tatters. Their patience with the Soviets now exhausted, the British, French and Americans decided to make Berlin and Germany work without the co–operation of their Russian ally.

February 1948. The Western powers proposed to a west European conference in London that the Germans draft a constitution for a semi–independent West German state, designed as an interim measure until there could be agreement with the Russians on a unified, autonomous Germany. To bolster the West German economy the Western Allies announced the introduction of a brand new Deutschmark, a sound currency that would be in use in the western sectors of Berlin by June 1948. It was this move that made Stalin snap. Through the early part of the year his forces had been interfering with road and rail traffic from the West, creating delays and causing electric power shortages. In March, the Soviet Military Governor quit the Allied Control Council, ending four–power government in Germany. On 5 April a British European Airways Vickers Viking was harassed by a Soviet Yak-3 fighter that performed aerobatics quite near the Viking as it approached to land at Gatow. Tragically, the Yak pilot collided with the BEA plane and both aircraft crashed, killing the BEA crew and all seven passengers as well as the Soviet pilot. The Russians attributed the crash to the Viking having rammed the Yak. From that date on, British and American transports were given fighter escort into Berlin, and the Russians hastened to say that no more interference was contemplated.

In mid–June the Russians pulled their representative from the Allied Kommandatura which was running Berlin, ending the four–power administration of the city. And on 24 June the Russians began a complete blockade of the western sectors of Berlin. More than two million Berliners

AIRLIFT

Left: Many of the airmen who participated in the Berlin Airlift had flown in World War II as RAF or USAAF bomber aircrew. Before the airlift began, US Army engineers built a twelve–foot–thick rubble–base runway at Berlin's Tempelhof airport. They covered it with pierced steel planking but, during the airlift, the PSP started to break up owing to the impact and weight of the various Allied transport aircraft landing on it with their cargoes of fuel, food and supplies. By late 1948 two new runways had been built at Tempelhof. The approach to the field was extremely difficult and hazardous as the cargo planes had to fly down a narrow slot between rows of five–storey apartment buildings just off the edge of the airfield. In the period of the airlift, three C-54s like the one pictured here were destroyed when they landed too far down the runway. The Douglas C-54 Skymaster carried most of the load ferried into Berlin by the US Air Force during the airlift. Powered by four Pratt & Whitney engines it cruised at 170 mph and had a payload of 19,500 pounds.

Right: A Douglas DC-6 civil version of the military C-54 Skymaster. Below: The venerable Douglas Dakota, also known as the C-47 or DC-3. Both military and civil Dakotas performed well in the airlift, with a 150 mph cruise speed and a payload capacity of 6900 pounds.

were at risk. The Russians must have believed that they could starve the western sectors and take them over, thus destroying West German recovery.

From the earliest interference by the Russians, US Military Governor General Lucius Clay had threatened that he would instruct his troops to open fire "if Soviet soldiers attempted to enter our trains". His approach, however, was vetoed by President Harry Truman who stated that the USA would never open fire unless first fired upon. The Western Allies had only 12,000 men in their Berlin garrisons. They were surrounded by as many as 300,000 Soviet troops. Even if the Allies had chosen to storm the city from the west, it meant risking a new war with Russia. They were in no shape to fight such a war, and in fact lacked the strength to prevent the Russians from advancing into western Germany should they have chosen to make that move. The Allies had but a single trump card... the atomic bomb, and no one thought that a reasonable option.

It seemed that the only solution to the problem of keeping Berlin supplied with food and fuel was a dramatic expansion of the British airlift. While the Allies did have access from their zones to Berlin via three twenty–mile–wide and 10,000–foot–high air corridors that had been allocated by the Russians in November 1945, the idea was fraught with complications. Berlin had two available airfields — Gatow and Tempelhof; each had only one runway and in both cases it was merely of temporary pierced–steel planking, a surface never intended to withstand the heavy landings of the laden transport planes that were required. There was the threat that the Russians would block the air corridors with barrage balloons or bring up anti–aircraft batteries in the Soviet Zone. Navigation was a problem, complicated by the fact that the Americans did not have the navigational aids the British used, and had to rely mainly on the radio compass. The

primitive ground control facilities at the Berlin fields were not up to dealing with heavy air traffic, and especially not in poor weather. Most worrying to the Allies, though, was the need to bring at least the 13,500 tons per day of food and fuels that they had been previously providing by road, rail and canal. Neither the British nor the Americans could quickly provide enough aircraft to mount the airlift on the scale required.

Despite the difficulties, Britain's Operation *Carter Paterson* (which soon became *Plainfare*) began on 28 June with an initial RAF Dakota taking off from Wunstorf, the first airlift base and the main feeder airfield in the British Zone, in very heavy weather to bring a maximum 7500–pound load to Gatow. The American effort, called Operation *Vittles,* was started on 26 June by 25 C-47s operating initially from the Wiesbaden and Rhein–Main airfields in the American Zone. These operations were launched primarily by British Foreign Secretary Ernest Bevin and US President Harry Truman who, to their credit, stood firm in the face of some determined domestic political and military opposition to the planned airlift. Many Generals believed at the time that, rather than expending the effort to provide the airlift capability, they should be concentrating all efforts on preparing for war with the Soviets. Many of the air crewmen who were to fly the airlift had already seen their share of war, having flown as bomber crew members with the Royal Air Force, the US Army Air Force, the Royal Australian Air Force, the Royal New Zealand Air Force, or the South African Air Force in World War II. In a great historic irony, some who only a few years earlier had been dropping bombs to destroy Berlin now found themselves delivering supplies to help keep its people alive.

The Berlin Airlift was simply a stopgap meant to buy time to keep the city supplied. Truman and Bevin hoped to save Berlin from a Russian takeover and to convince the Kremlin of the West's

"In our C-54, we had a flare chute under the navigator's table, where he could drop parachute flares to check his drift. We made small parachutes and tied candy bars in them, and would drop them to the kids lining the approach to the runways. There was only a brief time to do this as we were doing 120 mph on the final approach. We came over their heads rather fast. The kids loved it!"
— Joseph Anastasia, Berlin Airlift pilot

"There was an aircraft landing or taking off in Berlin every three minutes. You had to hit the airfield within 30 seconds of your allotted time, or turn back and start all over again."
— John Curtiss, former Berlin Airlift navigator

On the 50th anniversary of the start of the Berlin Airlift, 7000 Berliners, including German Chancellor, Helmut Kohl, gathered at Tempelhof Airport to commemorate the magnificent effort of the Britons and Americans who jointly planned and carried out the great blockade–busting operation to save the beleaguered populace in 1948. Among them too was Gail Halvorsen, one of the veteran bomber pilots who had flown the lift. Colonel Halvorsen is the "candy bomber", so–called because, in addition to the vitally needed supplies that he and his crew brought into the city, he is remembered for having dropped chocolate bars tied to handkerchief parachutes, to the people of Berlin.

I had just departed out of Celle and was in the outbound corridor at 4000 feet. I thought that I heard an unfamiliar sound. Of course, when you are flying you can imagine all sorts of things. But this sounded like a freight train coming down the tracks. It started with a low moan, then immediately changed into a high-pitched scream. Then all hell broke loose. The fire warning light on number two engine came on and the rpm went to the top of the gauge. Then came the damndest chopping, banging and a loud boom, boom boom. The number two propeller had come off the engine and its three blades had chopped holes in the side of the fuselage, and then gone up and over the airplane and disappeared. The propeller had chopped up the radio rack and cut all the wires on the left side of the aircraft. I immediately had the engineer cut the mixture to the carburetor and shut off the fuel to that engine. I pulled the fire wall shut-off lever for the engine. This slowed the engine down, but it was running wild and the vibration could have torn it off the mounts. All of this happened quickly and I was now calling 'Mayday,' Mayday.' I contacted the tower and told them of my predicament, and got clearance back to the airport. I set up the approach. We had been gone only fifteen minutes. We arrived back at Celle where it was clear to partly cloudy, and I landed. The crash crew met us and followed us in to park the airplane in the maintenance area. On inspection they found that the prop retaining nut had come loose because it had not been safety-wired by a mechanic. After filling out reams of paperwork, I was cleared to fly the Lift again.
– Joseph Anastasia, former Berlin Airlift C-54 pilot

strength and determination. They gambled that the Russians would not risk starting a war by shooting down one of the airlift planes. At the same time Bevin arranged for American B-29 Superfortress bombers, by then well known for their nuclear delivery capability, to be stationed in England.

It was all the Allies could manage to supply about 4000 tons of food and fuel a day. It was September before they could bring in 4500 tons daily, and January 1949 before a daily delivery of 5,500 tons was achieved. The Berliners were struggling to survive on this greatly reduced ration. The scope of the problem was simply overwhelming. Even with a massive infusion of York, Hastings and Sunderland aircraft by the British, and C-54s by the Americans, to augment the overburdened RAF Dakotas and USAF C-47s, as well as a mish-mash of civilian aircraft, they were still significantly short of airplanes and load capacity. Most of the crews who flew the airlift were former RAF and USAAF bomber air crew members.

Spare parts were in short supply, as were personnel for servicing and time to do the work. The state of the Tempelhof and Gatow airfields necessitated their upgrading for landing and unloading, which meant that heavy building equipment and materials had to be flown in, and a third airfield had to be constructed at Tegel in the French sector. The new facility was built by the Americans using mostly German female labour who were paid DM1.20 an hour and one hot meal per shift. The women had to do the work as the majority of German military prisoners of war had still to be repatriated. Work on Tegel was round-the-clock and the new airfield allowed a substantially greater quantity of supplies to be flown in to Berlin. All ground control facilities had to be modernized and nine new supply airfields had to be built; seven in the British Zone and two in the American. Much of the rubble used as hardcore for the new fields came from the

staggering bombed-out ruin of Berlin and was cleared mainly by women. Air traffic control had to be not just reformed, but revolutionized. Aircraft had to take off in timed departure blocks from the supply airfields, and the flights and landings had to be precisely timed to avoid chaos and collision.

RAF Sunderland flying boats were employed from 4 July to operate from the Havel See, a lake located just five minutes by car from the airfield at Gatow. The Sunderlands were special in that they could bring a 10,000-pound load on each trip, and because they were sufficiently corrosion-proofed to carry a cargo of salt to Berlin. The flying boats carried their salt to the city until the winter of 1948–49 ended their role, which was then picked up by converted Halifax bombers known as Haltons. They stored the salt in externally-mounted belly panniers. Soon more aircraft types were added to the airlift effort, including the Tudor, and the Lancastrian version of the Avro Lancaster.

The US Air Force had established a primary airlift operation at the Tempelhof airport in south central Berlin. Tempelhof now had three parallel runways, each more than 2000 yards long. The approaches to it were, however, still marred by the remains of some fairly tall buildings, requiring an attentive, on-your-toes landing. The Americans mainly operated Douglas C-54s capable of carrying a ten-ton load into Tempelhof. They had used C-47s until sufficient quantities of the larger planes were available. They also operated a small number of rear-loading Fairchild C-82 Packet cargo planes, mostly for the transport of vehicles and machinery.

The problem of how to haul coal for the essential fuelling of industry, for light and heat, was of great concern to the Allies. This heavy, bulky item had to be properly loaded aboard the planes or it could upset their trim and the dust from the coal could find its way into every area of the aircraft, making controls sticky and unresponsive. Similar

Left: All nine RAF squadrons of Avro Yorks participated in the airlift, making more than 29,000 sorties into Berlin and bringing in 239,000 tons of supplies to the isolated citizens. The York was developed from the design of the Lancaster bomber and cruised at 185 mph with a payload of between 15,000 and 20,000 pounds. Below: German labourers prepare to load sacks of coal aboard a C-54 at Fassberg Airfield prior to a flight to Berlin Tempelhof.

I crossed the Fatherland, to
take my place / in the swift-
wing'd swoop that all but
ended / the assay in one wild
and agile venture. I was
blooded then, but the wound
/ seared in the burnng
circlet of my spirit / served
only to temper courage / with
scorn of action's outcome.
— from 'Meditation of a Dying
German Officer'
by Herbert Read

problems were encountered with the transport of
flour. Vegetables and fruit were dried for lighter
shipment. Meat was boned to save on weight, and
then tinned or made into sausage to give it a
longer life. One such sausage product was
evidently so repellent that even the
undernourished Berliners could not tolerate it. It
is said that a civil servant then had the bright idea
that they could be bribed to eat it by offering
them a double ration. There were few takers.

   Through it all the hungry and courageous people
of Berlin carried on, feeling that as long as they
could hear the drone of aircraft they had hope.
Through it all the Russians continued to hassle and
harass the Berliners. They were only allowed four

hours of electricity a day and never knew when it
would be turned on. There was very little coal for
heating in that terrible winter and they broke up
their furniture to burn rather than accept Soviet
offers of free coal. They endured endless abuse and
harassment by the Russians but held fast to their
will to be free. And through it all they retained their
sense of humour: "Aren't we lucky? Imagine if the
British and Americans were besieging us and the
Russians were running the Airlift".

   The great airlift continued beyond 12 May 1949
when the Soviets officially ended their 318–day
blockade of Berlin. Scaled down from their peak
days, the British and Americans continued
Plainfare and *Vittles* through 23 September and 1

October respectively, to stockpile supply reserves for the Berliners. In the end the numbers were impressive. Royal Air Force aircraft delivered 394,509 tons, British civil aircraft delivered 147,727 tons and US Air Force aircraft brought in 1,783,573 tons, for a combined total of 2,325,809 tons. Of the load carried by the British, food amounted to 241,713 tons; coal 164,800 tons; military 18,239 tons; liquid fuel 92,282 tons and miscellaneous 25,202 tons. Of the total delivered by the USAF, food amounted to 296,303 tons; coal 1,421,730 tons, and liquid fuel 65,540 tons. The British also elected to bring loads back west from Berlin, a total of 35,843 tons. The French delivered 800 metric tons of supplies to the garrison in their

sector in 424 sorties. Both British and American aircraft were used to airlift passengers to and from Berlin; the British bringing in 36,218 and carrying out 131,436, while the Americans brought in 24,216 and carried out 36,584. In the course of the airlift British and American aircraft made 195,530 sorties to Berlin. The daily average tonnage carried was 4980. Aircraft used in the Berlin airlift included the Douglas C-47 Skytrain and Dakota, Avro York, Handley–Page Hastings, Handley–Page Halifax, Short Sunderland, Fairchild C-82 Packet, Handley–Page Halton, Avro Tudor, Avro Lancastrian, Douglas C-54 Skymaster, Avro Lincoln, Short Hythe, Consolidated Liberator, Bristol Freighter, Boeing C-97 Stratofreighter, Douglas C-74 Globemaster, and the Vickers Viking. During the airlift there were 31 American fatalities, eighteen British military fatalities and 21 British civilian fatalities.

The airlift was a kind of miracle. Even the weather seemed to co–operate to some extent with less frost and ice in Germany than in most winters. As the complex problems of the effort were gradually resolved, so too did the hoped–for effect occur. Stalin undoubtedly realised that West Berlin would come through his siege to the prospect of a bright and prosperous future thanks to the Marshall Plan and their rescue by the amazing airlift.

February 1949. Germany's political leaders met in Bonn to draft their constitution for a separate West German state. And in light of the burgeoning airlift the Soviet ambassador to the United Nations approached his American counterpart for conversations leading to a settlement of the Berlin crisis. There followed meetings of the western allies on the establishment of a new bond of nations to be called the North Atlantic Treaty Organisation, in which all members would come to the aid of any member nation that was attacked. The treaty was ratified on 9 May and the next day the Russians announced that they were lifting the Berlin blockade.

"The people of Berlin have never forgotten the debt they owe the Allied airmen and they have looked after the widows and educated the children of the 79 that were killed on the airlift. In addition, over the past year they have brought more than 1,500 veterans from all the participating nations to Berlin and have accommodated and entertained them at the city's expense.

"In an era when gratitude is somewhat rare this is a memorable example to us all." – John Curtiss, former Berlin Airlift navigator

Left: Berliners of all ages gathered around the perimeter of Tempelhof airfield during the airlift to watch the arrivals and departures of the C-54s and C-47s of Operation Vittles

THE NIGHTHAWK

CAN YOU keep a secret? Certainly, the United States Air Force can. For more than a decade it managed to hide the existence of its ultra–low–observable F-117A stealth fighter/bomber from the press, the public, the "other side" and, to a large extent, from the members of the US Congress.

In the mid–1970s, the USAF began a serious effort to develop a significantly less visible fighter/bomber aircraft, one that projected a dramatically reduced radar cross section or RCS. The Air Force was looking for an aircraft that would be inherently less visible to enemy radar and thus safer from radar–directed threats than conventional aircraft. It had to be able to approach and attack its target undetected to minimize the possibility of its being intercepted.

So–called "stealth" technology was developing during this time, and in 1975 two Lockheed engineers, members of Kelly Johnson's Advanced Development Projects Division, known as the Skunk Works group, made the key breakthrough. They solved the problem of predicting how a body of a given shape (an aircraft) would scatter radiation over all feasible angles of incidence, offering an extremely low RCS. That elegant solution came to be known as "faceting". One of these design engineers, Bill Schroeder, produced a drawing of a flyable, controllable aircraft that featured no curved surfaces at all, substituting instead small–radius straight edges on the wings and tail surfaces. The point was to show a finite number of edges and flat surfaces to the radar wave, and to achieve this Schroeder sought the help of software engineer Dennis Overholser. Overholser designed a program utilizing the Skunk Works' Control Data mainframe computer, to model the scattering of radiation from Schroeder's faceted shapes and predict their radar cross section relatively quickly.

Through trial and error, the Overholser program ultimately made it possible for the Lockheed designers to produce an aircraft shape which seemed capable of flight as well as the efficient management of incoming radar energy all at once.

Lockheed was then in a position to begin design of a faceted operational stealth combat aircraft that was to be all but undetectable by radar or infra–red capabilities. The plane would carry a pair of highly accurate 2000–pound bombs over a reasonable range and would combine the most effective uses of faceting and radar–absorbent material (RAM) possible in early 1976, when its first drawings were being made.

The people at Lockheed knew then that no one, and especially not the United States Air Force, would be likely to fund their stealth fighter development project. So, they opted instead for a "technology demonstration" programme; a relatively cheap effort which they expected would prove the viability and near–invisibility of their stealthy baby. They proposed construction of two prototypes scaled to 60% actual size and looking a lot like the real projected aircraft. They contained costs in the development of the prototypes by using, whenever possible, off–the–shelf parts from existing aircraft, and brought the two test aircraft in for about $35 million.

In 1976, Ben Rich, then head of the Skunk Works design team, persuaded the US Defense Advanced Research Projects Agency (DARPA) to pick up the tab for the stealth demonstrator programme. DARPA has historically supported relatively high–risk technology projects which appear to offer high potential, and often a multi–service application. The Lockheed project received DARPA funding in early 1977 and was given the code name, Have Blue, which probably meant something to someone somewhere.

During the time of the Jimmy Carter presidential administration, security concerns about the highly sensitive stealth project resulted in it being moved from DARPA, with its many civilian employees, to the control of the US Air Force Systems Command. It was set up in a secure project office at Wright–Patterson Air Force Base, Ohio, and the tightest of security nets was thrown over it. The design and fabrication of the two demonstrator aircraft was going ahead at Lockheed's Burbank facility. The planes were virtually made by hand, test pilots were selected, and flight testing of the completed scaled–down stealth prototypes began early in 1978 at the top–secret Groom Lake, Nevada base.

Groom Lake surely heads the list of America's least hospitable tourist attractions. Enclosed in an immense parcel of government–owned land about the size of Switzerland, the complex of hangars and support structures presents a bleak and bleached vista to anyone approaching. Not that doing so is advisable. The proprietors are never in the mood to receive callers, and the many prominent official warnings along the hundreds of miles of perimeter fencing make their attitude abundantly clear. Stay out, go away, don't come back. What goes on here doesn't concern you and if you try to gain entry to the area you'll wish you hadn't. That is the essence of the message from those who run the place where things like stealth aircraft have been tested. Fair enough. National security normally demands one or more layers of secrecy, and how many of us really have a need to know what happens at places like Groom Lake?

Through the test programme Lockheed and the Air Force learned about the subtleties of radar cross section reduction and the vital importance of radar–absorbent materials to their wondrous faceted fighters. As in any test programme, there were accidents and failures. But with them came understanding and the pair of Have Blue airplanes proved that an ultra–low–observable aircraft could fly and fly well.

With this proof in hand, the Carter administration moved quickly to fund the next phase of US stealth development. The new project, code–named Senior Trend, had as its goal to prove that a stealth aircraft could perform its combat mission. To do so, the programme was charged with the final design, development and production of the full–size Lockheed stealth fighter/bomber.

The idea behind the stealth fighter/bomber was that it should be capable of flying its mission, hitting at relatively small but important targets with a high degree of precision and minimal collateral damage, without much need for escort or support aircraft. It was to be developed as a single–seat night strike plane. It had to be deliverable virtually anywhere in the world where it might be needed by means of a giant C-5 transport, the outer wing sections of the stealth plane being removable.

An initial production order for twenty aircraft was placed and it included five planes designated as test aircraft. The Senior Trend airplanes entered production early in 1980 and in August of that year President Carter cancelled the B-1 bomber programme (revived in October 1981 by President Reagan). Carter had his reasons, of course, and one of them, the undisclosed key reason, was probably the rapidly developing stealth aircraft technology which seems to have changed a lot of minds in Washington and redirected a lot of 1980 developmental funding by the Congress. It then directed that research should begin immediately into the feasibility and design of a new Advanced Technology Bomber (ATB). The plan was to have the new bird operational by 1987. It was at this point that the Administration decided to disclose the existence of Have Blue, though not by that name. Some of the history of the programme was released, but no reference was made to work on the stealth fighter project which continued in its highly classified status for several years.

The stealth fighter/bomber was ultimately designated as F-117 and continued in test at the Groom Lake facility through 1982.

The big plane is impressive from any angle. It has the size and weight of the frontline F-15 Eagle. Its delta–like wing delivers low drag at high speed, easy handling at high attack angles and simplicity of structure and assembly. It takes off at about 180 knots and comes in on final at a fairly hot 150–175

"I went to training first in Tucson, Arizona to learn the A-7 and then immediately began training in January 1989 at the Tonopah Test Range (TNX) in the F-117. By the time I arrived at TNX the programme was emerging from the "black world" into what we referred to as the "grey world." In October 1988 the US Air Force had released that first grainy front–quarter photo [of the F-117], acknowledged the existence of TNX as a USAF base, and given some limited details of the airplane."
Dan DeCamp, former F-117 pilot

Sombre the night is. / And though we have our lives, we know / What sinister threat lurks there.
—from 'Returning, We Hear the Larks'
by Isaac Rosenberg

Far left: A stealth fighter/
bomber of the 415th Tactical
Fighter Squadron based at
King Khalid Air Base, Khamis
Mushait, Saudi Arabia gets in
position to refuel in Operation
Desert Storm. Left: An F-117
pilot greets a ground crewman
at King Khalid. Below and
below left: Patches of F-117
units that flew in the 1990–91
Gulf War.

"If the B-2 [stealth bomber] is
invisible, just announce you've
built a hundred of them and
don't build them."
— John Kasich, chairman, US
House Budget Committee,
opposing further expenditure on
the stealth bomber designed to
be virtually undetectable to
radar, July 1995.

Perhaps unfairly, the F-117 has at times been referred to as the 'Wobblin' Goblin', the result of rumours about the handling characteristics of the plane during aerial refuelling. Some F-117 pilots have denied that the aircraft can be less than stable when tanking and generously praise its flight qualities.

"We were like the rabbi who gets a hole–in–one on Saturday." – Ben Rich, Vice President and General Manager of the Lockheed special projects facility known as the "skunk works" on why he could not discuss the F-117 stealth aircraft for many years.

knots. Most modern fighters are not naturally stable and the stealth is no exception. It flies with a GEC Astronics analogue control system, artificially generating the necessary in–flight stability characteristics through fly–by–wire technology.

With the F-117 becoming operational in the early 1980s it was clear to the Air Force that the Groom Lake base, while perfectly adequate as a test facility, was no place to house an operational unit. The best option seemed to be a site within Nevada's immense Tonopah Test Range, another restricted area north–west of Las Vegas. Prior to 1983, the Range was where nuclear weapons drop–tests had been conducted and the existing airfield built in the 1950s for Sandia Laboratories offered an excellent foundation around which to build a new stealth base. The size of the test range area was to provide ample seclusion for the black jets and the security was so efficient that the location was not reported to the public until nearly two years after the base became operational.

When the Air Force began to comb its files for people to fly the stealth fighter/bomber operationally, it followed a criterion calling for pilots with roughly 1000 hours of flying time, mainly in fighter aircraft. Most of them would hold the rank of Captain and would have considerable experience flying air–to–ground missions in aircraft like the F-4, the A-10 and the F-111. The ideal candidate would be a very good pilot who was calm, serious and mature. When interviewed, the candidates were informed that they would be flying the A-7 aircraft, which in fact they would to some extent, that they would be in a location which would require them to be away from their families during the week and that, at the end of the interview, they would only be given five minutes to decide whether to volunteer for the programme.

The first of them were brought into the programme in mid–1982, and with no two–seat version of the F-117 to be trained on, each new pilot's first flight in the plane was also his solo. Their training progressed and in 1983 the new 4450th Tactical

Group took up residence at the Tonopah base where a more formal level of operational training was administered. At this time more and more key members of the US House and Senate armed services and appropriations committees were cleared to be briefed about the stealth programme. They liked what they heard, so much that they voted to increase funding for the programme and directed the Air Force to buy an entire four–squadron wing of 72 aircraft. The final purchase, however, was just 59.

The continuing security requirement of the F-117 activity made many demands on the pilots in the early months at the Tonopah base. All pilots in the programme were required to be housed with their families at Nellis AFB near Las Vegas, 190 miles from the TTR base. They had to commute to and from the job at Tonopah on Mondays and Fridays, flown back and forth in 727s operated by a company called Key Airlines, a charter line that was being kept quite busy by the US Defense Department.

Flying virtually all training missions at night during the week, and then having to adjust to a normal daytime routine on weekends with their families at Nellis, meant that the stealth pilots had to change their body clocks as much as eight or nine hours a week. Thus many of them were carrying a very high fatigue factor through their training as well as being chronically jet–lagged. One Thursday night during this period, Major Ross Mulhare admitted to another stealth pilot at TTR that he was tired and "just couldn't shake it." Still, he elected to fly, launching on one of the last missions of that night at 1.13 a.m. At approximately 1.45 Mulhare's aircraft was seen by an accompanying pilot to plunge into a mountainside in the Sequoia National Forest, north of Bakersfield, California. According to the other pilot Mulhare apparently made no attempt to eject and was killed in the crash. A cloak of security was dropped over the crash site by the Air Force. Firefighters called to the scene were made to sign statements declaring that they would say nothing about what they had seen at the site.

After the Mulhare crash things were different. When armed USAF personnel took charge of the area surrounding the crash site word of it got out and the press and media were on the scent of something unusual and important by early the next day. Reports about the stealth were beginning to leak now, though the Air Force still did not acknowledge the plane's existence. But the 800 or so civilian employees at TTR who lived in or near Tonopah were seeing the F-117 regularly, as were many residents of other nearby towns. Keeping a secret became more of a challenge to the service and events like the Mulhare crash added to the problem. Members of the Reagan administration believed in maintaining the veil of secrecy around the US stealth activity to the maximum, and resisted pressures to show the fighter to the press and public.

While continuing to believe that the secrecy was essential to the security of the programme, the Air Force was at the same time inhibited by its own restrictions on day flying of the stealth fighter/bomber and on the use of any bases for it other than the TTR facility. Finally, on 10 November 1988, after the recent Presidential election, the announcement came and with it a rather poor-quality heavily-edited photo of the plane, released by the Pentagon, which actually revealed very little about the design phenomenon the USAF had kept quiet about for so many years.

Now the news was out. The rumours were proven to be true, and the Air Force was at last able to fly its strange black fighter/bomber at all hours of the day and night from TTR and elsewhere.

16 January 1991. Some 45 combat-ready F-117A stealth fighter/bombers were housed in the brand-new hardened and blast-proof aircraft shelters of the Khamis Mushait base (nicknamed Tonopah East) in southern Saudi Arabia. Their deployment to the Gulf had begun on 19 August 1990 when aircraft of the 37th Tactical Fighter Wing's 415th Tactical Fighter Squadron were moved from their Nevada base as a result of Iraq's invasion of neighbouring Kuwait on 2 August. In addition to the aircraft, some sixty combat-qualified stealth pilots were on hand at the immaculate Saudi base.

When the Allied Coalition attacks began, the F-117As hit the vital Iraqi communications and command and control sites, which they took out with relative ease. Thereafter, the black jets were shifted to strategic targets including airfields, bridges, chemical and nuclear facilities as well as specialized targets within Baghdad. One third of the 1271 combat missions flown by the F-117As during the Desert Storm campaign were flown over Baghdad, penetrating the fire of an estimated 3000 anti-aircraft artillery pieces and some sixty SAM missile sites. No hits of any kind were recorded on any of the stealths.

The black fighter/bombers always attacked at night and each aircraft generally flew two missions a night, though each pilot usually flew only once. A mission from their Saudi base averaged 5.4 hours and required a number of in-flight refuelings. The planes flew in pairs but normally attacked singly. A typical stealth mission put the airplane inside Iraqi airspace for about thirty minutes. The stealth pilots flew their missions in radio-silence. The mission routes and altitudes were constantly changed to keep the Iraqis guessing.

The accuracy of the stealth's imaging infra-red weapons system amazed the world when CNN and other television networks showed the plane's laser-guided bombs targetting and destroying objectives as small as specific windows and ventilation shafts. The stealth's hit rate in the Gulf campaign was 80–85 per cent, compared to the 30–35 per cent that was typically achieved by other aircraft in the Vietnam war.

In time the stealth became known as Nighthawk. It had been created to bring stealth technology against high-value targets and, in the operations against targets in Baghdad, the airplane proved capable of delivering its load of sophisticated weaponry on such priority sites with remarkable efficiency, virtual impunity, and with minimal loss of civilian life.

Thou goest thy way, and I go mine, / Apart, yet not afar;
Only a thin veil hangs between
The pathways where we are.
"God keep watch 'tween thee and me;" / This is my prayer;
He looketh thy way, He looketh mine, / And keeps us near.
Although our paths be separate,
And thy way is not mine, / Yet coming to the mercy-seat, My soul will meet with thine.
"God keep watch 'tween thee and me" / I'll whisper there;
He blesseth me,
And we are near.
– Julia A. Baker

My centre is giving way, my right
is in retreat, situation excellent.
I shall attack.
– Maréchal Foch

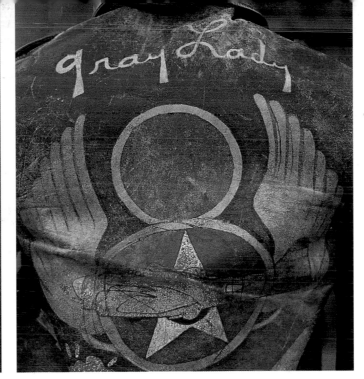

In the uniform environment of the military, it is only human to want to personalize your appearance a bit and display for your peers an icon you have taken as your own. Through much of military history, airmen (Americans in particular) have proudly worn leather flying jackets adorned with images of their choice that ranged from the frankly sentimental to the undeniably vulgar. World War II spawned the bulk of this jacket art and in the ensuing years many surviving examples have become high-priced, highly sought collectables.

"OUR CREW selected themselves RAF–style at the Operational Training Unit. It worked very well as far as personalities were concerned and was a typical [RAF] bomber crew in that the pilot came from Australia, I came from New Zealand, the rear gunner was Welsh, flight engineer Scots, and the bomb aimer, wireless operator and mid–upper gunner were English. We all got along famously and, as with most crews, went to pubs together.

"The pilot was the oldest at thirty. He was also the only married member of the crew, although this did not stop his off–duty activities in any way. He was not a very good pilot and I have always considered that my survival was in no small way due to the fact that he fell off his bicycle on the way back from the pub one night (the bomb aimer was on the handlebars) and broke his wrist. He was taken off flying. We got a new and experienced second–tour pilot. He was unfortunately killed in a training accident and we received our third pilot, with whom we finished the war.

"On one occasion on a fighter affiliation exercise our Australian pilot very nearly lost control of the aircraft, and boxes of 'window', left over from the night before, filled the cockpit and covered the windscreen with hundreds of metal strips. I had to get up beside him and clear the screen so he could see out. When we landed, we lined up and told him that if he ever did that again we would refuse to fly with him.

"The flight engineer had been a motorcycle speedway rider before the war. He had a silver plate in his head from a crash and was not very good at fuel calculations. We had a number of 'heart–stopping' incidents when he allowed engines to run out of fuel before changing tanks.

"The bomb aimer and I had most in common and we would box together and go out on dates as a foursome. We were the only public school boys, but that never affected our relationships with the other members of the crew, which were warm and close. We were all Sergeants at the start of our tour which meant we all lived in a Nissen hut together. This made for easy companionship. First awake in the morning had to stoke up the coke stove and put a record on my portable gramophone . . . usually the Mills Brothers singing 'I'll Be Around' or one of the jazz records from the collection I had bought from the effects of a squadron member who had been killed . . . Tommy Dorsey, Woody Herman, Bunny Berrigan, Artie Shaw, etc."
– John Curtiss, formerly with Nos. 578 and 158 Squadrons, RAF.

"Pocklington is up in the county of Yorkshire. A small farming community, it offered three pubs, an old Anglican church and two rather ordinary hotels which would serve you a very restricted wartime meal for five shillings. This was the top price allowed by the Government to any restaurant during the war years. It is strange that, to this day, I still dream of those meals. They usually consist of fried bread, egg, beans and sausage — this was always our pre–flight meal.

"On this particular day we had been briefed in the afternoon. The plan was to put as many bombs as possible, in the shortest time possible, on Berlin. This huge city seemed to represent all that was evil. I, personally, felt that at last I was in the action — frightened but fulfilled. Of all the targets, Berlin was the big one. The briefing finished at 1600 hours. Take–off was set for 2300 hours, seven hours of tension before we could get going. I decided to go to my Nissen hut and lie down for a while, pretending to sleep but finding my mind in a turmoil of dread. I stayed there for a couple of hours and then heard a loud rattling of the latch on the door followed by my Flight Engineer saying, 'What are you doing in there? Ops are scrubbed.' I don't think I've ever heard such welcome words."
– Peter Geraghty, formerly with No. 102 Squadron, RAF

CREW POSITIONS

Left: A B-24 gunner of the 93rd Bomb Group (H), Eighth USAAF, stationed at Hardwick, Norfolk, England in World War II. Above: Major–General Dale O. Smith who, as a Colonel, commanded the 384th Bomb Group (H) based at Grafton Underwood, in Northamptonshire, England from November 1943 to October 1944.

"I will always remember my 30th and last mission. I definitely was more nervous than on all the other 29 missions."
— Charles Bednarik, formerly with the 467th Bomb Group (H), 8 USAAF

"All pilots posted to 8 Group on Mosquitos had to complete a laid–down syllabus of 30 hours flying at 1655 MTU — ten in the Dual Flight and 20 in the Bomber Flight, the latter complete with navigator. No pilot was allowed to touch the controls of an 8 Group Mosquito until he had 1000 hours as first pilot under his belt and had been selected to fly Mosquitos.

"Having completed their prescribed time in the Dual Flight, the pilots of No. 15 Course now reported to the Bomber Flight and joined the navigators. The system of crewing up was easy — we were all assembled in the Crew Room and told to sort ourselves out. This we did fairly quickly and I soon found myself talking to a tall, rather quiet Flying Officer named John Hickox. He was known in the RAF as 'Bill'— after Wild Bill Hickok of American West fame. He told me that he had done his first tour of ops on 'Wimpies' and that he had been shot down and walked back through the desert. He did not relish the idea of being shot down in a Mosquito and walking back from Germany. I assured him that his thoughts accorded closely with mine so we shook hands and became a Mosquito crew.

"The next thing we did as crews in the Bomber Flight was to gather round a Mk IV bomber Mosquito for drill in abandoning aircraft. The Chief Ground Instructor, Squadron Leader Cairns, explained that if we were hit at high level we had about 45 seconds in which to get out. We had to disconnect our oxygen tubes and radio intercom plugs, release our seat belts, switch off engines if time permitted, jettison the bottom hatch and bail out. This sounds straightforward, but the Mosquito was a very small aircraft and the pilot and navigator

were intended to climb in, strap in and stay put.

"When Bill Hickox and I practised it the first time there was an unholy mix–up and after 45 seconds the CGI announced, 'You're dead'. The difficulty about getting out of a Mosquito wearing parachutes was that the navigator had to clip on his chest parachute and then manoeuvre his way through the main hatch in the floor of the aircraft. This hatch was scarcely large enough to get through without a 'chute. If the navigator got out safely, the pilot was supposed to follow him wearing the pilot–type parachute attached to his backside.

"Bill and I decided that bailing out was a dangerous business and we would stay with the aircraft if humanly possible. I resolved mentally that if all failed and we had to get out in a hurry I would wait until Bill was clear and then go out through the top hatch (which was the standard drill for the pilot seated in the left–hand seat of a dual Mosquito). Fortunately our agreed plan was never put to the test, but other crews had to jump out over Germany and did so successfully."
— J. R. Goodman, formerly with Nos. 37, 99, 139 and 627 Squadrons, RAF

"We didn't live in luxury. We lived in a wooden hut, down a hedge, two miles from the camp. They ran you in in transport if you needed it, or you had a bicycle. Four crews to a hut, 28 people, and you got to know them pretty well. But other than that, you didn't get to know many people on the squadron because you slept, flew, went out . . . the only time you were away from your own crew was when you went on leave. So now, when you go back to a reunion, you don't know many people. I know about two people, that's all. You just took things for granted. You were told to do something. You never bitched. You never asked why. You just did it and didn't query it. And it's only in recent years, with information coming out, that we've been able to find out why we went to certain

Right: Joe McCarthy (centre) and his No. 617 Squadron, RAF, Lancaster crew at RAF Scampton, Lincolnshire, England, after the famous raid of 16 May 1943 in which aircraft of 617 attacked the great dams of the Ruhr Valley in Germany. Above: *Royal Flying Corps Second Lieutenant Gilbert S. M. Insall, VC*, by Edward Newling.

Below: A 384th Bomb Group (H) crew on their way to interrogation after a World War II mission. Right: Members of the crew of the B-17 *Rose of York* meet Queen Elizabeth.

targets . . . synthetic oil, flying bomb sites, submarine pens, shipping and docks."
– Fred Allen, formerly with No. 158 Squadron, RAF

"The local villagers were always friendly. They always treated us with the greatest respect, even though I am sure we did not always warrant it."
– Nelson McInnis, formerly with No. 426 Squadron, RAF

"It was a bit upsetting when people you lived with didn't come back. There were four or five other

crew sleeping in the dorm with you and you'd just get off to sleep when the military police would come in . . .the RAF Regiment Police with all their kit bags. They would ask if it was so–and–so's locker and would pack up all his gear. They would ask if there was anything of yours among it, and if there were any of his belongings anywhere else. They'd just load it all up into containers and take it out. That was the last you'd see of him. He would never be spoken of again. We'd never talk about him after that."
– Jack Clift, formerly with No. 463 Squadron, RAAF

"We went to war with a mixture of apprehension, excitement and exhilaration, but we were young. War was a challenge and an adventure and we responded accordingly. While not as professional as we liked to regard ourselves, we had confidence in ourselves and our equipment although with retrospect we were ill–prepared to meet the challenges which lay ahead. But in war you learn fast.

"One lost many friends and they were grievous losses. When a friend went missing you always consoled yourself that he might be a POW. There was little time to dwell on these things, which was just as well, and you got on with the job. I think one automatically built up a form of immunity to safeguard your feelings.

"Although one faced danger on each mission, you always thought it would be the other chap who would get the 'chop.' Callous perhaps, but I suppose it was a form of self–preservation.

"The air battle was unique. We went to war for a few hours and then returned to live a near–normal existence. We could go to the pub, the cinema, see friends and family and then go to war again. A clean and comfortable way of fighting a war, but in many ways perhaps more stressful."
– Wilfred Burnett, formerly with Nos. 76, 49, 408, 138 and 148 Squadrons, RAF

Robert F. Cooper was a B-17 co-pilot with the 385th Bomb Group (H) based at Great Ashfield, Suffolk in 1944-45. "There were only six officers in our Nissen hut — Ray Shattenkirk (pilot), myself, and Howard Giberson (navigator) from our crew, and Alex Rusecky (pilot), George Burger (co-pilot), and Art Axelrod (navigator) from another crew. We arrived within a few days of each other and were constant companions and hutmates from late December until the end of February. We had friendly competitions, played softball, went on bike rides, told each other our life stories, went to the Officers' Club together, and often just huddled, all six of us, around the coal stove, trying to keep warm. I was especially friends with Burger, my fellow co–pilot, who was exactly my age and a happy–go–lucky type. On 1 March 1945, both crews were scheduled to fly, Rusecky as part of the Lead Section, Shattenkirk in the Spare Lead Section. We would not fly unless Rusecky (or another member of the Lead Section) had to abort. Even so, we had to go all the way through the starting procedure, including 'Start engines.'

"But Rusecky had developed a problem: he couldn't awaken his navigator, Art Axelrod. That was because Art was dead drunk! Art had been out on a bender

Here lies, beneath, with arms crossed on his breast, / A sergeant pilot, finally at rest, Not twenty Aprils sunshined his small life, / Before he took dark maiden Death to wife.
– from 'Epitaph'
by Anthony Richardson

Overleaf. Blenheim rear gunner Sergeant P. Kirk of No. 226 Squadron, RAF, as drawn by Sir William Rothenstein.

197

Wm Rothenstein
Wattisham
Oct 1941

the night before, even though he knew his crew was to fly a mission the next morning. He probably got in around midnight, worrying the hell out of Rusecky. When the Sergeant came in to awaken us at about 0300, he tried to wake Art but failed. His pilot said he'd take the responsibility to get him up. But Alex was unable to, and in fact, we all tried to. Art was totally out of it, and very quickly Alex realized he wouldn't be any good on the crew anyway. So pilot Alex had to call at the last possible moment for a replacement navigator, some poor guy from the Squadron who hadn't thought he would be flying that day. The rest of the five of us left for mission briefing, etc., leaving Art snoring away in his bunk. At the flight line, we started engines, but no one aborted, so we were able to come back to our barracks around 0600 or 0630, and pile back into our bunks for another few hours' sleep. Art was still snoring, still drunk, out of it.

"The bad news came to us at lunch — Rusecky's plane and Armbruster's plane had collided while assembling, and both planes had gone straight down. Of the eighteen men on both planes, only one parachuted safely — the tail gunner from Armbruster's crew. The other seventeen were dead. We all felt very badly indeed, but if we felt that way, imagine how Art felt. My pilot and I talked with him just a bit that afternoon. He said he was utterly devastated by the loss of his entire crew, but also utterly thankful that he hadn't been with them. Art didn't want to talk much about it, and he was gone almost immediately. The brass probably figured he wouldn't be welcome around the Squadron much. I don't doubt that this event (which just amounts to getting drunk one night at the wrong time — or perhaps the right?) changed Art's life forever. I never saw him again."

It was 17 July 1953 and B-29 Superfortress pilot Joseph Anastasia was flying from a 307th Bomb Wing field at Kadena Air Base, Okinawa to attack a target in North Korea in what he regards as "the mission to end all missions."

"The briefing was normal. We took off and flew at least fifteen minutes to cool the engines down and then began climbing to an initial altitude of 20,000 feet. As we climbed I had the gunners test–fire their guns to be sure they were working properly. They each had an extra 25 rounds for this purpose. Everything was going well. It was my sixth mission and I had no particular concerns about it. I had a flak vest under my seat and a steel helmet for my head. Now we were in the secondary climb and I was leading the last element of five airplanes up to 26,000 feet where we levelled off. This was to be our bomb run altitude.

"We were all set for the bomb run when suddenly the number four propeller went into an overspeed runaway condition. The only thing we could do was toggle it down electrically, and that didn't work. The engine would tear itself apart if we were unable to shut it down, so I ordered the engineer to feather it and he did so, I thought. We were on the bomb run and I had maximum power on (2600 rpm and 50 inches of manifold pressure) to keep the lead, and I was doing pretty well, except things were a little hectic.

"We came to 'bombs away' and released our load, but nine bombs were hung up and didn't drop. I was running on three engines but I called the Group Lead and asked permission to make a second drop. He OK'd it so I race–tracked my pattern around and came in for a second try.

"Now the enemy radar guns were all turned into me. They knew my altitude and where I was going, so all they had to do was blast away and the chances were they would hit me, and hit me they did. They knocked out the number three engine and set fire to number two. With number four out of commission I now had only one engine left. I ordered 'Salvo all bombs now' and they all dropped. At that point my airspeed was down to 150 mph and the bomber was about to stall. Then a burst of flak under the left wing lifted it up and

over we went . . . into a spin to the right. I shut down the number one engine and alerted the crew for a bail out.

"Boeing had built a good airplane. She was strong and reliable, and could stand a lot of stress on her airframe. She had done about one full turn when I rang the bail–out bell. From back in the airplane came the voice of the radar operator: 'We cannot move. We are plastered against the sides of the fuselage. Help us. Don't leave us!' Centrifugal force had pinned them to the interior of the airplane. I took my flashlight from the edge of the seat and looked at the darkened instrument panel. The artificial horizon was tilted and all the other instruments were out of action except for the turn needle and ball. With all engines off and the props feathered, there were no generators on line and the over–loaded electrical circuits killed all the power on the airplane. The waist gates, which close with power to keep the engines' turbo–chargers going, controlled the manifold pressure which gave power to the engines. Waist gates always failed in the open position, so I had four waist gates failed 'open.'

"The B-29 had Curtiss Electric four–bladed propellers which were set up to lose 35 rpm per 1000 feet of altitude lost. We lost 16,000 feet, from 26,000 feet to a bit under 10,000 feet, losing 560 rpm per engine. The only information available to me was from my pressure instruments, the altimeter, airspeed indicator, vertical speed, and turn needle and ball. Using my flashlight I restored the bail–out bell. Our navigator was standing on the nose wheel door, waiting to bail out. I told him to sit down.

"All this was taking place in about four to six minutes. I studied the instruments and using the needle and ball determined that we were in a right turn, and so went with the controls in that direction. I jammed the rudder and counted fifteen seconds, then popped the nose forward with the control wheel. It stopped the spin. We were now

To Tokyo Rose c/o Radio Tokyo. We've been listing to your line ever since you've been on the air. At times it was the best entertainment we could get. We don't know who you really are, what you look like, or where you get all those American records; but each of us has his own ideas.

With your sexy, silky soft–talk; a couple of innocent–looking syllables, a suggestive whisper, your microphone manner was something new to us. Your rumours, your melodramas of our girls taking to the primrose path, the 4–F'ers taking over, your descriptions of homy scenes, of chicken dinners, of moonlight strolls, of sodas at the corner drug, of petting in the park; your reproductions of beer–parlors, pool–rooms, of dancing to Glenn Miller, Dorsey, Goodman, Kyser. You flashed flickers of home, you talked across the breakfast table, you gave out with gossip; you were intimate, love–purring, cooing. That was your line, your technique. Why, you had a patent on it! And through all this chit–chat you played your old scratchy, corny records you brought over from the States.

"The Rose" has become a legend, a South Pacific yarn. Over our beers, in years to come, we will talk of you and smile and try to figure out just what kind of a gal you were. You were a part of our jungle life, a tropical whiff of amusement. Your programme was always good for a laugh! With all your subtle propaganda trying to scare us or make us homesick, you, in fact, gave us some of the most entertaining programmes we had till we got our own Jungle Network going with a taste of our real present–day America. For a while you were our only programme with a flavour of home. You filled the gap of loneliness, and we liked you. So orchids to you and thanks for the memories.
– from *We'll Say Goodbye*, the 307th Bomb Group (H) story

"I think, by common consent, we were all dedicated to surviving the tour. And to survive, we tried our best to be as professional as we could be. On the ground we all cleaned perspex, cleaned guns, belted ammunition, checked bomb circuits, practised manual release of hang-ups, ran through our dinghy and ditching drills, shot skeet, practised evasion tactics, ran through parachute drills without being told to, and exchanged information on our specialities. In the air we cross-trained ourselves so that if one or two were wounded or killed the remainder could get home and get down. I was second dicky and felt confident that I could land the Halifax on a crash drome (and there was one just a few miles north of our base at Lissett). But some of our cross-country trips, in which we all changed positions, were mad, wild and woolly. If nothing else, they gave each of us an appreciation of the other guy's problems."
— Ken Roberts, formerly with No. 158 Squadron, RAF

Right: RAF Bomber Command aircrew awaiting transport to their aircraft prior to a World War II operation. The photo is believed to have been made at RAF Bardney, Lincolnshire, England, home base for the Lancasters of No. 9 Squadron.

down to 13,000 feet and went right down to below 10,000 feet before the bomber levelled off. We then glided back up to 11,000 feet. I had recovered from a three—and—a—half—turn spin, a feat unheard of in the B-29. Fortunately, I was current in spins and spin recovery from flying P-51 Mustangs. I had a good number one engine, and, to my surprise, the number four engine was still running — the runaway prop had not feathered. So, I now had 1975 rpm on two engines, was doing 147 mph and descending in a 'stalled' or burbelling condition . . . a juddering airplane.

"I got the plane onto a 150 degree heading for Kimpo Air Base in South Korea. I was letting down to land there when a B-26 on final and on fire crashed on the runway. Kimpo was then out of the question for us. We went on toward Suwon which is about 40 miles south of Kimpo, and found it to be all fogged in, and, as we still had about 7000 feet of altitude, I decided to head for Taegu Airfield and when we arrived there, altitude 5000 feet, it too was fogged in and of no use to us. I continued south—east toward the next possible landing site, Pusan. All this time another B-29 was flying 'S' turns near us. It carried a boat on the bottom of the fuselage that could be dropped to us in the ocean if we should require it.

"We were in a constant descent as I did not have enough power to fly level. We arrived at Pusan with 4000 feet of altitude and solid fog and rain. At that point our alternative was to ditch in the Straights of Tsushima, islands between Korea and Japan. The airplane seemed to be shaking and vibrating severely and I commented on it to my co—pilot, who told me that it wasn't the airplane, it was my knees. I looked down and saw that my flight suit was quite bloody at my knees. I took my hands off the controls and held my knees to try to stop the shaking. We continued down toward the water to 1000 feet. We could get only 26 inches of manifold pressure on the engines, barely enough power to keep the airplane above the stall by a few

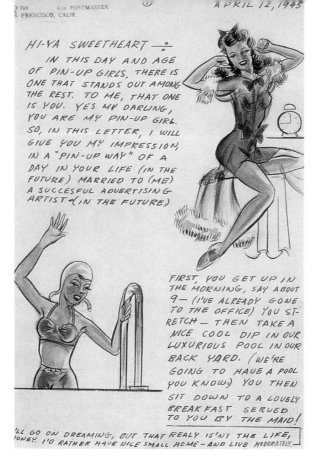

Above and right: Fred J. Kaplan served with the 307th Bomb Group (H), the "Long Rangers" on Guadalcanal and elsewhere in the western Pacific in WWII. An advertising artist, he always illustrated his letters home to his wife–to–be. Far right: Wartime wall art at Knettishall, the English base of the 388th Bomb Group (H).

APRIL 12, 1945

HI-YA SWEETHEART ⁞

IN THIS DAY AND AGE OF PIN-UP GIRLS, THERE IS ONE THAT STANDS OUT AMONG THE REST. TO ME, THAT ONE IS YOU. YES MY DARLING, YOU ARE MY PIN-UP GIRL. SO, IN THIS LETTER, I WILL GIVE YOU MY IMPRESSION, IN A "PIN-UP WAY" OF A DAY IN YOUR LIFE (IN THE FUTURE) MARRIED TO (ME) A SUCCESFUL ADVERTISING ARTIST (IN THE FUTURE)

FIRST, YOU GET UP IN THE MORNING, SAY ABOUT 9— (I'VE ALREADY GONE TO THE OFFICE) YOU ST- RETCH — THEN TAKE A NICE COOL DIP IN OUR LUXURIOUS POOL IN OUR BACK YARD. (WE'RE GOING TO HAVE A POOL YOU KNOW) YOU THEN SIT DOWN TO A LOVELY BREAKFAST SERVED TO YOU BY THE MAID!

I'LL GO ON DREAMING, BUT THAT REALY IS'NT THE LIFE, HONEY. I'D RATHER HAVE NICE SMALL HOME — AND LIVE MODERATELY.

THEN YOU'LL GO OUT AND PUTTER AROUND IN THE VICTORY GARDEN — (IF THEY HAVE "VICTORY" GARDENS THEN) IN FACT YOU'LL PROBABLY RAISE ALL KINDS OF "STUFF". IF YOU RUN INTO A SITUATION AS PICTURED ABOVE — YOU CAN ALWAYS JUST PHONE ME UP AT THE OFFICE, AND I'LL RUN HOME AND "SEW A BUTTON ON FOR YOU" ———!

③

AFTER THE VICTORY GARDEN, MAYBE YOU'LL JUST SUN BATHE IN THE BACK YARD (WHAT A LIFE!) WITH ALL THIS SUN — YOU'LL PROBABLY GET AS BLACK AS THE ACE OF SPADES — REMEMBER! WHAT I'M TRYING TO SAY IS THAT ALMOST ALL YOU'RE GOING TO HAVE TO DO — IS LOLL AROUND.

— EXCEPT FOR TAKING CARE OF THE KIDS. THIS IS THE YOUNGEST ONE — THE OTHER THREE ARE AT SCHOOL. YOU'LL PROBABLY PLAY WITH HIM A LITTLE BIT BEFORE HIS AFTERNOON NAP. — THEN, LET ME SEE, WHAT WOULD YOU DO NEXT. — YOU'D PRO- BABLY GO SHOPPING

AND BY GOBS OF CLOTHES AND THINGS THAT YOU REALY DID'NT NEED. BUT, WHAT THE HELL, WE'LL BE ABLE TO AFFORD IT.

THIS SCENE WILL TAKE PLACE ON OR ABOUT NOVEMBER 25?

DON'T MISS IT !!

miles per hour. We were just about level at 400 feet over the water when I heard a radio call: 'Skipper Crystal Control calling Glad 35, can you hear me?' I answered on the emergency channel: 'I read you loud and clear.' He said that we were only ten miles from Itazuke, Japan, and asked if we thought we could make it there. I said I would try. I had only 200 feet of altitude when I saw the breakwater at Itazuke. There were also two towers in the harbour. I aimed at the one on the left which aligned me with the runway. Seeing the green lights I called for gear down. We had no flaps and no electrical power, but the landing gear was a free–fall type. The main wheels touched the runway. The nose gear wasn't locked down, but it had an over–centre lock on it and when it touched down it locked just fine. I pulled the air brakes after the roll–out and we finally came to a stop. We all climbed out and kissed the ground. We were so happy to be safely on the ground that we wept for joy. They towed the airplane off the runway and we were transported to the billeting area where we all flopped into bed completely exhausted.

"The next day we went back out to the airplane to look it over. What a mess. All four engines needed to be changed as well as the oil coolers and two of the propellers, which had holes in them. The sheet metal work on the wings and flaps was so badly holed that in some places you could stand on a ladder and poke your head through the wing.

"All of our gunners were flown back to Okinawa on a courier flight. The officers, and our flight engineer, remained at Itazuke with the airplane while maintenance people there worked on it. We had no clothes with us other than what we had on, and there were no clothes available to purchase, but we met a group of Red Cross girls who loaned us some jeans, boots and sweatshirts. We looked a mess but we were clean and alive. We stayed in Itazuke for a week while the B-29 was being repaired. The Japanese maintenance people there were very efficient and the airplane checked out

OK when we flight–tested it. We then flew it back to Okinawa, landing at our home base, Kadena. We learned that we had missed three combat missions in the ten days' elapsed time that we had been away."

The Korean War ended on 27 July 1953. In that conflict B-29s dropped 167,000 tons of bombs on enemy targets in 21,328 sorties. They accounted for the destruction of 30 enemy aircraft. Thirty–four B-29s were lost.

"We went back to Nuthampstead in 1962, and had trouble finding it. We turned in at the Woodman Inn. I never even went to the Woodman when I was stationed there. I used to go into Hitchin or Royston, and after Helen and I met, I used to go down to London all the time. So, we went into the Woodman and I asked them were the airfield was They said to just walk down the path about half a mile and we would see it. We did, and we found a few of the old Nissen huts still there. We then met an old guy who asked us if we would like to come on the field, and told us how to drive around and come on through the village. We then drove onto the remains of the runways. I couldn't orient myself at all. I didn't even have any idea where the main gate had been."
– Bill Ganz, formerly with the 398th Bomb Group (H), Eighth USAAF

Former B-17 pilot Bill Harvey was assigned to the 384th Bomb Group (H) at Grafton Underwood, Northamptonshire in World War II. "I have never forgotten the green. 'Farty shades of green,' the Irish would say. After months of training in the western deserts of the US, I couldn't believe how beautiful Ireland and England looked then.

"We arrived at Grafton on a beautiful Saturday morning in early June, 1943, two to three weeks after the rest of the crews. By this time they were old hands with a mission or two under their belts. The next day, Sunday, was another beautiful day so

USO camp shows gave us Bob Hope, and we laughed. He and his gang put on the best show we'd seen. Thanks, Bob. Though the show was three hours late, heat and discomfort were forgotten when Bob stepped on the stage. The hit of the show, lovely Patty Thomas danced her way into our hearts and gave us something to talk about. Like all good things, the Hope show ended too soon.
– from We'll Say Goodbye, the 307th Bomb Group (H) story

Left: Eighth USAAF air crewmen in World War II England.

Wake, friend, from forth thy lethargy; the drum / Beats brave and loud in Europe, and bids come / All that dare rouse, or are not loath to quit / Their vicious ease and be o'erwhelmed with it. / It is a call to keep the spirits alive / That gasp for action, and would yet revive Man's buried honour in his sleep life, / Quickening dead nature to her noblest strife. / All other acts of worldlings are but toil / In dreams, begun in hope, and end in spoil.
– from 'An Epistle to a Friend, to perswade him to Warres' by Ben Jonson

Look at those beauties / Hanging on the racks, / With bright, shiny fuses / And olive–drab backs.

my navigator, Dick Sherer, and I decided to go to Kettering, the closest town of any size, then take a train to Leicester, a nearby city, and be tourists for a day. At the Kettering station, I read the schedule and there was a train returning at six that night, which was perfect, getting us back to the base before dark. After a looksee at downtown Leicester we stopped in a hotel and they were having a tea dance. This turned out to be our first chance to see English girls. They were pretty and friendly and we had a great time. Five–thirty came all too soon and we had to leave for the station. I checked at the ticket window to see if the six o'clock train was on time and was advised that this being Sunday there was no six o'clock train and the next one was at midnight. I never could read a train schedule. Back to the dance. We took two of the pretty girls to dinner and the movies, arriving back at the station in time for the midnight train. Our only thought was, we'll never get a taxi so late at night, so we'll have to walk out to the base — which we did. As we got near, we could hear the roar of many engines. Deciding there must be a mission on, we walked down to the flight line to watch the planes take off. We had only been there a couple of minutes when our Squadron Operations Officer saw us and said, 'Where the hell have you fellas been? We've been looking all over for you. Your plane and crew are on this mission and we've had to find a replacement co–pilot and navigator to go in your place.' We couldn't believe it! We had only arrived yesterday. We hadn't even had an orientation flight. How could they send our crew? We weren't ready. Not even one practice mission. This is crazy. Crazy or not, there was our plane taking off and we were sick. He told us to go to our quarters until the Squadron Commander could see us. It wasn't long before we were standing at attention in his office. We felt terrible. We knew we hadn't done anything wrong, but he told us that the Group CO was really upset. After hearing our explanation, he said, 'I'll do my best to save your

asses.' We were sent back to our quarters and told to stay there until the Colonel could see us.

"Hours later the mission was due to return and we said, 'To hell with it, let's go down to the flight line and watch the planes land.' One after another the Forts came in and landed. Two didn't make it back — one of them was ours. God, then we really felt terrible, thinking that, if we had been along, maybe we could have done something to bring the plane back. Just then the Colonel spotted us and called us over. He said, 'I was all for court martialling you two, but I can't because you really haven't broken any rules and I know how bad you feel. Anyhow, your Squadron CO was the one who really saved your asses because I wanted to make an example out of you.' What a way to start a tour of duty! As badly as we felt, we also knew that we were damned lucky to be alive. I would let someone else read the train schedules from then on.

"The next three months were the most frustrating of my life. Whenever a co–pilot was needed for a crew, I was picked. Seven times I started a mission and seven times we aborted and returned to base. There were, of course, many reasons for these abortions . . . engine problems, control problems, weather, but the really bad one was mental problems. Some pilots just lost their nerve when they got close to enemy territory and they would use any pretence to turn back. This was rare, but it happened. That was my luck on my fifth, sixth and seventh aborted missions. My pilot must have had a premonition that he was going to be shot down. He would drop out of the formation and turn back for the least little reason. After his second abort, I went to the Squadron Commander and asked to be taken off the crew. I didn't want to fly with that pilot again. The CO said, 'Harvey, fly with him one more time. If he aborts again I'll relieve him. I reluctantly agreed and a couple of days later we were off on another mission. We hadn't even reached altitude when the pilot said, 'Look at the RPM indicator, it's jiggling all over the place.' It

After 27 months' continuous work, the bulk of our veteran ground men got their first rest. Ten-day leaves were finally allotted in a little country town of 10,000 population, in Queensland, Australia, named Mackay.

We stuffed ourselves with fresh fruit and vegetables, ice cream, milk, "Styke'n aygs." We cleaned the town of souvenirs, drank all available beer and liquor, legal and otherwise, and generally raised as much hell as we could. The American Red Cross had a full week's schedule of horse back and bike rides, river picnics, moonlight cruises, and swimming parties at the beach, plus nightly dances in their rec. hall. Young and friendly junior hostesses attended all these functions, did their best at jitterbugging, and swapped slang expressions with us.

Combat men got a better break, they went to Sydney on their rest leaves. There was the real deal! Everything under the sun in the recreation line. Ample night spots and plenty of good-looking women. Ten days' "rest" in Sydney and we went back to the jungle—tired but happier men.
– from *We'll Say Goodbye*, the story of the 307th Bomb Group (H)

looked OK to me, but he said, 'We are going back to base.' I pleaded with him to let me take the controls, but all he would do was shake his head. That was the last time I spoke to him. After landing and taxiing to our hardstand, I got out of the plane and reported to the CO. The pilot was removed from command and a few days later was flying co-pilot for another crew. His premonition was right. He never came back. I vowed that if I ever made first pilot I would never abort.

"One day the CO called me in and said, 'Harvey, you've had enough experience now so I'm going to make you a first pilot, but I'm not giving you a crew. We need some experienced instructor pilots to fly with the new crews, anywhere up to five missions. If you think the pilot and crew are ready before that, that's OK too. Teach them well.' Then he added, 'As you know, most of our losses are on the first five missions. We should cut those losses with an experienced pilot aboard.' I was so happy to be a first pilot that I didn't even think about having to fly with inexperienced crews all the time. I thought about it many times later.

"Slowly I was getting my missions in, over France, Germany, Holland, even up to Norway. They were all tough; some tougher than others. In those days in England you had to fly 25 missions to complete a tour of duty. I had been looking at that magic number for months.

"April 24, my 25th mission. This was the sixth crew I had trained and my second time out with them. They were about ready to go on their own under their pilot, Bob Brown. The target for the day was an airfield and manufacturing plant in Oberpfaffenhofen, a suburb of Munich.

"We were leading the low squadron that day with Colonel Dale O. Smith leading the group and the wing, which consisted of three groups. The high squadron in our group was led by Bud MacKichan, who was married to a girl from Saginaw, Michigan, where my parents lived. Bud's wife and my mother had become friends.

"The take-off was normal, but shortly after beginning our climb to altitude we lost the supercharger on one of the engines and as a result my low squadron began to lag behind the group. Colonel Smith radioed to close it up, but I just couldn't do that while climbing. I thought that once I reached altitude we'd be all right and I could close up then. During this time I began to think about aborting the mission, something I had never done as a first pilot. I had had enough of those as a co-pilot. Also, I had five planes flying formation on me and they were all inexperienced pilots with very few missions. I probably should have aborted, but I didn't. We finally got to bombing altitude and, little by little, we were closing in. I could see Paris far below and to the south of us. It was a perfect spring day, not an enemy fighter in sight and our own escort of Mustangs and Thunderbolts all around us.

"Suddenly the sky below was filled with little black puffs, those innocent-looking little clouds were anti-aircraft shells exploding just beneath our group. A few seconds later the Germans found our range and the puffs were all around us. Just then our B-17 lurched and I knew we had been hit. I looked around and the back of the cockpit was on fire. This had happened to me on a previous mission and I had been able to put it out, so I told Brown to take over and I would go back and try to put out the fire. No luck this time, so I rang the alarm and told the crew to bail out, grabbed Brown by the arm and said, 'Let's go.' The bombardier and the navigator already had the forward escape hatch open and were waiting for my signal. A thumbs-down sign did it and the four of us were out and away.

"When we were lectured on how to parachute, three things were stressed. Number one:'free fall' as long as possible so the enemy fighters can't follow you down and shoot you. Number two: free fall so that the ground forces can't follow you down and be there to meet you as you land, and

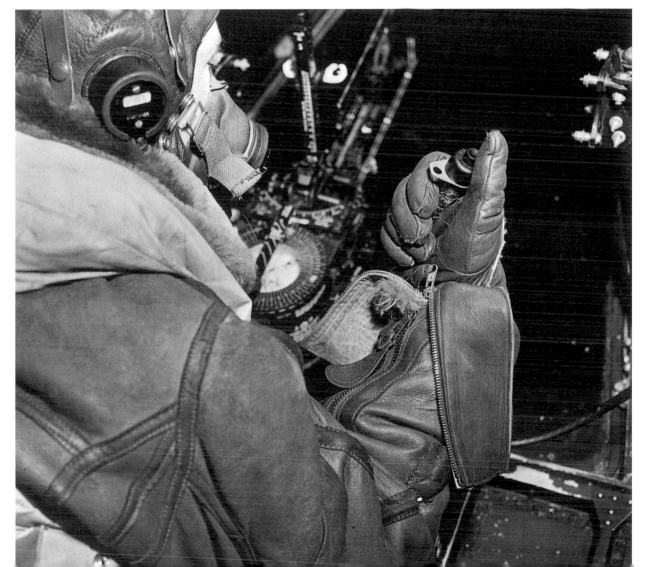

If I were fierce, and bald, and short of breath, / I'd live with scarlet Majors at the Base, And speed glum heroes up the line to death. / You'd see me with my puffy petulant face, / Guzzling and gulping in the best hotel, / Reading the Roll of Honour. 'Poor young chap,' / I'd say – 'I used to know his father well; / Yes, we've lost heavily in this last scrap.' / And when the war is done and youth stone dead, / I'd toddle safely home and die – in bed.
– 'Base Details'
by Siegfried Sassoon

Above: Wellington pilot Nick Kosciuk was one of the Polish Air Force airmen to fly with the RAF in World War II. Above left: An RAF Lancaster wireless operator and below left, a Lancaster bomb aimer.

Right: A memorial to the men of the 34th Bomb Group (H), Eighth USAAF, who flew from Mendlesham airfield in World War II. Below: The shoulder patch of the Eighth USAAF on a dark olive WWII uniform shirt.

number three: save the ripcord ring as a souvenir. The first and second, I did, the third I didn't. When the 'chute opened, and I thought it never would, it gave me a hell of a jerk. I realized I hadn't tightened my leg straps enough and they were really cutting into me. I would lift one leg at a time to relieve the pressure which helped, but in the meantime I was swinging back and forth and starting to get airsick. I couldn't see any other parachutes in the sky no matter where I looked, but I thought that Bud MacKichan must have seen what happened and would be able, through his wife, to tell my family that the plane didn't explode, that he had seen parachutes and that I probably would be OK. That report never got home, however. Bud was killed a few minutes later."

Forty–three years after the end of World War II, a group of 305th Bomb Group veterans and their wives went on a kind of pilgrimage to England, a sentimental journey to the Northamptonshire airfield where the vets' old outfit had been stationed during the war. Most of the men were in their late 60s or early 70s. For most, their working lives were behind them, their children long since grown with familes of their own.

In the States, they gathered annually to renew acquaintances, retell their war stories and raise a glass or two to comrades who never came home from their war. Now they returned to Chelveston, scene of what for most of them had been the greatest adventure of their lives. From its runways, now back to grazing land, they had flown their 25 or 30–mission tours of duty, bringing loads of high explosive and incendiary bombs by B-17 Flying Fortress to dozens of targets in Germany and German–occupied Europe. Their mission memories, filed away for all the intervening years, now stirred and came to the fore. They were driven in a fleet of meticulously restored World War II jeeps, trucks, weapons carriers and an ambulance, all carefully maintained by a group of English WWII enthusiast collectors, to the old airfield.

They entered at the place where the main gate, Military Post, and Group Headquarters had once stood. This was the base of the 'Can Do' boys; a group that produced two Congressional Medal of Honor winners and earned two Distinguished Unit Citations by its last combat mission of the war, 25 April 1945.

Brigadier General Brian Gunderson, USAF (Ret), once a B-17 navigator at Chelveston, remembers: "A strange feeling overtook most of us. Regardless of what we had hoped or expected to find there, the shock of seeing only one large hangar, and the old, crumbling runways, perimeter track and aircraft hardstand, which had lost the battle to weeds and grass pushing up through the cracks, was very real and almost devastating.

"As we approached the hangar, we noticed a large WWII engineering chart of the airfield posted on one of the doors. Someone had carefully identified and marked all the important sites, such as the squadron living areas, Officers, NCO and Service clubs, the PX, theatre, HQs, main gate, hangars, squadron operations and maintenance buildings, the flight line, control tower, bomb dump, etc. Suddenly, everyone began talking at once; the map had hit a nerve in the memory chain of each returnee. They remembered where they had lived and worked while at Chelveston and they wanted to see the old locations even if there was nothing there but a mossy green grazing ground for cattle and sheep. We raced for the jeeps and trucks to start a tour of the old airfield. For us Chelveston had suddenly come alive again.

"The jeeps and trucks split up to take small parties to their particular squadron areas, and we began thinking about life in the Nissen huts. Those huts, built as living quarters, had been sixteen feet wide, with a maximum height of eight feet and a length of between 24 and 30 feet, with a slab of concrete for a floor. At Chelveston both officers and enlisted men lived in them, and the enlisted quarters were definitely overcrowded. Double–deck bunks were used as opposed to the single cots for the officers. The mattresses were three–piece affairs, each section called a 'biscuit.' They were filled with excelsior, a very uncomfortable base on which to get much–needed sleep. The hut was heated by a small, coal–burning stove in the middle of the room. It generated only enough heat to keep those within five feet of it comfortably warm. Those unlucky enough to live at the ends of the hut often had to sleep with their clothes on and their overcoats on top of their blankets to survive the damp, chilly nights. Coal was rationed and unless you used it carefully, the fire would go out before dawn. The practice of 'midnight requisitioning' from the coal yard was honed to a high art. The latrines, showers and washstands were located in a building in the middle of several Nissen huts, and the frequent lack of hot water made such visits torture. Pity the poor enlisted men who lived in the more crowded huts where the cold, damp air mixed with the smell of bodies, sweaty clothing and stale cigarettes made life all but unbearable.

"As we toured the living site someone mentioned the mess hall and the jokes started about powdered eggs, whose texture and eatability depended so much on the expertise of the cook. We recalled the chalky–flavoured powdered milk and the ever–present Spam, and I remembered my evening meal the day I arrived at the base, Spam coated with a solution made of powdered eggs. In those days Spam was known as 'ham that had failed its physical.'

"Someone remembered how going to the club or taking a 'liberty run' to a nearby town were the only ways to escape the depressing boredom, loneliness and cold of life in the Nissen huts. Some went to drown their sorrows and fears, to relax and forget for a few hours. Once a month, usually on a Saturday night, dances were held in the clubs. There were female officers and WAC enlisted

TO THE AMERICAN AIRME
OF THE '34TH', WHO, IN VALO
GAVE THEIR LIVES TO THE VICTO
THAT MADE REAL THE CHALLEN
FOR WORLD PEACE AND UNI

4TH HEAVY BOMBARDMENT GROUP
NIT   OF THE UNITED STATES
EIGHTH AIR FORCE
IN WORLD WAR II,
APRIL, 1944 TO JUNE, 1945
MENDLESHAM AERO
DROME, SUFFOLK

"For our dances at the officers' club, we arranged for local girls to be picked up at the Red Cross office in town. It went well for a while until the townspeople complained. They couldn't understand how it was that while we sent ten trucks in to town to pick up these lovely English girls, only three or four trucks returned after the dance. Finally, our commander issued a memo: ALL GIRLS PICKED UP FOR SATURDAY DANCES MUST BE OFF THE PREMISES BY THE FOLLOWING WEDNESDAY!"
— Sam Young, formerly with the 452nd Bomb Group (H), Eighth USAAF

Left: A B-24 Liberator about to take off for the United States in June 1945, one month after the end of the war in Europe. The residents of a nearby Norfolk, England village turn out to witness the departure of some of "their Yanks" who have been flying missions from the local air base for the past three years.

Below: Technical Sergeant Lawrence Cuthiel aboard an engine of *Son of Satan*, a Ninth USAAF Martin B-26 medium bomber. Right: The crew of *Piccadilly Lilly II*, a 100th Bomb Group (H), Eighth USAAF B-17G Flying Fortress, photographed at their Thorpe Abbotts, Norfolk base on 27 January 1944. The 100th flew its first WWII mission on 25 June 1943 and its last on 20 April 1945. The mission total for the group was 306, including six food drops for the people of the Netherlands. The average combat life of a B-17 in the ETO was 11 missions. The 100th lost 177 B-17s in combat and 52 in additonal operational losses.

women, as well as nurses and Red Cross girls, but they were all vastly outnumbered by the men, and English girls were bussed in from the nearby cities, towns and villages. So at least one evening a month, the clubs came alive and everyone forgot their worries and fears. On paydays the clubs turned into casinos with poker and crap games thriving. A guy could lose all his money or make a small fortune, just like that.

"We turned toward the flight line and the conversation turned to that odd phenomenon most of us had experienced when, in moments of extreme danger, we had somehow felt quite indestructible. Maybe it was our youthful naïvety making it possible for us to ignore the realities of the situation. It was only after the mission, when we had returned to the base and lay exhausted in our huts, staring at the ceiling and replaying in slow motion the frantic moments we had endured a few hours earlier, that we'd begin to shudder and feel the fear and panic.

"After our tour of the airfield, we regathered by the big hangar and boarded our buses. Several of the group managed to talk their driver into making a stop at their favourite wartime pub, The Chequers, where they kept the now—energized conversation going over several ales.

"For those of us who had survived the war and had returned to Chelveston these many years later, there was a special poignancy about our memories and about this day. Many realized that this would be their last visit to where so much had happened to change their lives in a brief period long ago. Why had we come? Were we just incurable romantics who loved to live in the past? Had we felt some sort of reawakening and wanted to recapture the excitement of days long gone? Did we really think that after drifting through the years with blurring memories we could come back here and 'relive history' for one brief moment? Whatever our reasons, we were all glad that we had returned for one last look."

HOW WELL have bomber aircraft been employed in the many conflicts since World War I? How effective have campaigns such as the Combined Bombing Offensive against Germany in World War II been, and in what measure did aerial bombing actually contribute to ultimate victory in that and the other wars of the twentieth century?

Throughout World War I bombing was fascinating to the participants as a concept, but in practice it was not particularly effective. Many attempts were made by the air arms of the combatants to strike decisively at their enemy through aerial bombardment, but nearly all such efforts fell short of acknowledged victory in battle. The relatively fragile and underpowered aircraft of the time were simply incapable of the energy and the bomb–carrying capacity needed to make a significant impact on their targets. With the exception of the effective attacks aimed at destroying enemy aircraft sitting at their aerodromes, and thus ensuring at least temporary control of the air–space above a battle zone, little was actually achieved by the majority of airmen operating in the pure bombing role.

Bombing did, however, make a powerful psychological contribution to the efforts of the First War combatants. Stark visions of terror bombing in the years to come raised the level of fear in world capitals and many military leaders correctly predicted horrific future raids.

In World War I, the most effective bombing was done by tactical aircraft. Relatively light, small and fast, these machines proved the most successful in support of their ground forces in the battle zones.

While it is true that the bomber was born in World War I, and that its development and evolution gathered momentum in that conflict, so too were its vulnerabilities then identified and exploited. Progress in the development of fighter aircraft and in anti–aircraft defences was equally impressive. Probably the most interesting portents of the bomber's role in future wars, though, were the early indications that it would be of greatest effect when applied against enemy airfields and other targets relating to the suppression of enemy air power and the control of enemy airspace. Where the planners seem to have erred repeatedly since 1914 is in their assumption that saturation attacks on essentially civilian targets would be as effective as hitting industrial, supply or communications targets, or enemy airfields. Most evidence to date suggests that bombing civilians invariably fails to destroy their collective morale. Nearly all nations who have mounted significant campaigns of aerial bombardment in all conflicts since World War I have discovered, but failed to learn, that bombing civilians actually tends to harden their resolve.

The Spanish Civil War in 1936 revealed what Germany would soon bring to the air action of World War II. When Nationalist General Francisco Franco requested assistance from Adolf Hitler in the form of Ju 52 transport planes, the German leader not only complied, sending twenty, but also supplied crews to operate and maintain them, as well as reinforcements. In August of that year, he provided the first elements of the Kondor Legion, a force made up of a bomber and fighter *gruppe*, a reconnaissance *staffel*, three air signals units and a marine *gruppe*. Kondor was initially led by GeneralMajor Hugo Sperrle, who was later to command Luftflotte 3 in the Battle of Britain. The Kondor Legion was relatively ineffective until the summer of 1937 when it was re–equipped with the newest Me 109B fighters and the Dornier Do 17 and Heinkel He 111 bombers. Spain became the test bed for the new German bombers as well as the 109. Their strengths and deficiencies were quickly spotlighted and several important tactics were devised in this period. The Heinkel, in particular, performed well, hinting at somewhat more promise than it would actually deliver in the greater war to come.

To their dismay, the Germans found that they

RESULTS

Left: Ruins at Kaiserlautern, Germany where repeated heavy attacks on bridges and rail marshalling yards by Eighth USAAF bombers and medium bombers of the Ninth USAAF contributed significantly to halting the German offensive in the Ardennes in December 1944.

Above: An electrical rheostat used in bombers of the US Army Air Forces in World War II. Right: North American B-25 bombers in the airplane graveyard at Davis–Monthan AFB in 1968. D–M has long been the repository for US military aircraft deemed surplus to current service requirements. Many planes there are cocooned and preserved for future re–use. Others are sold to friendly foreign governments, and some are chopped up and smelted to re–claim the metals.

had committed one of the major errors of World War II in an early stage of the Battle of Britain in August 1940. They suddenly relented after a week of bombing Royal Air Force fighter airfields that were key to the defence of the UK. Instead of continuing to pound these vital bases, they turned their attention to essentially civilian targets and in so doing allowed the RAF precious time to regroup, repair and recharge itself for the rounds to come.

In the period between the two great world wars, opportunities for testing new and improved bomber types, including the Junkers Ju 86 and the Heinkel He 111, came for Germany with the Spanish Civil War. That war exposed dramatic deficiencies in both German aircraft. In the far east the Sino–Japanese war, which broke out in 1937, afforded the Army Air Force of Japan the chance to put their new Mitsubishi Ki-30 and Kawasaki Ki-32 single–engine monoplane bombers to the test. These machines, together with the Mitsubishi Ki-21, and the Mitsubishi G3M (built for the Japanese Naval Air Force) were used in a series of highly effective attacks against Chinese airfields in which most of China's military aircraft were destroyed. They were considerably less successful, however, in 1939 when they went up against the Soviet Union and a multitude of Russian fighters.

Meanwhile, design and testing of a range of new bombers for the French Air Force, including the Breguet 693-AB2, the CAO 700, the Potez 63-II, the Bloch 174 A3 and the LeO 451, many of them showing promise in their early development, was largely to no avail. By the time they were operational, they were obsolete.

Italy proved to be a significant player, fielding three bombers of impressive quality and performance, all of them emanating from the mid–1930s. Undoubtedly the best of these was one that emerged from its earlier airliner origins to become a superb land–based bomber, the Savoia–Marchetti SM 79. Built mainly of wood and powered by three

750 hp Alfa Romeo engines, this 267 mph lightweight was able to deliver a 2750–pound bomb load over a range of 1180 miles with a service ceiling of more than 21,000 feet. It proved extremely effective in the Mediterranean, the Balkans and North Africa. Additionally, the Italians produced significant machines in the twin–engined Fiat BR 20 and the somewhat shorter–lived Savoia–Marchetti SM 81, the latter operating successfully in both the Ethiopian campaign and the Spanish Civil War.

The two best Russian bombers of World War II were the long–range Ilyushin Il-4 and the Petlyakov PE series beginning with the Pe-2 tactical bomber. The Pe-2 was an outstanding combat aircraft originally planned as a fighter. It was adapted as a high–altitude bomber which, like the De Havilland Mosquito, evolved through many refinements and, with its clean aerodynamic design, was always fast enough to be difficult for the German fighters to intercept. Speed was its great asset and Russian Hurricanes, flying in the escort role for the Pe-2s, were frequently unable to keep up with them. The Pe-2 was easily one of the most effective, efficient and high–achieving weapons on the Eastern Front.

The other principal bomber aircraft of World War II and the developmental periods before and since have been considered in the earlier chapter, *Delivery Systems*.

Ethical and political issues aside, the argument over the effectiveness of aerial bombardment in war rages on. The most devout advocates of aerial bombing insist that air power alone, properly directed and utilized, can achieve victory. At the other extreme are those who feel that bombing per se, even highly precise bombing of the most legitimate targets, is prohibitively expensive in all ways. They believe that in the end it accomplishes very little and that ground and sea forces are the only real means to a win. While it may be a stretch

Right: Devastation wrought by Allied bombing attacks on the rail centre at Neustadt, Germany in February 1945.
Below: The wreckage of twin–engined Me 262 jet fighters in the shattered Messerschmitt assembly plant at Obertraubling, Germany after raids by B-17s and B-24s of the Eighth Air Force on 21 July 1944.

to suggest that bombing alone actually won World War II, it is demonstrable that the delivery of two atomic bombs on Japan by American B-29s in August 1945 certainly ended it.

Statistically, RAF Bomber Command's bombing accuracy progressed during World War II from the early days through late 1941 when, using as a measure bombs striking within three miles of their aiming point, accuracy had risen from almost nil to 16 per cent. It actually increased to 96 per cent by late 1944.

Two significant surveys were launched near the end of, and just after World War II, to establish the effects, statistically and in real terms, of the Allied bombing offensive against Germany. The Americans set up the US Strategic Bombing Survey in November 1944 to begin to assess the results of their bombing campaign. By the end of the war in Europe, the USSBS employed some 500 military enlisted men, 350 officers and 350 civilians who represented a range of disciplines. The British Bombing Survey Unit was administered by the Royal Air Force and was comprised of personnel from the RAF, the British Army and the Royal Navy, as well as civil servants and civilians from business and industry.

Both the American and British survey units were viewed with some suspicion and mistrust by some in high places within the American Air Force and the British Air Ministry. In both cases, direct and indirect attempts were made to influence the results in the reports of these survey units.

The work of the US survey team, and the publication of more than 60 reports (of more than 200 prepared) went on through the spring of 1947. It involved the responses to questionnaires given to some 8000 industrial managers in fifty German cities, along with interviews of local and central Government officials, as well as extensive field research in several key locales. According to Norman Longmate in his fine book *The Bombers*: "Every possible aspect of the effect of bombing

was studied, from the suicide rate — people killed themselves just as frequently in the lightly–bombed areas as in the devastated places — to the effect of religious and political background on attitudes to the war. 'The more actively religious cities . . . had a lower war morale', it appeared, than the more godless districts, while the largest 'incidence of voluntary participation in war activities and . . . the smallest number of people ready to accept unconditional surrender' was in the North Central Region, containing Hamburg and Bremen, which had been more badly bombed than anywhere else in Germany."

Longmate continued: "The immensely thorough US survey bore out to a remarkable degree the conclusions of the British team: 'The major cities of Germany present a spectacle of destruction so appalling as to suggest a complete breakdown of all aspects of urban activity. In the first impression it would appear that the area attacks which laid waste these cities must have substantially eliminated the industrial capacity of Germany. Yet this was not the case. The attacks did not so reduce German war production as to have a decisive effect on the outcome of the war.' " The British survey report further stated: "The effects of town area attacks on the morale of the German people were, with the exception of one estimate, very much over–estimated by all other ministries and departments throughout the course of the war . . . There is no evidence that they caused any serious break in the morale of the populations as a whole." From a report of the US survey: "Bomb damage to the civilian economy was not a proximate cause of the military collapse of Germany. There is no evidence that shortages of civilian goods reached a point where the German authorities were forced to transfer resources from war production in order to prevent disintegration of the home front." In its final conclusion statement, however, the US Strategic Bombing Survey report stated: "Allied air power was decisive

The real importance of the air war consisted in the fact that it opened a second front long before the invasion of Europe. That front was the skies over Germany. The fleets of bombers might appear at any time over any large German city or important factory. The unpredictability of the attacks made this front gigantic; every square metre of the territory we controlled was a kind of front line. Defence against air attacks required the production of thousands of anti-aircraft guns, the stockpiling of tremendous quantities of ammunition all over the country, and holding in readiness hundreds of thousands of soldiers, who in addition had to stay in position by their guns, often totally inactive, for months at a time. As far as I can judge from the accounts I have read, no one has yet seen that this was the greatest lost battle on the German side. The losses from the retreats in Russia or from the surrender of Stalingrad were considerably less. Moreover, the nearly 20,000 anti-aircraft guns stationed in the homeland could almost have doubled the anti-tank defences on the Eastern Front.
— from *Spandau: The Secret Diaries* by Albert Speer

Below: RAF wireless operator/air gunner Douglas Radcliffe with his mother in 1942. Radcliffe served with No. 142 Squadron at RAF Waltham. Right: The charred and battered tower of the church of St. Nicholai in Hamburg. The ruined church is preserved as a war memorial.

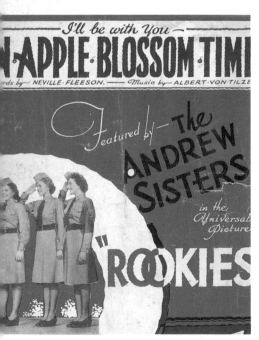

in the war in western Europe. Hindsight inevitably suggests that it might have been employed differently or better in some respects. Nevertheless, it was decisive. In the air, its victory was complete; at sea, its contribution, combined with naval power, brought an end to the enemy's greatest naval threat — the U-boat; on land, it helped turn the tide overwhelmingly in favour of Allied ground forces. Its power and superiority made possible the success of the invasion. It brought the economy which sustained the enemy's armed forces to virtual collapse, although the full effects of this collapse had not reached the enemy's front lines when they were over–run by Allied forces. It brought home to the German people the full impact of modern war with all its horror and suffering. Its imprint on the German nations will be lasting."

Longmate: "The decisive facts came from the show–place of area bombing, Hamburg. The 1943 raids left 'more than 750,000 homeless . . . At the end of 1943 there was still a backlog of 80,000 unfilled requests for housing. Of the 81,000 industrial and commercial buildings in the city . . . more than 48 per cent were completely destroyed.' But though production dropped by 50 per cent in August, it was back to 82 per cent of normal by December. 75,000 of the industrial labour force of 250,000 had 'failed to return to work' by then but 'war industries were least affected and later transfers of workers from non–essential plants . . . were generally sufficient to offset the slight shortage which did exist'. All Bomber Command's most destructive operations had achieved was 'a loss of 1.8 months of the city's industrial production, about half of which was intended for the German armed forces'. The Americans' main conclusion was the same as that already reached by the British: 'Although attacks against city areas resulted in an overall production loss estimated at roughly 9 per cent in 1943 and perhaps as much as 17 per cent in 1944 this loss did not have a decisive effect upon the ability of the German nation to produce war material . . .The direct loss imposed was of a kind which could be absorbed by sectors of the German economy not essential to war production, while the indirect loss fell on industries easily able to bear the burden'."

In their impressive historical volumes *The Army Air Forces in World War II* Wesley F. Craven and James L. Cate state: "The air offensive against German oil production was the pride of the US Strategic Air Forces. Initiated through the insistence of its officers, effective immediately, and decisive within less than a year, this campaign proved to be a clear–cut illustration of strategic air war doctrine. In April 1944, Germany possessed barely adequate supplies of crude oil and was producing a growing volume of synthetic oil. In the following year the Eighth Air Force aimed 70,000 tons, the Fifteenth Air Force 60,000 tons, and RAF Bomber Command 90,000 tons at oil targets. By April 1945, when Germany was being over–run by the ground forces, her oil production was 5 per cent of the pre-attack figure. She had been starved of oil, as her captured commanders and officials testified, often with genuine emotion, for the last year of the war. Her air force seldom flew after the first concentrated attacks on synthetic oil plants, which produced aviation gasoline. Tanks and trucks had to be abandoned. Toward the last, even the most august Nazis in the hierarchy were unable to find gasoline for their limousines. Germany's industries were badly crippled, and an enormous amount of effort was absorbed in the furious attempt to defend and rebuild oil installations. The Allied oil offensive had been quite as devastating as [General] Spaatz had predicted in March 1944, but it had taken longer than he and the British had expected to produce collapse. The Germans, never easily beaten, used passive and ground defences skilfully in protecting their oil producers, and they reconstructed their bombed plants faster than the Americans anticipated. Nevertheless, the offensive had gone on as first priority until the desired results were attained."

On morale, the US survey went on to state: "Continuous heavy bombing of the same communities soon led to diminishing returns in morale effects. The morale in towns subjected to the heaviest bombing was not worse than in towns of the same size receiving much lighter bomb loads. War production is the critical measuring rod of the effects of lowered morale in the German war effort. Allied bombing widely and seriously depressed German morale, but depressed and discouraged workers were not necessarily unproductive workers . . . Armaments production continued to mount till mid–1944, in spite of declining civilian morale, but from that point on, arms production began to decline and dropped every month thereafter at an increasing rate."

In conclusion, the British Bombing Survey Unit report stated: "Three major factors were associated in Germany's defeat. The first and most obvious was the over–running of her territory by the armies of the Allies. The second was the breakdown of her war industry, which was mainly a consequence of the bombing of her communications system. The third was the drying–up of her resources of liquid fuel, and the disruption of her chemical industry, which resulted from the bombing of synthetic–oil plants and refineries . . . If none of these factors had operated, another less decisive, but nevertheless potential war–winning event was looming on the horizon — the damage to the Ruhr steel plants, which would have shown itself in a decline in the output of armaments in the second half of 1945."

Of the bombing campaign against Germany, Sir Arthur Harris said in his memoirs: "If we had had the force we used in 1944 a year earlier, and if we had then been allowed to use it together with the whole American bomber force and without interruption, Germany would have been defeated outright by bombing as Japan was . . . The Allied

war leaders did not have enough faith in strategic bombing . . . We were always being diverted from the main offensive by the demands of other services . . . Without these diversions . . . there would have been no need for the invasion." And in Nazi wartime Minister of Armaments Albert Speer's view: "The real success of the bombing of the Royal Air Force is in fact that you succeeded in tying up tremendous forces. Those forces, if they had been free, would have caused great damage to the Russians. I doubt if with them [in action] the Russians would have succeeded in their offensive at all. We had to pile ammunition everywhere, because we never knew where the attacks would take place. We were forced to increase the production of ammunition of the anti–aircraft guns larger than 8.8 centimetres in 1940 to 1944 by 70 million rounds. And this was much more than we could produce for the anti–tank guns, which we could provide only with 45 million rounds. You had a second front already from the beginning of 1944 and this second front was really very effective."

In his excellent book *Bomber Command*, on the RAF bombing campaign against Germany in World War II, Max Hastings takes the view that: "Beyond any doubts, the area offensive punished Germany terribly. It destroyed centuries of construction and of culture, the homes and property of Germans who for the first time experienced the cost of Nazism. At the end of 1942 Göring had said: 'We will have reason to be glad if Germany can keep the boundaries of 1933 after the war.' By the end of 1943 production in every critical area of war industry — tanks, U boats, guns, aircraft — was still expanding at a gigantic rate. But it had become apparent to the German people that they were beyond the hope of mercy. After three years of terrible sacrifice, this was the principal achievement of Bomber Command." Hastings further states: "The two great achievements of the Allied strategic air offensive must be conceded to the Americans:

In peace there's nothing so becomes a man / As modest stillness and humility: / But when the blast of war blows in our ears, / Then imitate the action of the tiger.
– from *Henry V, III, I* by William Shakespeare

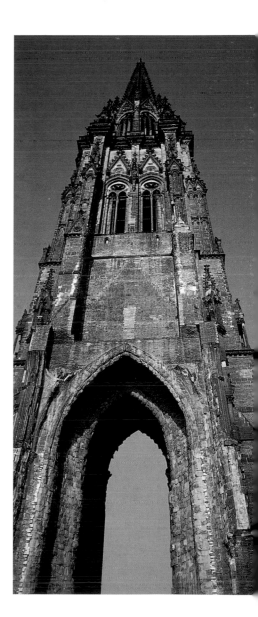

the defeat of the Luftwaffe by the Mustang escort-fighter, and the inception of the deadly oil offensive."

Albert Speer: "In the burning and devastated cities we daily experienced the direct impact of the war. It spurred us to do our utmost. Neither did the bombings and the hardships that resulted from them weaken the morale of the populace. On the contrary, from my visits to armament plants and my contacts with the man in the street, I carried away the impression of growing toughness." Speer was amazed by what he referred to as "the inconsistency of the Allied air attack" (in ironic similarity to that of the German bombing attacks during the Battle of Britain). He believed that "the vast but pointless area bombing had achieved no important effect on the German war effort by 1944." Referring to the American attacks on the ball-bearing works at Schweinfurt, and the combined raids on Hamburg, he was astonished by the failure of the Allied bomber forces to return to these and other targets of such great importance... "at intervals the bombers had stumbled on a blind spot, a genuine Achilles' heel, only to turn aside and divert their attack elsewhere when they had done so." Considered by many to be the most valuable German source on the effects of the strategic bombing, Speer stated emphatically that, in his opinion, such bombing could have won the war without a land invasion. Other notable Germans offered comment and opinion at war's end. Colonel General Alfred Jodl stated that the winning of air superiority altogether decided the war and that strategic bombing was the most decisive factor. Field Marshal Wilhelm Keitel gave credit to the Allied air forces for the victories in the west, and Reichsmarshall Hermann Göring told USAAF Generals Carl Spaatz and Hoyt Vandenberg that the Allied selection of targets had been excellent and that American precision daylight bombing had been more effective than the night raids. Grand Admiral Karl Dönitz said that the air

power of the Allies was the decisive element in the failure of the Nazi submarine war, and Field Marshal Gerd von Rundstedt ranked Allied air power first among several ingredients in the triumph of the United Nations.

The cost of the Allied bombing offensive against Germany and German–occupied target areas in pounds sterling and in dollars is all but impossible to calculate, there being so many variables and indirect expenditures involved. The cost in lives of airmen alone: 47,268 RAF Bomber Command aircrew were killed on operations or died in captivity, the total rising to 55,573 when it includes those airmen killed in accidents. In addition, 8403 airmen were wounded and 9784 became prisoners of war. RAF Bomber Command lost a total of 10,724 aircraft, of which 6931 were heavy bombers. It dropped a total of 954,958 tons of bombs on enemy targets in Europe between September 1939 and May 1945.

44,472 aircrew of the American Eighth Army Air Force were killed in the air war. The Eighth lost 8857 aircraft, of which 5857 were heavy bombers, most of the rest being fighter escorts. It destroyed 9472 enemy aircraft and dropped a total of 726,923 tons of bombs on German targets. Operating from bases in Italy, the American Fifteenth Army Air Force suffered 2703 aircrew killed, 12,359 missing in action or captured and 2553 wounded. It lost nearly 3400 aircraft and destroyed 1946 enemy aircraft. The Fifteenth dropped a total of 303,842 tons of bombs on enemy targets in twelve countries. A total of more than 100,000 Allied aircrew involved in the bombing offensive against Germany lost their lives. The raids on German cities killed upwards of 305,000 people and seriously injured 780,000. More than 25,000,000 Germans experienced the terror of the bombing.

Between the summer of 1940 and the end of the war, the German Air Force dropped a total of 74,172 tons of bombs on the United Kingdom.

In the bombing campaign against Japan, between

Left: The results of a major American attack on German synthetic oil production facilities at Misburg, Germany in early March 1945. Shown is the hugely cratered plant and oil storage farm.

On the question of pyrotechnics, one might imagine that the situation was simple. I would therefore like to explain to those who had not had the pleasure of bombing Germany, that the enemy went to extreme lengths to divert the fall of bombs from the proper targets on to spots which were more attractive from his point of view. This was done in a number of different ways. Both before and after the advent of the Pathfinder Force, one of the most common customs was to create a target area adequately surrounded by defences and searchlights, and to let off dummy incendiaries, like our own, on the ground, so as to look as if there was a town being bombed and defended. Many a crew would drop their bombs into the middle of it all, fondly believing that they were giving the real target a real pounding. Unfortunately, all too frequently this was simply a dummy town — in the open fields. The realistic nature of these dummies was quite staggering, and it is no reflection that many crews were caught by them. With the advent of Pathfinders we expected that the enemy would try to copy the markers which we used. Illumination, useful in opening attacks in good weather but useless once the smoke and dust of bombing had started, had certain advantages in the matter of identification of genuine surface landmarks. This, however, only applied to the early *continued*

Bottom: The main
Hamburg WWII flak tower
in 1945. Right: The same
structure in 1985.

Pathfinder crews, and it was quite clear that the main force had to aim at pyrotechnics of some sort. The intensity of the target indicators, which we subsequently referred to as TIs, was very great, and indeed right to the end of the war the enemy never really produced a very good copy. As we expected trouble, we arranged for all sorts of combinations and variations of colours and the like. We were prepared to use different colours for different purposes, and indeed to change colours if necessary during a raid so as to ensure the correct aiming point even if the enemy were sufficiently alert to watch and copy. In addition, the bursting of the Target Indicators was carried out by barometric fuses, usually set to burst at relatively low levels between 200 and 500 feet. This meant that there was a slight cascade onto the ground, but that the main burning period was right on the ground *continued*

June 1944 and August 1945, the American Twentieth Army Air Force dropped 178,700 tons of bombs on enemy targets and the combined efforts of the US Navy and the Fifth, Seventh and Thirteenth US Army Air Forces accounted for an additional 13,801 tons of bombs dropped on Japanese targets.

On 14 September 1944, control of the strategic bomber forces in the European Theatre of Operations was shifted to Sir Norman Bottomley, Deputy Chief of Air Staff, RAF, and General Carl Spaatz, Commander of US Army Air Forces, Europe. In a letter to Bottomley on 29 March 1945, RAF Bomber Command's Sir Arthur Harris wrote: "I have always held and still maintain that my Directive, 'the progressive destruction and dislocation of the German military, industrial and economic systems', could be carried out only by the elimination of German industrial cities and not merely by attacks on individual factories however important these might be in themselves. This view was also officially confirmed by the Air Ministry. The overwhelming evidence which is now available to support it makes it quite superfluous for me to argue at length that the destruction of those cities has fatally weakened the German war effort and is now enabling Allied soldiers to advance into the

heart of Germany with negligible casualties. I assume that the view under consideration is something like this: 'no doubt in the past we were justified in attacking German cities. But to do so was always repugnant and now that the Germans are beaten anyway we can properly abstain from proceeding with these attacks'. This is a doctrine to which I could never subscribe. Attacks on cities like any other act of war are intolerable unless they are strategically justified. But they are strategically justified in so far as they tend to shorten the war and so preserve the lives of Allied soldiers. To my mind we have absolutely no right to give them up unless it is certain that they will not have this effect. I do not personally regard the whole of the remaining cities of Germany as worth the bones of one British Grenadier."

In his memoirs of World War II, Winston Churchill wrote: "In judging the contribution to victory of strategic air power it should be remembered that this was the first war in which it was fully used. We had to learn from hard—won experience . . . But although the results of the early years fell short of our aims, we forced on the enemy an elaborate, ever—growing but finally insufficient air—defence system which absorbed a large proportion of their total war effort. Before the end, we and the United States had developed striking forces so powerful that they played a major part in the economic collapse of Germany."

It was 4 a.m., Sunday, 25 June 1950 and the weather in Korea was predicted to be fine and hot. The forces of the North Korean Army began moving south across the 38th parallel into the Republic of Korea, the start of a conflict between the two Koreas that would last until 27 July 1953.

As US Air Force General Hoyt Vandenberg put it in a report to the Congress: "The proper way to use air power is initially to stop the flow of supplies and ammunition, guns, equipment of all types, at its source." The problem, in the case of

the North Korean People's Army, was that their primary Communist sources of supply lay beyond the borders of Korea and were declared off–limits to the American strategic bomber force. Thus, the B-29s of the US Far East Bomber Command were ordered instead to attack the five major industrial centres of North Korea, which would at least have the effect of denying such direct 'local' support to the Red Korean Army.

These industrial targets, with the exception of Pyongyang, were all located on Korea's north–eastern coast. Within these large complexes lay the petroleum refineries and tank farms, the seaports, rail hubs, rail–repair, manufacturing and locomotive shops, the arsenals and armament plants for the manufacture of weapons, ammunition and vehicles, as well as the aircraft maintenance and repair facilities, chemical, aluminium and magnesium production facilities, iron and steel works, explosives plants and their principal naval bases. Also located in this same coastal region were Japanese–built dams and one of the world's major hydroelectric systems.

Yet another consideration remained on the table for the US strategic bombing planners — whether to use incendiary bombs predominantly in attacks on the key northern industrial targets. These fire–bomb raids, the bombing planners believed, would be the most efficient, economical and expeditious means of destroying both the major targets and the adjacent subsidiary facilities as well. It was not to be. The Administration in Washington was concerned that the North Korean Communists would gain propaganda capital which they would exploit on a massive scale if, in the course of such fire–raids, unnecessary civilian casualties resulted. The FEAF bombers were then prohibited from the use of incendiary munitions in their forthcoming raids on the North Korean targets. They were also ordered to fly leaflet missions notifying the civilians to leave the industrial areas before the impending US attacks.

On 10 August 1950 the attacks began with a raid on the Wonsan railway shops and oil refinery. In his determination to carry on the bombing at the specified rate of sorties and tonnage, General Emmett O'Donnell let his B-29 crews know that he would not wait around for favourable weather conditions to mount his strikes. Instead, he sent an airborne mission commander in a weather aircraft in advance of the striking force, a senior officer with authority over the method of attack. This officer would also decide if the primary target could be bombed by radar or if the bombers should be redirected to an alternate target. By these means the Americans were able to conduct the missions with a minimum of interference from the weather.

By mid–September, Lieutenant–General George Stratemeyer, Commander of Far East Air Forces, announced: "Practically all of the major military industrial targets strategically important to the enemy forces and to their war potential have now been neutralized." On 26 September the final attack of the strategic bombing campaign on the northern industrial targets was flown when eight B-29s struck the Fusen Hydroelectric Plant near Hungnam. Following this raid, Washington called a halt to the strategic attacks and ordered that the

itself. Each TI consisted of a large number of these pyrotechnic candles, ignited by the initial bursts, which meant that the fire–fighters on the ground would take a considerable time to get around to the job of putting them all out. Moreover, their burning period was relatively short anyway, and so there was no question of their being dealt with in that manner. Continuity of marking was achieved by replenishing from above.

In addition to these target indicators for ground use, we prepared something which was ridiculed and laughed at by a good many people. These were sky markers, and consisted of parachute flares of various colours throwing out stars (or not, as the case may be) so that we could mark a spot in the sky for a limited period, usually three to five minutes. I had done a few calculations on the use of such a method for blind bombing through thick cloud. These rough calculations seemed to me to indicate that the results to be achieved by such an apparently difficult method would probably prove just as effective as the slap–dash visual bombing that I had so often seen in the past. Roughly speaking, the idea was that the sky markers would be put down by a marker aircraft using Oboe or H2S, in a position so that after it had burned half its time it had drifted, in accordance with the wind found by the navigator, to the correct point through the line–of–sight of a bomber on to the aiming point, assuming that the bomb sight was set to the normal height and that the bomber was approaching the target on the correct heading. This latter point was, of course, the most difficult one to achieve, but as we hoped that the relative accuracy of the fore and aft position would be greater than normal, the error in line was, we felt, acceptable.
—from *Pathfinder* by D.C.T. Bennett

air forces of the United Nations were to be employed against tactical objectives from that date forward.

According to Robert F. Futrell of the USAF Historical Division, writing in *The United States Air Force In Korea 1950-1953*: "The FEAF Bomber Command strategic air attacks destroyed none but legitimate military targets in North Korea, and the bombing was so accurate as to do little damage to civilian installations near the industrial plants."

There followed a campaign to neutralize North Korea's airfields, utilizing the B-29s with their large bomb load capacity. These were essentially night attacks and by 1952 the North Koreans had developed a well—co—ordinated radar air—defence intercept system which effectively interferred with the bomber missions.

In general, most historians tend to conclude that the various uses of air power employed in the Korean conflict — strategically, in interdiction and in support roles, were never truly decisive. The total air combat losses of the Far East Air Forces were 139, including 78 F-86 Sabres. The total of US Navy and Marine Corps aircraft losses was 1183. The total of FEAF airmen killed was 1180; 368 were wounded and 220 became prisoners of war.

Whether you perceive it as a wind—down, a cease—fire, a settlement, a disengagement or a defeat, the key results of the Vietnam war when the Americans left it in 1973 included the fact that the North Vietnamese Army remained on the territory of South Vietnam, as committed as ever to a Communist victory. Without a further air and naval campaign by the US, the armed forces of South Vietnam were simply incapable at that point of strategic defence, and the fate of the country appeared sealed. Still, fighting continued, mainly in guerrilla and sapper activity, into 1975, ending in a decisive Spring offensive and a Communist takeover.

For seven years, beginning in 1965, US Air Force

B-52 strategic bombers were utilized in a most unconventional way: bringing and delivering millions of iron bombs in a tactical function. The giant bombers operated routinely in support of ground forces, against North Vietnamese bases and offensives, and interdicting the enemy infiltration routes into the South. Finally, in December 1972, they played their most significant role in an operation called Linebacker II in which they achieved spectacular success. The eleven days of bombing attacks against the Hanoi and Haiphong areas of North Vietnam were highly instrumental in persuading the North Vietnamese to return to the Paris peace talks which resulted in a settlement of the lengthy war in January 1973.

In the eleven days of Linebacker II, the big B-52s flew 729 sorties — 340 from U-Tapao, Thailand, and 389 from Guam. Fifteen of the bombers were lost, all to SAM missiles, and nine others were damaged. Twenty-nine crewmen were killed and thirty-three were captured and later returned. A further twenty-six were rescued in courageous post-mission efforts. The bombers struck at thirty-four separate targets, dropping 49,000 bombs with great accuracy amid determined and effective defences. Many military analysts believe that the prolonged and costly repairs to the targets damaged in this Linebacker operation significantly delayed the North Vietnamese invasion of South Vietnam in 1975.

More than eight years of American bombing in South-East Asia ended on 15 August 1973 when the US Congress halted funding for the air campaign, which had shifted in January to Laos, and then in April, to Cambodia. 2,633,000 tons of conventional bombs had been dropped in eight years and two months and 124,532 successful sorties were flown. In all B-52 operations eighteen of the bombers were lost to enemy action, and thirteen in mid-air collisions or other accidents. In the entire Vietnam and South-East Asia conflict, from January 1962 through August 1973,

the US Air Force lost 2257 aircraft to combat and operational causes. 2118 airmen were killed and 3460 were wounded. 586 were reported missing or captured. US Air Force operations in Vietnam and South-East Asia in that period cost the American tax payer $3,129,900,000. Of the B-52's contribution in that war, General William C. Westmoreland, Commander, US Military Assistance Command, Vietnam, later wrote, "The use of this weapon has won many battles and made it unnecessary to fight many more."

In the spring and early summer 1982 South Atlantic conflict, usually referred to as the Falklands War, the Argentine forces lost a total of 100 fixed-wing and helicopter aircraft, while aircraft losses of the United Kingdom numbered 34. The action, known as Operation "Corporate", saw significant contributions in the areas of low-level ground attack, reconnaissance and air interdiction on the part of RAF Harrier GR.3s, which also proved themselves to be tough against the small arms fire of the Argentine defences. Prior to the Falklands conflict, the Royal Navy's Sea Harrier had been perceived by some in the British military establishment as not really up to the tasks it was intended to perform. The airplane rose to the challenge, however, and operated in the South Atlantic with distinction. Its reliability and high state of readiness was exceptional among combat aircraft, and the level of confidence it inspired in its pilots was unparalleled.

Vulcan B.2 bombers from RAF Waddington participated in "Black Buck" sorties, mainly runway denial attacks, operating from Ascension Island during the Falklands campaign. The initial Vulcan sortie on 30 April took a load of 21 1000-pound bombs to hit the Stanley airport runway, thus beginning the six-week British air action. The attack was only marginally successful, and was followed on 3 May by another of equally unremarkable result. The big RAF bombers were

Now, there was another, and unwritten, declaration of courage in Mr. Simpson's BUSINESS AS USUAL sign. Like all the others in this small-tradesman's street (men and women who defied disaster to make them fold up and clear out), Mr. Simpson had already lost some 60 per cent of his customers. The wealthy, retired people in the neighbourhood, who had no useful reason for remaining in London, had long since gone to live in the country. The wives of men who had positions, or felt it their duty to remain, had also been shipped out, and the men were eating as far as it was possible in restaurants or their clubs. The breakage of the gas mains in the neighbourhood, too—a stoppage of some weeks—had also practically ruined the business of the butcher, who could not find many people with even an oil-stove to cook his meat. And then it was only chops.

Now, in thousands of instances, that is what a BUSINESS AS USUAL sign means in London these days. It is far more than patriotism: it is just another example of the indomitable pluck which will, one day, give this great city the slogan: "You can't beat a city that won't be beaten."
– from *Bomber's Moon*
by Negley Farson

Left: A 1944 7th Photo Group, Eighth USAAF reconnaissance photograph of a main bridge on the Rhine river at Koblenz after an Allied bombing raid.

Above: Staff Sergeant Clarence Johnson, an Eighth Air Force Liberator waist gunner in WWII. Above right: A WWII US Army Air Forces D–2 Time and Distance computer. Below right: Short Stirlings of No. 1651 Heavy Conversion Unit, stationed at RAF Waterbeach in Cambridgeshire, April 1942. Far right: The position of the bombardier in a Boeing B-29, the last US heavy bomber type to see action in World War II.

then modified to carry Shrike missiles and were redeployed to Ascencion to begin anti–radar missions. They finished up with a final raid on the Stanley airport facilities on the night of 11 June. While the results of this last attack were considered good, the overall performance of the Vulcans in the Falklands arena was not impressive.

The level of technology brought to bear on Iraq in the Gulf War, which was triggered when Saddam Hussein's Republican Guard entered Kuwait on 2 August 1990, must have been startling and unimaginable to him and his people. The ferocity of the air campaign mounted against him and his forces by the United Nations coalition was historically unprecedented.

The Gulf War may have been the most interesting proving ground for aircraft, tactics, weapons and technologies since the Spanish Civil War. The Iraqis found themselves blind–sided in attacks by the world's deadliest helicopter, the AH-64 Apache, which was turned loose on Iraqi armour with utterly devastating effect, unseen from stand–off range. For the first time, the F-117A stealth fighter/bomber appeared in combat and in 1271 sorties, all of which were flown at night from the Khamis Mushait base in Saudi Arabia, proved itself beyond any doubt. The black jets, or "ghosts" as the Iraqis called them, drew the most difficult and dangerous assignments of the conflict, attacks on heavily defended command and control targets in downtown Baghdad. They also struck at airfields, bridges, chemical and nuclear sites, and evaded the Iraqi SAM and triple–A defences so well that not a single F-117A was even damaged during the entire conflict. More than 2000 laser–guided GBU-10 and GBU-27 Paveway bombs were delivered by the stealths.

A literally ground–breaking assignment for the Royal Air Force and Royal Saudi Air Force Tornados was the dropping of runway–cratering bomblets, and anti–personnel mines to discourage the repair of the runways, thus denying Saddam facilities from which to launch aircraft against those of the coalition. Flying at a height of 180 feet, the JP-233—equipped Tornados scattered their bomblets with great effect and made a major contribution to the ultimate result for the coalition force.

US Navy A-6 Intruders and US Marine Corps F/A-18 Hornets were employed in an iron–bombing role against Iraqi railyards, airfields, bridges and a power plant, performing creditably, while French and RAF Sepecat Jaguars carried their share of ordnance to war in the coalition cause with distinction. The vital 'Scud–hunting' mission was the province of the magnificent USAF F-15E Strike Eagles. It proved how effectively they could surround the enemy missile launch units with very destructive cluster bombs, when they weren't busy taking out Iraqi bridges.

From RAF Fairford in southern England, from airfields in Egypt, Saudi Arabia and Spain, elderly B-52 Stratofortresses were once again pressed into service as the coalition's pre–eminent haulers of bomb tonnage. The huge bombers regularly brought up to 51 750–pound bombs each on their sorties from as far away as the UK, targeting the Iraqi leader's elite Republican Guard personnel in saturation attacks. The B-52s tended to operate in 'cell' units of three aircraft, dropping their combined total of 153 iron bombs silently, from a high altitude, causing maximum terror and psychological trauma among the targetted troops when the weapons arrived without warning. The effect on the morale of those on the receiving end was undoubtedly profound and resulted in many of them surrendering by the start of the ground offensive in late February 1991.

In the Gulf War coalition losses to all causes, combat, non–combat, and accident, came to 88 aircraft of various types. 106 airmen were killed; 15 were rescued; 26 were captured and later released, and 5 were missing in action.

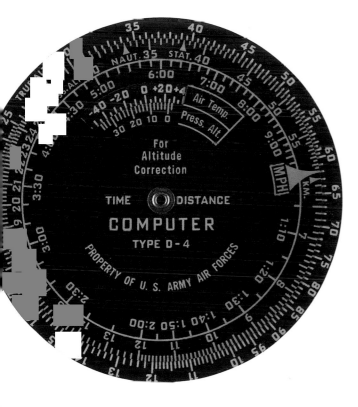

For
Altitude
Correction

TIME ⬤ DISTANCE

COMPUTER

TYPE D-4

PROPERTY OF U.S. ARMY AIR FORCES

231

The mother does knitting
The son fights the war / She
finds this quite natural the
mother / And the father what
does he do the father? He
does business / His wife does
knitting / His son the war / He
business / He finds this quite
natural the father / And the
son and the son / What does
the son find the son? / He
finds absolutely nothing the
son His mother does knitting
his father business he war
When he finishes the war
He'll go into business with his
father / The war continues the
mother continues she knits
The father continues he does
business / The son is killed he
continues no more / The
father and the mother go to
the graveyard / They find this
quite natural the father and
mother / Life continues life
with knitting war business
Business war knitting war
Business business business
Life with the graveyard.
– 'Familial'
by Jacques Prévert

Far right: B-29s of the
500th Bomb Group (VH),
Twentieth USAAF, based at
Isley Field, Saipan, unload
their incendiaries on a
Japanese target. Right:
Incendiaries rain down on
the docks of Kobe, Japan's
sixth largest city. This attack
by US B-29s took place on
5 June 1945.

Right: Boeing B-52 bombers await scrapping in 1983 at the airplane graveyard, Davis–Monthan AFB near Tucson, Arizona. Below right: B-52H bombers from the Second Bomb Wing at Barksdale AFB, Louisiana and the Fifth Bomb Wing at Minot AFB, North Dakota are shown in operation against Serbian targets in May 1999. The B-52s were based at RAF Fairford, Gloucestershire, England, along with five B-1Bs. In addition to air–launched cruise missiles, the American bombers carried the 3000–pound AGM Have Nap long–range precision–strike missiles on their nightly operations. They also struck frequently with conventional Mk 82 500–pound general–purpose bombs in their bomb bays and on underwing racks. In addition to that ordnance, some of the B-52s carried cluster bombs containing leaflets intended to convince the Serbs to quit their fight with the Kosovo Albanians.

In spring 1999 a major air campaign was conducted by the nineteen member nations of the North Atlantic Treaty Organisation. They were engaged in a series of conventional, cruise and other missile attacks on Serbian targets in the Albanian province of Kosovo and in Yugoslavia. The effort was intended to degrade and, ultimately, end the ability of the Serb leader, Slobodan Milosevic, to threaten, displace, terrorize and murder Kosovars in his programme of so–called "ethnic cleansing" in the region.

Argument raged around the world about the wisdom and morality of the NATO bombing raids, and, after 79 days of concerted attacks (the majority of the sorties were flown at night), Milosevic yielded and agreed to abandon the Serb positions within Kosovo. NATO forces began to occupy the province and several hundred thousand Kosovar refugees, who had been forced to flee their homes and villages in the wake of the Serb terror, began their journey home.

Whether or not NATO's detractors were right in their condemnation of the air campaign, whether or not some alternative approach to halting the activities of Milosevic's army and police forces might have been employed, the debate continues at the time of this writing. It seems clear, however, that the cumulative effect of the bombing campaign did, ultimately, cause the Serbs to give up.

Bombing and aerial attack may or may not be perceived as an ethical and appropriate means of warfare; it may or may not prove effective when applied in particular situations, but since the first time it was tried it has been perpetuated and has continued to evolve. It is simply a fact of warfare.

234

In 1942, when Sir Arthur Harris presented his idea for mounting a thousand–bomber raid on a German city, Winston Churchill and Chief of the Air Staff Sir Charles Portal welcomed and accepted it. Harris then had the problem of actually assembling that enormous bomber force for use on such a mission. RAF Bomber Command had at the time barely 400 front–line bombers with experienced crews. To these Harris added aircraft from conversion and training units, as well as from Coastal Command and Flying Training Command. Utilizing the then–new "bomber stream" procedure, with the application of the Gee system for navigational aid, he designed a plan for the giant raid that would become a pattern for Bomber Command raids for the rest of the war. Key to the plan was the ability to get the entire bomber stream across the target city in a mere 90 minutes, in order to minimize exposure to enemy flak and fighter defences, and to concentrate the pattern of incendiary bombs in the shortest time span possible, for maximum effect. The effort was complicated when the Royal Navy denied the participation of the Coastal Command aircraft. This meant that Harris had to reach deeper into his training units and, in the end, 49 aircraft participating in the raid were flown by student pilots. In late May the plan and the force were ready and on 30 May Harris selected Cologne as the target for that night. A total of 1047 aircraft participated including 602 Wellingtons, 131 Halifaxes, 88 Stirlings, 79 Hampdens, 73 Lancasters, 46 Manchesters and 28 Whitleys. Of these, the Night Bombing records of Bomber Command *continued*

Picture Credits Photographs by Philip Kaplan are credited: PK. Photographs from the author's collections are credited: AC. Photographs from the United States National Archives and Records Administration are credited: NARA. Jacket front: NARA; jacket back: Imperial War Museum. Jacket back flap: Margaret Kaplan. Front and back endsheets: AC. P2: NARA, PP4-5: AC, P6: AC, P8: AC, PP8-9: NARA, P11 top: PK, P11: NARA, P12 top left: NARA, P12 top right: AC, P12 bottom: AC, P14 both: AC, P15: NARA, P16: PK, P17 right: courtesy R. F. Cooper, P18: AC, P19 top both: AC, P19 bottom left: AC, P19: bottom right: courtesy Jack Woods, P20 top: AC, P20 bottom: courtesy Paul Connelly, P22: PK, P23 both: courtesy Dave Hill, P24: USAF Museum, P26 both: courtesy Dave Hill, P27: courtesy Merle Olmsted, P28: NARA, P31 all: courtesy R.D. Cooling, P32: AC, P34 top: courtesy R.D. Cooling, P34 bottom: AC, P36: NARA, P38: courtesy Brian Gunderson, P39 top left: courtesy R.D. Cooling, P39 top right: PK, P39 bottom: courtesy Brian Gunderson, P41: USAF, P42 all: NARA, P43: AC, P44: courtesy Quentin Bland, P45: Toni Frissell–Library of Congress, P46 top left: courtesy Sam Young, P46 all colour: PK, P47 both: PK, P48: NARA, P50: PK, P51: PK, PP52-53: AC P54 both: PK, P55 all: PK, P56: Mark Brown–USAF Academy, P58 both: RAF Museum, P60: courtesy Nick Brown, P61 top: courtesy Jonathan Falconer, P61 bottom: AC, P62: courtesy Michael O'Leary, P63 both: PK, P64: AC, P66: AC, P69: USAF, P70: PK, P72 centre and bottom: NARA, P72 top right: courtesy Cliff Shirley, P73 all: NARA, P74 top: AC, P74 bottom: PK, P75: courtesy Frank Wootton, P76: AC, P77: AC, PP78–79: courtesy Robert Bailey, P80: AC, P82 both: AC, P83: AC, P84: NARA, P86 both: AC, P87 both: AC, P88 both: NARA, P90: Imperial War Museum, P91: AC, P92: NARA, P93: NARA, P94: courtesy Sylvan Lieberthal, P95: USAF, PP96–97: NARA, P98: NARA, P99: PK, P100: Mark Brown–USAF Academy, P101: AC, PP102–103: courtesy Lloyd Stovall, P104: Mark Brown–USAF Academy, P106: PK–courtesy Douglas Radcliffe, P107: Mark Brown–USAF Academy, PP108–109: AC, P110: both: AC, P112: courtesy Joseph Anastasia, P113: USAF, P114: PK, P115 both: Mark Brown–USAF Academy, PP116–117: Len Morgan Collection, P118 both: AC, P119 top: NARA, P119 bottom: AC, P120 top: courtesy Horst Petzschler, P120 bottom: RAF Museum, P121: AC, P122 both: AC, P124: USAF Museum, P125: AC, PP126–127 all: Mark Brown–USAF Academy, P128: courtesy Michael O'Leary, P129 both: AC, P130: PK, P131 both: PK, P132 all: AC, P133: courtesy John Turnbull, P134 top left: courtesy Fred Allen, PP134–135 all colour: PK, P136: NARA, P137: NARA, P138 both: PK, P139 both: PK, P140 both: USAF, P142: AC, P143: AC, P144: USAF, P145: USAF, P146 both: PK, P148–149: USAF, P150 left: AC, P150 top: courtesy Quentin Bland, P150 bottom right: NARA, P152: USAF, P154: PK, P156: AC, P158 both: PK, P159 both: PK, P160–161: NARA, P162: AC, P164 both: NARA, P167 both: NARA, P168: NARA, P169: NARA, P170: NARA, PP172–173: NARA, P174: courtesy Quentin Bland, P175: AC, P176: NARA, P178 both: PK, P181 top: AC, P181 bottom: NARA, PP182–183: NARA, PP186–187 all: USAF Academy, PP190–191 all: PK–jackets coutesy Dave Hill and Greg Parlin, P192: Toni Frissell–Library of Congress, P193: NARA, P194: Imperial War Museum, P195: Imperial War Museum, P196: courtesy Quentin Bland, P197: AC, P198: AC, P199: AC, PP200–201: AC, P202 all: AC, P203: PK, P204: Toni Frissell–Library of Congress, P205 top: Toni Frissell–Library of Congress, P205 bottom both: Mark Brown–USAF Academy, P206: courtesy Bill Graham, P207: AC, P209 top and bottom left: AC, P209 right: courtesy Nick Kosciuk, P210: AC, P211: PK, P212–213: NARA, P214: NARA, P215: Mark Brown–USAF Academy, P216: Mark Brown–USAF Academy, P218: PK, P219: PK, P220 both: NARA, P222 top: courtesy Douglas Radcliffe, P222 bottom: AC, P223: PK, P224: Mark Brown–USAF Academy, P226: AC, P227: PK, P228: USAF, P230: USAF, P231 all: AC, P232: NARA, P233: NARA, P234 both: PK, P239: NARA.

Acknowledgments The author is especially grateful to the following people for their generous help in the development of this book: Joseph Anastasia, Robert Bailey, John M. Bennett, Jr, John S. Bennett, Quentin Bland, JoAnne Bromley, Piers Burnett, Paul Connolly, R.D. Cooling, Robert F. Cooper, Kate and Jack Currie, Sir John Curtiss, Dan DeCamp, Ella and Oz Freire, Bill Graham, Nick Grey, Stephen Grey, Brian Gunderson, Bill Harvey, Don Haynes, Larry Henderson, Dave Hill, John Howland, Claire and Joe Kaplan, Hargi and Neal Kaplan, Margaret Kaplan, Ruth and Fred Kaplan, Karen King, David C. Lustig, Missy Marlow, Judy and Rick McCutcheon, Tilly and James McMaster, Michael O'Leary, Merle Olmsted, Robert Owen, Douglas Radcliffe, Duane Reed, Dale O. Smith, Lloyd Stovall, Ann and John Tusa, Raymond Wild, Mary K. Wiley, Frank Wootton, Hub Zemke.

The author greatly appreciates the kind help and inspiration of: Fred Allen, Mark Aragon, Roger Armstrong, Philip Avery, Ian Bain, Ray Beckley, Charles Bednarik, Mike Benarcik, Gordon Bennett, Larry Bird, Oscar Boesch, Morfydd Brooks, Nick Brown, Wilfred Burnett, Geoffrey Butcher, M.A. Clarke, Don Clement, Jack Clift, Verne Cole, Harry Crosby, James Dacey, Scotty and Clayton David, Harold Davidson, Louis DelGuidice, Lawrence Drew, Jonathan Falconer, Ray Fletcher, W.W. Ford, Roger A. Freeman, Royal Frey, Bill Ganz, Peter Geraghty, J.R. Goodman, Kenneth Grantham, Sol Greenberg, Ed Haggerty, David Harper, John Hersey, Larry Hewin, John Hill, John Holmes, Alfred Huberman, John Hurd, Franc Isla, Markus Isphording, Walter Ketron, John Kirkland, Walter Konantz, Nick Kosciuk, Edith Kup, John Lamb, E.F. Lapham, Ed Leary, Curtis E. LeMay, Sylvan Lieberthal, Walter Longanecker, Wlater Lybeck, Ron MacKay, Roger MacKenzie, Ken Manley, Nelson McInnis, Brian McMaster, John McQuarrie, Edgar Moore, Douglas Newham, Keith Newhouse, Steve Nichols, Geoffrey Page, Greg Parlin, David Parry, John Pawsey, Reg Payne, Len Pearman, Horst Petzschler, Gerald D. Phillips, R.H. Powell, George Reynard, Ted Richardson, J.G. Roberts, Ken Roberts, Lynn Seabury, Dave Shelhamer, Cliff Shirley, Robert Silver, Jerome Solomon, Stan Staples, Ken Stone, Robert Strobell, Stephan Stritter, Alfred Tarry, Leonard Thompson, Robert Thompson, John Turnbull, George Unwin, John Vietor, Douglas Warren, A.L. Wilson, Robert White, Jack Woods, and Sam Young.

Grateful acknowledgment is made to the following for the use of their previously published material.
Ian Allan Ltd: Excerpts from *Bomber Pilot 1916-1918*, by C.P.O. Bartlett.
Frederick Muller Ltd: Excerpt from *Pathfinder*, by D.C.T. Bennett.
Goodall Publications Ltd.: Excerpts from *No Moon Tonight*, by Don Charlwood.
Hutchinson & Co. Ltd: Excerpt from *Bomber Pilot*, by Leonard Cheshire
Houghton Mifflin Company: Excerpt from *The Second World War*, by Winston S. Churchill
The University of Chicago Press: Excerpt from *The Army Air Forces in World War II*, by Wesley F. Craven and James L. Cate.
Macdonald & Co: Excerpts from *Yesterday's Gone*, by N. J. Crisp.
Kate Currie: Excerpt from *Lancaster Target*. by Jack Currie, reprinted by permission.
Harper & Row: Excerpt from *Bomber*, by Len Deighton.
Victor Gollancz Ltd: Excerpts from *Bomber's Moon*, by Negley Farson.
Duell, Sloan and Pearce: Excerpt from *The United States Air Force in Korea 1950–1953*, by Robert F. Futrell.
Goodall Publications Ltd: Excerpts from *Enemy Coast Ahead*, by Guy Gibson.
McClelland and Stewart Ltd: Excerpt from *Boys, Bombs and*

Brussels Sprouts, by J. Douglas Harvey.
Michael Joseph Ltd: Excerpt from *Bomber Command*, by Max Hastings.
USAF Museum: Excerpts from World War II diary of Don Haynes.
John Hersey: Excerpts from *Hiroshima*, by John Hersey.
Alfred A. Knopf Inc: Excerpts from *The War Lover*, by John Hersey.
McGraw Hill: *The Fighters queued up like a bread line and let us have it*, by Beirne Lay, Jr.
Ballantine Books Inc: Excerpt from *12 O'Clock High!*, by Beirne Lay, Jr and Sy Bartlett.
Random House: Excerpts from *Thirty Seconds Over Tokyo*, by Ted W. Lawson.
Doubleday: Excerpt from *Mission With LeMay*, by Curtis E. LeMay and MacKinlay Kantor.
Hutchinson & Co Ltd: Excerpts from *The Bombers*, by Norman Longmate.
Missy Marlow and John S. Bennett: Excerpts from *Letters From England*, by J. M. Bennett, Jr, reprinted by permission.
A special acknowlegment to Richard Rhodes, author of *The Making of the Atomic Bomb*, published by Simon and Schuster, for the fine reference it has provided.
The Viking Press: Excerpts from *Once There Was A War*, by John Steinbeck.
Leo Cooper: Excerpts from *The Eighth Passenger*, by Miles Tripp.
J.B. Lippincott Co: Excerpt from *Heritage of Valor*, by Budd J. Peaslee.
Wartime News: Article on No. 617 Squadron reproduced by kind permission of Wartime News and Robert M. Owen.

Bibliography

Armstrong, Roger W, *USA The Hard Way*, Quail House, 1991
Barker, Ralph, *The Thousand Plane Raid*, Chatto & Windus, 1965
Bartlett, C.P.O., *Bomber Pilot 1916–1918*, Ian Allan, 1974
Bekker, Cajus, *The Luftwaffe War Diaries*, Doubleday, 1968
Bennett, D.C.T., *Pathfinder*, Frederick Muller, 1958
Bennett, John M. Jr, *Letters From England*, 1945
Bowyer, Michael J.F., *The Stirling Bomber*, Faber & Faber, 1980
Brown, G.I., *The Big Bang*, Sutton, 1998
Butcher, Geoffrey, *Next To A Letter From Home*, Sphere Books, 1987
Caidin, Martin, *Black Thursday*, E.P. Dutton, 1960
Caidin, Martin, *Flying Forts*, Meredith Press, 1968
Campbell, James, *The Bombing of Nuremberg*, Doubleday, 1954
Charlwood, Don, *No Moon Tonight*, Angus & Robertson, 1956
Cheshire, Leonard, *Bomber Pilot*, Hutchinson, 1943
Collier, Richard, *Eagle Day*, Hodder & Stoughton, 1966
Cooper, Bryan, *The Story Of The Bomber 1914–1945*, Octopus Books, 1974
Crisp, N.J., *Yesterday's Gone*, Viking Penguin, 1983
Crosby, Harry, *A Wing And A Prayer*, Harper Collins, 1993
Cumming, Michael, *Pathfinder Cranswick*, William Kimber, 1962
Currie, Jack, *Lancaster Target*, New English Library, 1977
Currie, Jack, *Mosquito Victory*, Goodall Publications, 1983
Currie, Jack, *The Augsburg Raid*, Goodall Publications, 1987
Deighton, Len, *Bomber*, Harper & Row, 1970
Dugan, James, and Stewart, Carroll, *Ploesti*, Random House, 1962
Ellis, John, *The World War II Databook*, Aurum Press, 1993
Ethell, Jeffrey L, and Simonsen, Clarence, *The History of Aircraft Nose Art, WWI to Today*, Motorbooks, 1991
Falconer, Jonathan, *The Bomber Command Handbook 1939–1945*, Sutton, 1998
Farson, Negley, *Bomber's Moon*, Victor Gollancz, 1941
FitzGibbon, Constantine, *The Blitz*, Allan Wingate, 1957

Frankland, Noble, *The Bombing Offensive Against Germany*, Faber & Faber, 1965
Freeman, Roger A, *The Mighty Eighth*, Macdonald, 1970
Freeman, Roger A, *Mighty Eighth War Diary*, Jane's, 1981
Freeman, Roger A, *Mighty Eighth War Manual*, Jane's, 1984
Futrell, Robert F, *The United States Air Force in Korea 1950–1953*, Duell, Sloan and Pearce, 1961
Glines, Carroll V, *The Doolittle Raid*, Orion Books, 1988
Gibson, Guy, *Enemy Coast Ahead*, Michael Joseph, 1946
Green, William, *Famous Bombers of the Second World War*, Macdonald, 1959
Harvey, J. Douglas, *Boys, Bombs and Brussels Sprouts*, McClelland and Stewart, 1981
Hastings, Max, *Bomber Command*, Michael Joseph, 1979
Hersey, John, *The War Lover*, Alfred A. Knopf, 1959
Holder, Bill, *Northrop Grumman B-2 Spirit*, Schiffer, 1998
Howland, John W, *Diary of a Pathfinder Navigator*, 1999
Jablonski, Edward, *Flying Fortress*, Doubleday, 1965
Kaplan, Philip, and Smith, Rex Alan, *One Last Look*, Abbeville, 1983
Kaplan, Philip, and Currie, Jack, *Round The Clock*, Random House, 1993
Lay, Beirne, Jr, and Bartlett, Sy, *12 O'Clock High!*, Ballantine Books, 1965
Lawson, Ted, *Thirty Seconds Over Tokyo*, Random House, 1943
Longmate, Norman, *The Bombers*, Hutchinson, 1983
Lyall, Gavin, ed. *The War In The Air*, William Morrow, 1968
Mason, Francis, *The British Bomber since 1914*, Putnam, 1994
Maurer, Maurer, *Air Force Combat Units of World War II*, Franklin Watts, 1959
McCrary, John, and Scherman, David, *First of the Many*, Simon and Schuster, 1944
Merrick, Ken, *By Day & By Night*, Ian Allan, 1989
Middlebrook, Martin, *The Nuremberg Raid*, Penguin, 1973
Middlebrook, Martin, and Everitt, Chris, *The Bomber Command War Diaries*, Viking, 1985
Morris, Eric, *Blockade: Berlin & The Cold War*, Hamish Hamilton, 1973
Moyes, Philip, *Bomber Squadrons of the R.A.F. And Their Aircraft*, Macdonald, 1964
Pearcy, Arthur, *Berlin Airlift*, Airlife, 1997
Peaslee, Budd, *Heritage of Valor*, J.B. Lippincott, 1964
Penrose, Harald, *Architect of Wings*, Airlife, 1985
Reynolds, Quentin, *A London Diary*, Random House, 1941
Rhodes, Richard, *The Making of the Atomic Bomb*, Simon and Schuster, 1986
Robertson, Bruce, *Lancaster—The Story of a Famous Bomber*, Harleyford, 1964
Rust, Kenn, *The 9th Air Force in World War II*, Aero, 1967
Saward, Dudley, *'Bomber' Harris*, Cassell, 1984
Shores, Christopher, *Duel For The Sky*, Doubleday, 1985
Sloan, John S, *The Route As Briefed*, Argus Press, 1946
Smith, Dale, *Screaming Eagle*, Algonquin Books, 1990
Steinbeck, John, *Once There Was A War*, Viking, 1958
Stiles, Bert, *Serenade To The Big Bird*, W.W. Norton, 1947
Sunderman, James, *World War II In The Air: The Pacific*, Franklin Watts, 1962
Tripp, Miles, *The Eighth Passenger*, William Heinemann, 1969
Truman, Harry S, *Memoirs—Year of Decisions*, Doubleday, 1955
Vietor, John, *Time Out*, Richard R. Smith, 1951
Verrier, Anthony, *The Bomber Offensive*, B.T. Batsford, 1968
Watry, Charles, and Hall, Duane, *Aerial Gunners: The Unknown Aces of World War II*, California Aero Press, 1986

show that 868 aircraft bombed the primary target while an additional fifteen aircraft hit other targets. 1455 tons of bombs were dropped, two–thirds of them being incendiaries. 1700 large fires were started, according to German records, and 3330 buildings were destroyed, with 2090 being seriously damaged. Approximately 470 people were killed and slightly more than 5000 were injured. Some 45,000 people were made homeless. The RAF lost 41 planes and crews. The Cologne raid was considered a significant success and the results of the area bombing provided a model for what the RAF could expect in future raids.

Below: RAF ground crews preparing their Lancasters for an upcoming operation.